What Every Child Needs

Best Wishes

Lil

What Every Child Needs

Lillian Peairs and Richard Peairs

HARPER & ROW, PUBLISHERS

NEW YORK, EVANSTON, SAN FRANCISCO,
LONDON

1817

Designed by Lydia Link

Library of Congress Cataloging in Publication Data

Peairs, Lillian.
  What every child needs.
Bibliography: p.
  1. Child study. 2. Children—Management.
I. Peairs, Richard, joint author. II. Title.
BF721.P36   649'.1'019   73–14281
ISBN 0–06–013309–0

Preface

This book is meant to challenge you to search for better ways to help your children grow. Your care and affection must provide the nutrition necessary for the proper development of your child's mind. All parents want emotionally healthy, happy children. No one deliberately seeks to make children dull, shy, anxious, or delinquent, but many of us are handicapped by the results of our own authoritarian upbringing and by a lack of reliable information. Probably our biggest problem is that we want to be friends with our children but don't know how to be that and at the same time set limits on their conduct. Today's creative, spirited, and sometimes disrespectful youngster creates problems difficult to handle.

Although behavioral science has accumulated much evidence on how children develop best, it is not readily available to most parents. The information is reported in the special literature and language of psychology, which is largely technical and difficult for the layman to understand. This volume, which results from the authors' own search for child-rearing information, brings together a great deal of those data in an easily understandable and condensed form. For many everyday emotional problems it provides answers that have hitherto been, as a practical matter, virtually inaccessible to the general public.

Your child's formative years pass quickly, and you will not get a second chance to shape personality. The subjects covered will help you provide the early environment needed for your child to become a creative, self-fulfilling person. Parenthood may not be easy, but it can be rewarding.

With regard to the more serious behavioral pathologies with which some children are born, the information herein may help parents develop the understanding and tolerance needed for living with what they cannot totally control or modify.

The material is not graded according to age levels, as the authors believe that most of it is pertinent regardless of the youngster's age. Although this book should be most helpful in earlier years, it also ought to be quite useful in the teens, especially in dealing with the problem of rebellion. Communication is less of a problem for parents who learn how to react to their teen-agers as friends. Valued as individuals, treated with respect and dignity while struggling through their search-for-identity years, they are less likely to become alienated.

The sections on anger and hostility are intended to help you understand how reduced feelings of self-esteem often cause anger in both parent and child. Anger is a natural reaction with the objective of protecting one's self-feelings. It can be helpful or destructive to a child's personality development. When we understand this, we can react to a hostile child with sympathy rather than anger.

Teen-agers, too, may benefit from a reading of this material. The sections on sibling rivalry should help them understand how brothers and sisters affect each other's personalities. From the discussion of self-image development they can learn how opinions that they form very early about themselves can, even if incorrect, become patterns to which they try to shape themselves and their lives. Increased understanding of their parents' problems should help them handle their own problems more effectively.

Parents will, we hope, read this book through as a text and

then keep it on hand to read and reread when they feel the need for reassurance or guidance on specific problems.

Students will find in it an extensive bibliography as well as suggestions for new areas of research. (The sources of passages quoted in the text will be found in the bibliography, which is alphabetically presented by authors' names.)

Our three children supplied both the incentive and the background information for the compilation of this work. We owe our thanks to Mark, John, and Anne for their tolerance and express our deep gratitude that they have been ours.

Acknowledgment must go to the authors cited in the bibliography who provided a great amount of information. Reflected and noted throughout this volume are ideas contributed by many scholars. The various cooperative nurseries our children attended were especially valuable sources of information. Our thanks go also to the many parents of our children's friends who read and commented upon the ideas presented here. Finally, appreciation goes to the scholars who read this manuscript and offered advice and opinions: Dr. Frank J. Vattano, assistant academic vice president, Colorado State University; Dr. Leo Pirojnikoff, professor of psychology, California State University, Northridge; Dr. Helen Giedt, professor of psychology, California State University, Northridge; Dr. Anita Fisher, chairman of the Department of Psychology, College of San Mateo; Dr. Roger Myers, professor of psychology, Teachers College, Columbia University; Henry S. Richanbach, M.D., Burlingame, California; Dr. Luther Jennings, professor of psychology, Occidental College; Dr. John Dackawich, chairman of the Department of Sociology, California State University, Fresno; Dr. Leona Tyler, president of the American Psychological Association; Dr. Stanley Coopersmith, chairman of the Department of Psychology, University of California, Davis; Mrs. Sherrie Epstein, school psychologist, Millbrae, California.

Particular thanks go to Dr. Virginia Voeks, professor emeritus of psychology, California State University, San Diego, for her enthusiasm, interest, and advice. Her very careful observations, in combination with her special warmth and sensitivity, produced many improvements in the manuscript. We are deeply indebted to her.

L. G. P.
R. H. P.

Introduction

What contributes most to the development of emotionally healthy children? It's not wealth or poverty, not one parent or two, not the absence of a working mother or the amount of attention a child receives from an at-home mother, but the quality of the parent-child relationship. Hence this book is as much concerned with parent behavior as with child behavior. It will help you understand how your own personality took shape, thus enabling you to interact with your children in more positive ways.

Putting to use the knowledge gained from self-education is difficult. Our own well-established feelings and attitudes tend to block recognition and practice of new knowledge and to confine us to ways of the past in rearing children for the future. Few people are aware of the number of myths that succeeding generations of parents have projected upon their offspring. It may seem "natural" to believe that:

A child owes obedience to his parents in return for his care.
Praise is boastful and will make a child conceited.
Children must be kept under strong control or they will surely become unruly.
Good manners and common sense must be learned while one is young or they never will be.
Harsh treatment will toughen a child.

Too much love and attention will spoil children.
There are "mean streaks" that must be taken out of them.
It's disrespectful to talk back to one's parents.

Parents want the best for their children, yet few fully comprehend the seriousness of their responsibility—the molding of a human personality. Parents seek the latest and best that medical science has to offer for a child's physical ills, but emotional problems may not receive equal concern. We keep up-to-date on the latest fiction, politics, music, business, fashion, sports, theater, but we learn little about child behavior. How-to-do-it books are easily available for cooking, building a home, planting a garden, or even fixing a bicycle, but not for the emotional problems of raising children. Family therapist Thomas Gordon writes:

Preparation for parenthood in our society does not go much beyond buying the new bassinet, repainting a borrowed crib, or purchasing a paperback by Dr. Spock. . . . Girls in high school can learn cooking, but not how to be an effective parent. Even the small percentage of students who take a course in child psychology in college discover that it is generally a course about how the child's mind and body develop, not about parenthood. How to discipline a child is seldom covered, nor is much of anything else a parent actually needs to know. . . . Almost none of the vast literature even deals with conflict and conflict resolution. [1970, *a*, p. 408.]

Burton White observes:

I have been to many conferences in recent years where practitioners have literally begged academicians for our pearls of wisdom. It is very disconcerting to have to admit that the cupboard is nearly bare, but it is. [1971, p. 132.]

A wide range of psychological research—experimental and clinical, group and individual, human and animal—has identified many factors affecting child behavior. The literature of

behavioral science can be a source of many practical suggestions useful in solving the kinds of problems parents face daily.
But for most parents this storehouse of knowledge might just as
well be nonexistent. It is hoped that this book will ease your
search for answers.

ONE

What Every Child Needs

A PLEASANT EARLY ENVIRONMENT

Created by Parents

Yes, we are the major architects of our children's personalities, with mother carrying the greatest responsibility in early infancy. The improvement of our social climate, of our behavioral environment, awaits a wider recognition of these simple, fundamental facts. From one generation to another, we have accepted with too little skepticism inaccurate, untested, unexamined beliefs about child-rearing. Children are far too often raised according to whatever ideas we parents just happen to pick up along the way. Children are far too important to have the haphazard memories of our own childhood serve as principal reference and guide in our handling of their development.

A youngster's first years, spent almost entirely with parents, affect his personality throughout life. From birth—perhaps even before birth—he receives impressions about the world in which he lives. The home's intimate and pervasive emotional atmosphere is crucially important to how he conceives life. Routine daily activities to which parents may give little thought provide him with pleasant and meaningful experiences from which he draws the conclusions that will shape his personality. Every new day's experiences are perceived in the light of what has gone before. If past experiences have been pleasant and rewarding, he will expect new ones to be the same, if unpleasant or threatening, he will tend to see his future world as untrustworthy and menacing.

The infant is learning as he observes those who care for his bodily needs. As he nurses, notice how he searches mother's face with his eyes. Eye-to-eye contact and smiles are signals of the beginning of his intense attachment to mother. When he learns to crawl, he strives on his own to see and be with her. He will cry if she disappears from view. Parents' tone of voice, their facial expressions, as well as the adequacy of his nourishment, contribute to his sense of well-being. A powerful bond of attachment develops. He will attempt to copy his parents' behavior. To a degree, he will act and think like them. The qualities they criticize in him, he will criticize in himself. If respected, he learns respect for himself. If a recipient of sympathy, he can give it in return. He will respond to and recall the pleasure or lack of it that parents display when they are with him. He learns to love by being loved. He will grow to value himself and others to the extent that he feels valued and loved by his parents.

In startling or frightening situations we can most easily observe how a child adopts parental feelings as his own. He looks directly to mother's face when he seeks comfort and reassurance. If he sees that mother remains calm, he is likely to stay calm. When he sees her dealing effectively with a problem, he may learn a valuable lesson in dealing with reality. In the preschool years, observations of his parents guide his learning. More permanent emotional learning takes place at that time than in all the remaining years of life. "All areas of the child's personality are deeply influenced by the child's interaction with his mother. . . . She reacts more or less differently to the various areas of the child's behavior (speech, play, motor activities, social interplay, separation behavior), thereby shaping their development" (David and Appell, 1969, p. 183).

By the age of three an identifiable personality is clearly apparent. The child has listened repeatedly to his parents' views of the world and has observed their relationships in it. He has noticed their emotional reactions in many kinds of situations. From these observations, he will have concluded that the world appears generally comfortable, friendly, pleasant, and reliable— or unfriendly, punishing, restricting, inconsistent, and unstable.

Your Most Important Task

Creating a home environment that will shape a well-adjusted, competent personality is one of the most difficult and important tasks for which you ever will have responsibility. It requires great devotion, with a generous measure of patience and self-discipline added.

A contented and happy early childhood strengthens a child against the hazards and insecurities of a lifetime. It can be provided most effectively by parents who themselves have overcome the adversities of their own early experiences. What was good enough in our childhood may not be enough for our children. As Bettelheim describes the opportunity of this period, "Never again in your life will you be so important to another human being" (1962, p. 203).

From the moment of birth the infant is learning. At first, feelings make up his world. He learns through his sense of touch and, in particular, his parents' gentleness. Being rocked, cuddled, and cared for are some of his most satisfying first impressions about life. Research indicates that handling of the newborn may increase his later ability to tolerate emotional stress. Handled infants have been found to learn faster and grow better, emotionally and physically (Scott, 1962; Levine, 1969; Denenberg, 1969). Some of the effects of extra-attentive mothering are noted in Marcelle Geber's research with over three hundred East African babies:

Babies remain with their mothers day and night. They are talked to, cuddled, and stroked; they are fed whenever they wish to eat; and they are watched for cues as to what they want to do—sit up, for instance—and are then helped to do it. The Uganda mother is wholly child-centered. . . . And the child she produces is noticeably superior to Western European or American children. At seven weeks, for example, he can sit up unaided and watch himself in a mirror; at seven months, for another example, he can walk to a box and look inside it for toys. These accomplishments occur in our children at about twenty-four weeks and fifteen months, respectively. [Description by Beadle, 1970, pp. 59–60.]

The research of Harold Skeels helps us comprehend even more fully the importance of early love and attention:

Thirteen mentally retarded children under three years of age, with an average IQ of 64 were transferred from an orphanage, where they received only minimum care, to an institution for the mentally retarded. Here the women inmates loved, cuddled, and played with them for an average of four years before they were transferred back to the orphanage or adopted. Tracing these children twenty-three years later, Skeels found that all had finished high school and were self-supporting. Four had one or more years of college. One had a B.A. degree. Eleven were married. Nine of the eleven had a total of twenty-eight children.

Thirteen other children, with slightly higher IQ's, who had never left the orphanage, were also followed up as adults. One had died in adolescence, four were still wards of institutions, one in a mental hospital, and three were in institutions for the mentally retarded. A median of less than third grade was completed. Those working, with the exception of one, who had acquired the skill of a typesetter, were dishwashers or groundsmen. The typesetter was married with four children. One other subject was married and had a retarded child. (Summarized from 1966, pp. 8–10, 33, 40–42, 44–45.)

The major difference in the experience of these two groups of children was the attention, gifts, and affection bestowed by the women inmates. The children remaining in the orphanage experienced relatively little attention. They showed a loss of 26.2

IQ points over a two-year period as compared to a gain of 28.5 for the children cared for by the women inmates.

TRUST

In Infancy

Trust in the reliability of mother is vital as the young infant begins to seek independence. Mother's dependability gives him the confidence he needs to reach out and explore. Even for the baby monkey subjected to a frightening stimulus, "clinging to mother provides enough safety feeling for the baby to tolerate looking at a frightening object" (Sandler and Joffe, 1968, p. 289).

Mother functions both as a part of and as an extension of her child. The young infant becomes frightened when she disappears from view and unhappy when she looks disturbed. Through her he comes to know and communicate with the outside world. She is the base from which he feels free to explore. If afraid that she will disappear, blame, rebuff, or not love him, he will cling to her, seeking to protect his source of security and affection. Self-assertion and exploration are abandoned when security is threatened. Trust in himself and others may never develop if his early environment is one that he can seldom depend on. On the importance of this period, Sandler adds: "A child who is able to explore his environment freely and fairly aggressively, without diminishing his sources of basic safety feeling, may retain this freedom to explore (in activity or in thought) throughout his life because he has found appropriate techniques for doing this. . . . In contrast, a child who has had to cope with too severe and extreme safety-pleasure conflicts in early life may restrict himself to stereotyped types of behavior because he is frightened by his drives and exploratory impulses" (1968, pp. 291–292).

Trust first develops as the infant observes that when he is hungry, tired, wet, or cranky, parental care and understanding are dependable and predictable. His need for love is partially met by much close physical contact. Love and approval seem unconditional. Discipline is not prolonged. He is not judged too quickly in any circumstance. He finds support and encouragement when faced with failure, distress, or fears.

In Older Children

Trust continues to grow as parents demonstrate faith that their older, more active child is genuine and good. Friendship is not given or taken away because behavior of the moment may not be up to standard. They accept less than desirable behavior as a passing thing, natural to his development. Severe reprimands, commands, and physical punishment display no such confidence and can be particularly harmful if they occur as statements of expectation, as predictions of future misbehavior. Parental trust helps him come to trust himself. Every day, in numerous ways, your confidence in your child can be manifested. Here are some of the ways:

IN YOUR POSITIVE EXPECTATIONS

Finding a quarter in the car, five-year-old Jane says, "I'm going to keep it." Big brother says, "No, you aren't. It belongs to Tom. He lost it here yesterday." The disagreement continues with "Yes, I am" and "No, you are not." What can the parent say? *Stating a positive expectancy* seems most effective: "No

more arguing. Jane knows who it belongs to. She will return it."
In this way, sister has an opportunity to change her own behavior. Parental demands for the immediate surrender of an attractive object are frustrating, as well as an assault upon Jane's right to be a separate individual with judgments of her own.

Then there is five-year-old Beverly, who eagerly expresses her wish to accompany you on a brief errand. You chill her enthusiasm with "What do you want to come for?" or "You can come, but I'm telling you right now that I'm not going to buy you anything. If you touch one thing, we'll come right home." An excursion begun on such a note appears unlikely to encourage companionable feelings. The parent, perhaps preoccupied with his own needs, has not shown an interest in being accompanied but has displayed an expectancy that problem behavior will occur. Children learn about themselves and start their own expectancies about themselves from our expectancies. How much better to say, "I'd like you to come. I'm only going to be at the store for a few minutes, so we won't have time to stop and look this time."

Five-year-old Mary has taken father's place at the dinner table and stubbornly refuses to move. Ordinarily, she does not challenge his position; thus, to ignore the immediate situation seems more appropriate than a disturbed evening meal and an exaggeration of the assault. Showing no fear of loss of your paternal position displays trust in her essential goodwill. Making an issue out of it would have given her an example of how to suspect others of deliberately trying to put something over on you.

IN YOUR COMFORT AND SYMPATHY

Missing for some time, eight-year-old Billy is discovered hiding beneath the covers of his bed. Mother learns that he has run the considerable distance home after dropping a glass figurine in the variety store. Further discipline seems unreasonable. He has already shown strong conscience. What he really needs is comfort and sympathy to ease his fright and concern: "That's all right. We know you didn't drop it on purpose. I'm sure that stores expect things to get broken occasionally. We'll stop on our way to the market tomorrow and pay for it." Thus the child learns to deal with his guilt by making some form of restitution.

IN YOUR CONCERN

A very angry ten-year-old walks away from home. When he returns two hours later, what do you do? He has already spent considerable time being miserable, returning home only after strong feelings of anger, distress, and isolation have subsided. Added reproach and punishment rekindle anger and aggression. Instead, try showing your sensitivity and concern for his welfare: "I was very worried about you. I had almost decided to have the police help me find you." Now your child knows you care (provided he has learned to like and trust the police). Knowing you care may be all he was seeking in the first place. Next step might be to help him explore his feelings: why he left home, how he feels now, and what he and his parents can do about such feelings in the future.

IN YOUR PATIENCE

The noise of small children prevents completion of many a telephone conversation. Children often appear to plan such interference, as though their distress occurs only when mother is busy. Perhaps it does. Having come to anticipate a customary pattern of behavior from mother, they are frustrated when she does not meet their expectancies as usual. When we can't hear, it is probably wise to postpone our call.

Trust your child to want to be fair. It's his natural self-centeredness, not his lack of respect or concern, that makes him continue to harass us when we have told him to stop. He does not know how things look from our adult point of view. We can try to discuss the situation with him. Depending upon the child, he may be mature enough to understand.

RESPECT

Respect means treating a child in ways that communicate that he is worthwhile and important. His approval of himself as a person of value largely depends upon the respect conveyed by the way we respond to him—our willingness to let him be as he is, to make mistakes, to have opinions. Every experience with our love and displeasure affects his image of himself. Right or wrong, he tends to adopt our feelings about him as his own. They may remain with him always. As Missildine puts it: "The 'child of our past' actually continues, with all his feelings and attitudes to the very end of our lives" (1963, p. 20).

Parental respect counts for more in this type of development than the economic status of the home. Neither poverty nor wealth can excuse lack of respect for children. In the economically deprived home and in the home of comfortable means, a child can develop a rich and full personality if his parents have the time and concern to promote his welfare. Parents are a powerful force. Neighbors, siblings, teachers, friends all contribute to this end but not so pervasively as do parents.

Conveyed by Parents

Acts and words are the vehicles through which we convey respect and trust. We need to give thought and attention to routine daily communication. Our children deserve the same consideration that we display in our relationships with adult friends and associates. For example, seldom would we:

Belittle a friend for being awkward or making a mess in our home.
Act indignant should a friend interrupt our conversation.
Fail to keep a date with a friend.
Tell a friend who makes a simple request: "Do it yourself."
Be abrupt, domineering, or arbitrary with a friend.
Punish with resentment a friend who fails to go along with our ideas.
Fail to say "Thank you," "Excuse me," "Beg your pardon," or "Sorry" to a friend.
Call a friend "stupid," "silly," "dumb," or "liar."
Question a friend's behavior with "What did you do that for?"
Slap a friend who talks back.
Force a friend to eat the food placed in front of him.
Ridicule a friend's choice of clothing, possessions, or companions.
Tell a friend not to touch the display on the living room table.
Answer a friend's request for the spelling of a word with "You ought to know how to spell that."

Yet too often parents act as though they have the right to express irritations harshly and directly to children, while in similar circumstances they would go to considerable lengths to avoid offending adult friends.

Parents sometimes see their child more as a responsibility than as a friend. Too busy to seek out his love, they miss what could be one of the greatest enjoyments in life. Treated with consideration and the respect that one ordinarily reserves for a valued friend, a child can give a depth of devotion, of faith and trust, that is unparalleled. The confidence that love, respect, and understanding give to the child yields to parents a rich

Seven-year-old Susie is having dinner with a friend. Slightly nervous, she puts her fingers in her mouth. The observing mother asks, "Do you bite your fingernails?" When Susie answers "Yes" everyone laughs. The comment, probably made without an intent to be critical, has nevertheless had its effect. At home, little Susie is distressed at any mention of fingernails. When mother finally isolates the trouble and it is talked about, the subject becomes less of a problem for her.

SECURITY

Security is the "feeling of all rightness" that a child has for his parents when they are entirely satisfied with him; when they accept him as he is and feel that no alterations are necessary in his basic makeup (Beverly, 1941). Many difficulties that adults experience in their personal relationships occur because they are ultimately looking for a certain something (perhaps an escape from insecurity) that they should have acquired in infancy from their parents and which seems impossible to achieve in adult relationships (Storr, 1968, p. 80).

Security arises from various favorable influences in the child's daily environment. Of these, parental empathy—the ability to sense how a child feels—seems vitally important. Parents who can see things from a child's point of view tend to have children who cry less, who have greater ability to tolerate frustration and delay, and who are easier to get along with. Being sympathetic (not to be confused with pity or feeling sorry for him) lets him know he's not alone and lessens distress. An understanding parent or friend can greatly ease disturbing situations, such as when:

At school he sits half the year between two girls who make him feel uncomfortable.
He is disciplined by the teacher.
Rude and hurtful comments are made by a friend.
A beloved pet is lost.
He is afraid to speak to the teacher about the bully behind him.
A particular class at school leaves him miserable each day.
His new bike is stolen from the parking lot at the city park.
He is afraid of being left alone in the dentist's office.
He mislays his reading glasses.
He comes in last at the track meet.

As parents, we sometimes try to erase such difficulties with a single statement of fact. We may deny that a problem exists, perhaps hoping it will go away. At other times, we suggest that our child accept the situation without help. Or we may remark as follows (imagine how these comments sound when spoken in a sarcastic and ridiculing tone):

That shouldn't bother you.
What did you do to make the teacher angry?
You're just imagining. He wasn't trying to hurt your feelings.
We'll get a new cat.
Tell your problems to your teacher.
You'll just have to make the best of it.
You learned your lesson, didn't you?
What are you afraid of?
Wait till your dad hears about this.
If you had practiced more, you could have done better.

Try to understand the effects on a child when we respond in these ways. How can he see us as a source of support if his feelings are not of sufficient worth to be discussed in a nonjudgmental, nondemeaning atmosphere? The ability to influence the behavior of parents is necessary if he is later to believe in his ability to persuade others. When adults take the time to understand and show genuine concern, as in the following contrasting examples, a greater sense of security develops:

I agree. You deserve a change. Let's talk to the teacher.
How unhappy you must have been when the teacher called you a "tattletale" in front of the class.
You must have been surprised and disturbed to have your friend suddenly speak to you that way.
I think he was a grand pet, too.
Maybe I can stop in with you after school and we can talk to the teacher together.
Your counselor would want to know how uncomfortable you are in Miss Baker's class.
I know how disappointed you must be to lose a brand-new bike.
You feel afraid to see the dentist without mother? I'll be glad to stay with you as long as you need me. I'm sure we can find a dentist who will be agreeable.
I know how you feel about losing your glasses. We'll do our best to help you find them.
You feel angry with yourself because you didn't do better?

Security permits a child the freedom to confide in parents. He knows that his feelings will receive consideration and protection. Whether he is right or wrong, their concern and regard for him are not reduced by judgments of friends, school, or community. If faced by unfairness or the lack of concern of others, with whom he feels unable to cope, *they* rightfully will support him. Knowing this, he can speak freely about many of his feelings of distress or unhappiness. Don't misunderstand. It is not that the child is always "right" no matter what he has done, but rather that we help him correct his mistakes, his faulty perceptions, his unwise behavior, and we do it in the respectful way we would help a friend.

TUNED-IN PARENTS

DO YOU RECOGNIZE YOUR RESPONSIBILITIES?

To live as part of a congenial family puts limits on parents' right "not to be bothered." Before children are in bed for the night, parents' hours may not be completely their own. When watching TV or reading, do children usually get only a swat if they persistently demand your attention? When you see a problem—a toy someone can't reach, a shoelace that won't stay tied, an uncomfortable wet diaper—are you reluctant to offer assistance? When trouble brews, do you try to settle it with commands issued from a reclining position on the couch or from behind the newspaper in your favorite rocker? Do you make an active effort to help resolve conflicts only after your temper has reached the exploding point? If so, you're not unusual.

Parents willing to exert themselves for the growth of their children accomplish much more than those who are unseeing or customarily resort to threats. Assistance with emotional and physical needs as they arise is necessary if children are to grow well. Effectively meeting children's difficulties requires participation of an active sort, at frequent intervals, to restore calm and reorient behavior to less aggressive or disruptive play. Children need and demand much. They may be irritable and tired when parents feel the same. Only as they mature through elementary school do they begin to show self-sufficiency along with a heightened, more accurate sensitivity to the needs and feelings of others. Dismissing their efforts to gain attention in a superficial way conveys lack of interest. If we don't pay attention to a child's problems, we cannot know whether a situation merits our concern or assistance.

ARE YOU TUNED IN TO THE NEEDS, FEELINGS, AND MOODS OF CHILDREN?

Can you sense how a child feels when:

A parent continues reading the newspaper after having agreed to listen to a story?

A parent gets up and leaves the room without comment while a child is still talking to him?

A child speaks directly to the parent and the parent fails to nod, look up, comment, or make any sign of hearing?

A child, asked to describe his day at school, finds himself not being listened to?

A child gets put to bed as soon as daddy comes home?

A parent is too busy to meet a child's request for assistance, but is free to spend a half hour on the phone with an adult friend?

A parent frequently sides with little sister in children's quarrels?

A parent, arriving home from work, is too busy to talk for a few minutes with the child who has waited for him all day?

The family's dinner table conversation is dominated by adult talk?

Father takes off after dinner for the den, his own TV, or the newspaper for the remainder of the evening?

Dad has only ten minutes for his son, but five hours for golf with his friends?

A parent gives away his favorite hobby horse because he has out-grown it, without asking him?

Parents get rid of a beloved pet (perhaps his only trusted friend) because they can't be bothered with the mess it makes?

Parents postpone promised activities or frequently leave his
requests until last?
His fine report card or first prize in the art show is ignored?

Except for occasional needs for privacy, adolescents seldom
tune out parents who have been close to them over the years.
Fond parents who have been tuned in know what to expect of
their children. Behavior builds on previous behavior. Children
who have enjoyed a companionable relationship with parents
during their early years don't suddenly become problem teen-
agers.

Of course children also grow without attention, but for
maximum development of their potentialities, they need an
early start in a warm, interested, respectful environment. Creativity, self-confidence, a sense of responsibility, the ability to
love and be loved do not unfold without assistance.

WHAT ARE YOUR INTERESTS?

Before getting around to the promised reading, the game of
chess, or other planned activity, do you frequently explain that
you must finish one or more of your own tasks and then another
and another, make a necessary phone call, empty the wastebaskets, put the dishes away? If so, isn't it possible that by the
time you are underway, the children may no longer feel that
you really desired to join them but are capitulating to harass-
ment? Consistent procrastination, as well as forgetfulness, is one
way of suggesting to others that you don't really care. This does
not mean that we should always drop everything. It's the way
we cooperate most of the time that counts.

Do you genuinely enjoy the time you spend with your children? Or are you often aiming at "getting it over with" as soon
as possible so that you can get back to your other interests? Of
course being a parent doesn't necessarily make you interested.
Nevertheless, when education gives you greater insight into the

role you play in personality development, your concern for your child's full development will help you become interested. You'll discover how much more important they are than the dusting. Children need our interested attention. When they enjoy communicating with their parents, they also relate well to other people.

DO YOUR CHILDREN KNOW YOU?

Some parents seem unknown to their children. The parents' pleasant personalities may be more familiar to their adult friends than to their children. Involved and satisfied with their work and other interests, parents sometimes provide attention only to their child's physical needs. Unaware of any deeper needs, communication tends to become merely a series of orders: "It's time to get up." "Eat your breakfast." "Did you brush your teeth?" "Are you ready for school?" "Comb your hair." The child may not discover that beneath the seeming indifference there exists a parent who really cares. He certainly will not discover this if the parent assumes exclusively the role of first sergeant!

How often do you engage in friendly conversation when a child happens to be in the same room with you? Is it difficult to speak without directing or teaching? Do you frequently pass through a room, or generally work, sit, or stand beside your child without comment, unless someone lets out a yell, teases the dog, makes a mess, or hurts himself?

A child learns quickly the techniques that will get his parents to turn around, stop talking on the phone, put down the newspaper, and perhaps even relate to him. When he wants recognition, any kind of attention, even anger, irritation, or a spanking seems better than none. And one thing is certain: it comes more quickly. Children need the love and attention of their parents, with whom they seek to identify. The extra effort of a warm greeting, of conversation, is a small price for a child's added feeling of self-importance and rapport. Communication isn't difficult to initiate:

> Hi, how did your Spanish test go today?
> Say, I like the way you organized your room.
> How's my pal?
> Talk to me while I peel potatoes.
> Would you like to ride along to the store with me?
> Let's have a game of checkers.

Of course if one feels that all conversation must be intellectually meaningful, it may prove difficult. However, just chatting about trivial things can do a great deal to keep children in touch with you. Talk informally about yourself. Talk about household activities in progress: the foods being prepared, the housework, various features of the clothes in which you may be dressing him. Note how children enjoy hearing or talking about pleasant experiences that have happened to them when they were tiny. As your child matures, you will begin to see how experience in communication with you helps him meet the demands of his other social worlds.

WHERE ARE YOU?

Do your children usually spend their after-dinner hours in one part of the home while you retire to another? Their security comes not only from parental expressions of affection and care but from simply being able to see and hear you in your activities around the home. Direct interaction is not all that counts. The sight and sound of congenial parents provide comfort and increased security.

In earlier days most of a family's activities were often conducted in the same room. Children realized a great deal of "nearness comfort" from the familiar presence of their parents. Father could be seen and heard behind the evening newspaper, while mother tended pleasant kitchen sounds and aromas. After dinner she probably joined them in the living room with her sewing or reading. Grandparents were apt to be more in evidence as a source of added companionship and security.

Our modern homes often are planned with a family room for children and a den or living room for parents. Parents' bedrooms are far removed from those of the children, reducing even nighttime security. Children desiring to speak with parents must find them first; and chances are that they may feel they are interrupting or intruding. No doubt adults enjoy the increased freedom that today's home provides. They seem in a way less pressured than their predecessors, who did not have home conveniences or TV entertainment. Today's children, however, live increasingly by themselves even while actually at home at the same time as their parents.

Children need to feel needed. Today's parents do not necessarily share this need, as their security is not vested in the child. With all the social arrangements parents provide, they may not sense any dissatisfaction, may even less comprehend that their children are emotionally neglected. Willingness and good intentions, however, fail to take the place of real companionship. Parental involvement and commitment are necessary. Children value the companionship of their parents more than the substitutes parents find for themselves. They will live emotionally separate from parents who treat them as objects.

Not only do parents spend less time with their children when they actually are at home, but they are home less frequently. They have become increasingly more interested in community affairs and opportunities for their own self-fulfillment. Educational advancement, drama, art, politics, professional organizations, charity work, social clubs, and longer business hours all take larger portions of parents' time and energies. With less of their parents available, children must learn to be satisfied with the attention they do receive, or seek companionship elsewhere.

It must be added that increasing parental companionship proves valuable only if the overall quality of that relationship is good. No special benefit is derived from increased companionship with a parent who nags, judges, or blames continuously, or where compatibility is nonexistent. If a choice is necessary, quality remains more important than quantity.

HOW DO YOU EXPRESS AFFECTION?

Parents usually love their children, but how do they demonstrate that love? Some do it by excessive rules, inflexible limits, frequent punishment and taunts. Relationships between almost any two people would be endangered under these conditions. When a child expresses affection at inopportune times, is he turned aside? If so, he soon learns to withhold future affectionate impulses.

Love is expressed most fully in unplanned giving of oneself, in a spontaneous abiding interest in the thoughts, feelings, and happiness of the child. Love means respect for the child as an individual—an affectionate respect of what he says and does. It means courtesy and unwavering honesty, and taking the time to talk to him about his problems and interests. You show that you care by the way in which you ignore many of his mistakes, knowing that they are lessons in themselves. You show your love by the way you offer guidance unaccompanied by debasing judgment, blame, or punishment.

Hugs and verbal reassurances of love are desirable, but they are not all that is necessary to help a child feel that he is loved. The strength of a child's attachment to either parent is related to the readiness with which that parent responds to the child's crying and social advances, as well as the extent to which the parent initiates social interaction with him (Schaffer and Emerson, 1964). A child becomes more closely attached to the parent who is interested in his interests, who smiles and plays with him, who gives sympathy, who cares for his needs. Bettelheim tells of a young child who defined love as "pick me up, hug me, kiss me, carry me, and put me down" (1950, p. 27).

The young child cannot thrive on being loved solely for his parents' pleasure. He feels loved to the extent that parents take time to concern themselves with his numerous needs and interests without his persistently having to ask or beg for such assistance. Briefly summarized, he needs a parent who will:

Understand him.
Sympathize with his problems.
Listen to his stories.
Read to him.
Play with him.
Cuddle him.
Smile and give approval.
Help him find his important lost Teddy bear.
Get for him the things he cannot reach.
Help him bathe, dress, and care for his personal needs.
Accept without anger his lack of interest in some of the
  parents' suggestions.
Persuade him to conformity with imagination rather than
  domination.
Accept and value him as a separate individual.

These are ways of showing love. These are ways to help our children grow. Fromm reminds us: "Love is the active concern for the life and growth of that which we love" (1956, p. 26). We cannot expect our children to thrive or to show many signs of love if we have neglected much of the above.

A DEMOCRATIC HOME ENVIRONMENT

The professional literature of psychology discloses evidence that self-fulfillment needs are most favored by a democratic home environment, where parental influence is displayed by example in a companionable atmosphere of acceptance and partnership.

Democratic parents are companions who spend much time with their children—including the setting of necessary limits. They should not be compared with permissive parents who may set no limits at all. Permissive parents avoid putting on pressure or making demands. They avoid setting limits or indicating boundaries. "Anything goes." They may appear to do much "for" their children, but not "with" them.

In the democratic home, the rights of children are respected. Appreciated for their uniqueness, children are neither overcontrolled nor undercontrolled. Their basic integrity is not questioned. Guidance and direction are provided in nonpunitive ways. The warm and positive relationship that exists in the home is reflected in the child's developing personality. Researchers have found that children entering nursery school from such homes participated more freely, were more socially accepted by peers, showed healthy aggression and self-assertion, and were more creative and constructive (Baldwin, 1948, 1949, 1955, and Marshall, 1961). Children's emotional health is closely related to the emotional relationships that exist between parents—a fact fully supported by the careful research of Westley and Epstein (1969) and others. A democratic relationship permits children, adults, and nations to grow, and reduces conflict. "Given [*as a child*] a climate of respect and freedom in which he is valued as a person, the mature individual would tend to choose and prefer these same value directions" (Rogers, 1964, p. 166).

Authoritarian parents, on the other hand, believe in keeping the child in his place. They give orders without explanations, dominate, and make all the decisions. Discipline may be strict and harsh. The child's behavior is frequently subjected to adverse judgment and debasing evaluations, and seldom to favorable, encouraging evaluations. There is little support and acceptance of the child as an individual. Authoritarian child-rearing techniques primarily satisfy parental needs for control. Self-expression necessary for the achievement of a growing child's identity and self-fulfillment is apt to be much restricted. "Authoritarianism is great training for children who will live under dictatorship, but far from adequate for children who will be expected to think independently" (Briggs, 1970, p. 237). Gordon gives us an account of what he regards as the existing situation today:

> While the authoritarian method of conflict resolution is rapidly losing ground in labor-management relations, in boss-subordinate relations, in relations between husbands and wives, and even in relations between nations, the parent-child relation is one of the last strongholds for the advocacy of power to settle conflicts. The teacher-student relationship is one other that has steadfastly resisted change. . . . The idea of not using power in the parent-child relationship comes as a real shock to parents. . . . It provokes initial resistance because it threatens one of the oldest and most sacred beliefs in our society, namely, that parents must exercise their authority over their children. [1970, *a*, p. 420.]

Of course parents must exercise some authority, but it need not and should not be exercised continuously, without consultation and without respect.

We can study ourselves to see what authoritarian and democratic traits we possess. In the following lists are characteristics that most commonly differentiate democratic from authoritarian parents. These are presented together with the traits most likely to be found in the personalities of the children from such homes. Keep in mind, of course, that few homes can be characterized as entirely authoritarian or entirely democratic. Every family is a combination of democratic and authoritarian traits, but with the emphasis on one or the other. Each child's personality develops along the lines of the unique combination that exists in his particular environment.

Authoritarian parents often appear:

Low in expressions of warmth.
Inflexible, strict, and disciplinarian.

Inconsistent in their use of harsh and permissive discipline.
Demanding of respect and appreciation.
To expect children to do as they are told without question.
To spend less time with their children, especially father.
Not to consult children about family affairs.
To emphasize home restrictions and household
    responsibilities.
To highly value order, structure, and smooth functioning.
To stress early independence from parental care.
To more frequently judge, blame, and criticize.
High in aggression toward children; father most aggressive.
To punish child aggression toward themselves.
To permit and encourage aggression toward other children.
To avoid or deny the problems of children.
To describe their children as uncooperative or inconsiderate.
Punitive in their attitudes about sex.
Not to provide opportunities for intellectual stimulation.
To discourage verbal give and take.
In frequent discord with each other.
To live in an atmosphere of tension.
Low in emotional adjustment and sociability.
To have come from broken or rejecting homes.
To admire power and strength.
To be submissive to people with greater status than their own.
High in social conformity.
Delinquent or highly moralistic.

Their children are likely to be: overdependent, socially with-
drawn, noncompetitive or excessively competitive, neurotic,
sensitive, low in self-confidence, obedient, rigid, low in creativity and originality, high in inner hostility, more hostile and
aggressive outside the home, delinquent, more dependent upon
peers, frequently low in academic proficiency, resentful of
authority, low in ability to sustain interest and effort.

Democratic parents often appear:

Respectful, concerned, sympathetic.

Openly affectionate.

To have a warm and positive parent-child relationship.

To spend more time with their children, both father and mother.

Low in hostility, nonpunitive, flexible.

To model good behavior.

To accept child hostility toward themselves.

To use reasoning, example, and explanation rather than punishment to discipline.

To use encouragement and appreciation rather than punishment to encourage learning.

To accept slow growth of impulse control.

To have well-defined limits and rules of conduct.

Respectful of the child's individuality.

High in the amount of freedom they allow.

Open to a child's viewpoints.

To encourage decision-making, curiosity, and exploration.

To share ideas and activities with their children.

Nurturing in early infancy.

Not to force early independence.

To provide opportunities for creativity and intellectual growth.

High in reasonable aspirations and expectations for their children.

To provide emotional support for their children's problems.

High in emotional adjustment and self-esteem.

Better able to relate to each other, their children, and others.

To have come from calm, happy, and generally well-adjusted homes.

To be more highly educated.

Free in their verbal communication about sex.

Their children are likely to be: curious, expressive, self-reliant, self-confident, cooperative, friendly, happy, sociable, accelerated in schoolwork, high in spontaneity and originality, imaginative and creative, high in leadership ability, highly motivated, competitive, low in inner hostility, somewhat aggressive in the home, unprejudiced, democratic in their relations with others, nonconforming to a degree in thought and behavior, nondelinquent.

A POSITIVE SELF-IMAGE

A Child's Picture of Himself

By self-image we mean a child's picture of himself. As this picture takes shape so does his personality. It becomes gradually defined and molded as he repetitively evaluates himself and his capabilities from the clues parents and others give as they respond in a tender, indifferent, or angry way. Observing their reactions, he learns about himself and draws conclusions about his nature, often very sweeping conclusions. Following their expectations, he pursues certain goals and activities and abandons other prospects. Right or wrong, the values of others strongly tend to be accepted and regarded as his own. How he reacts toward the world is governed by the ways they have caused him to see himself—not necessarily how he, or the world, actually may be. What he believes about himself becomes more important than his real physical, social, emotional, or intellectual capabilities. Stated more simply: it's not so important what he is as what he thinks he is.

IT'S LIKE A PUZZLE

The labels, attitudes, and views that go into the making of our self-images are as numerous and varied as the intricate parts of a gigantic jigsaw puzzle. Each piece is a gift, sometimes received unwillingly, from friends, neighbors, and relatives. Piece by piece the parts are carefully fitted together. Ultimately we have what appears to be a complete self-picture. Nevertheless, like a puzzle, it remains a collection of pieces. Feelings evoked by frequent and intense criticism of even one of the pieces, such as disapproval of one's speech, forgetfulness, a thumb-sucking habit, restlessness, or dependency, reflect upon the total picture. At any point in time we may feel that one defective piece has turned our whole picture bad.

The early experiences that helped design our self-pictures are largely forgotten, though they continue throughout life to influence our behavior and thinking. Self-image, basically designed in the preschool years, is highly resistant to change. Nevertheless, some alterations do occur as over the years situations change and we continue to pile up successes and failures.

IT'S COMPLICATED

We rarely have a clear understanding of our own personalities. Broad and diverse concepts, some of which may be below our level of awareness, have gone into the making of our total self-picture:

Body image: Views about one's body (handsome, ugly, or plain; graceful or clumsy; strong or weak; tall, short, or medium).

Social image: Views about one's social adequacy (likable, unlikable, or partially likable; tactful or untactful; a leader or a follower; popular or unpopular).

Ability image: Views about one's ability to dance, sing, write, draw, read, tell stories, cook, sew, climb, run, swim, jump, play ball.

Intellectual image: Opinions about one's capacity to learn (remembers well or forgets easily, knows very little or a lot, catches on slowly or very quickly).

Personality image: Concepts of oneself as cheerful, self-confident, friendly, lovable, aggressive, negative, shy.

Character image: Concepts about one's integrity, loyalty, honesty, trustworthiness, morals, reliability, competence, perseverance.

Idealized image: Ideas about the kind of person one would like to be.

As parents, one of our goals should be to see that each child receives a range of *positive* experiences—intellectual, emotional, verbal, social, and motor—sufficient to ensure the development of a healthy self-picture. When success and pleasure experiences outnumber or have greater impact than our unavoidable negative experiences, an emotionally healthy and self-confident person is more likely to emerge.

An overabundance of unpleasant experiences causes a child to view himself and his world negatively. He may withdraw from human contacts. As Kelly (1962) notes, he denies himself the social communication that would help him learn to feel like an adequate and significant individual. Living out his life according to the dictates of his self-image, his expectations are likely to be confirmed.

IT BEGINS AT HOME

Society will find it increasingly difficult to deny that a child's personality is largely shaped at home. Psychologists are well aware of this fact. Parents are not yet fully convinced. It's not easy to understand how our own learned attitudes, opinions, and preferences, colored by the way others reacted to us in childhood, govern the ways in which we respond to our own children, thus shaping their reactions to themselves. While genetic factors have some effect in that they set limits upon a child's capacity for growth, the family enhances or damages his opportunity to make full use of his potential.

"It is not true that heredity is responsible for maladjustment, delinquency, or poor character. Those things are the products of learning and experience" (Bernhardt, 1970, p. 5). Approval and disapproval determine which personality traits are encouraged or discouraged. Personality is greatly influenced by the way parents and others respond to:

Inherited temperament, activity level, responsiveness, passivity, physical appearance, intelligence, artistic ability, mechanical dexterity, motor ability.
Abnormal body shape, biological impairment, state of health.
Rates of physical, emotional, or intellectual maturation.
Even the fact that the child exists.

The living conditions in the home also have an effect, as well as the social and cultural conditions of the school and community, but not as great an effect as the quality of his early "human" relationships.

While a child is born with certain physiological tendencies, these need not become problems to him. The extent to which they are rewarded or punished, and the other ways in which they are responded to, influence the degree to which they become fixed. For instance, the quiet, passive child who is ignored may become more passive and quiet. The aggressive, hyperactive child who arouses frequent parental anger may show an increase in these tendencies. Intellectual and physical abilities remain underdeveloped or are accelerated by the absence or addition of parental interests. With correct family attitudes, a handicap can become an asset. When we help the child keep the door of his self-concept open, he continues to seek new experiences, discovering more about himself and finding greater self-fulfillment.

Informed parents control their reactions, reassured by the knowledge that they can shape development through experiences tailored to an understanding of their child's potential. They give attention to the passive child when he joins activities, speak to him whether he speaks or not, and engage him in conversation whenever possible. They provide sufficient outlets for the energy of the high-activity child, restraining much of their own frustration. They provide numerous opportunities for physical and intellectual development.

Children give us glimpses as to how these multiple self-images are taking shape in the reflections they occasionally make about themselves. Note how various preschoolers disclose their self-feelings:

POSITIVE	NEGATIVE
See me ride my scooter.	I might fall.
My mommy loves me.	I'm always making mommy mad.
Let's draw pictures.	I don't draw very well.
I eat lots of things.	I don't like to eat.
See the pretty flower on my slip.	I don't want you to see my slip.
I can write my name.	I don't know how to write my name.
My daddy says I'm pretty.	I'm too skinny.
Let's play dolls.	Your doll is prettier than mine.
My mother says I'm a good girl.	I'm bad.
I helped mommy set the table.	I get in mommy's way.

A child isn't born with such self-perceptions. They evolve from his everyday personal experiences. Although others may be less than perfect as judges, he has no effective alternative. He himself is even less qualified as a source of reference. The things that parents and older brothers and sisters say about him, he seems compelled to accept as an accurate picture of himself.

IT'S DIFFICULT TO CHANGE

Influenced first by the way in which others respond to him and later by his own observations about his various competencies, the preschooler paints his self-portrait at a time when he is far from able to look at himself objectively. Although his portrait may contain marked distortions, this fact is seldom evident to him. Regardless of its lack of authenticity, once constructed, it resists alteration.

His relationship with others then begins to follow a circular pattern:

The opinions he holds about himself he believes to be identical with those of others—perhaps because they were earlier supplied by persons of apparent authority and wisdom.

He uses his self-image as a guide for his behavior.

Thus influenced, he acts out his self-picture, increasing the possibilities that its reality will be verified (whether originally right or not).

Thereafter, he has difficulty comprehending that others might see him differently from the way in which he sees himself. His self-portrait, designed largely to the specifications of other persons in his early environment, persons upon whom he had to depend, becomes the pattern for himself and his actions and thereby becomes self-fulfilling:

If he believes himself a poor reader, he will tend to avoid reading and thereby will become a poor reader.

If he believes himself socially inadequate, he will avoid social situations or feel awkward in them and self-conscious, thereby becoming more inept socially than he otherwise would be.

If he believes himself impossible to manage, he will behave
that way.

Although conditions in his life may change and he may sense
himself better than his self-picture dictates, he will tend to
continue acting out the design as he first perceived it to be. This
can be tragic.

In physical size he may grow without obvious handicap, but
not so in other ways. His intellectual competence and his emotional maturity lag or move forward to the degree that his environment is stimulating and favorable, and only to the extent
that he sees himself capable. At a most inopportune time, he
makes long-lasting, inelastic decisions about himself. While
struggling with a world where doorknobs and tabletops appear
above his head and where privileges belong mainly to grown-
ups, he's not at all well-equipped to make such important judgments about himself. "While still unskilled in reasoning, unprac-
ticed in evaluating other people's judgment, inexperienced in all
aspects of living, unable to go outside his family to any great
degree, he builds his self-image on what his family and a few
friends and neighbors say and do. He lays the foundation for his
life" (Voeks, 1973). Without the aid of protecting, praising, accepting, and loving parents, a child has little opportunity to
develop an effective image of his best potential for use in an
expanding future. To see his potentialities and understand his
limitations, he must have someone who has faith in him—faith
in his ability to learn and grow.

How a Positive Self-Picture Is Formed

When a child grows up in a democratic home with genuinely
affectionate, usually approving, and understandingly responsive
parents, he accumulates many positive self-images—important
equipment for later social adjustment and enjoyment of life.

Respecting himself, he holds few doubts that others could feel differently. He respects others and values them. He's happy, with energy readily available for creativity, initiative, and leadership. Without a need for energy to defend himself against fear of losing the love and protection of others, he is free to direct his personal resources toward the infinitely greater satisfaction of self-fulfillment and outgoing interaction with others.

BELITTLEMENT IS NOT OF SIGNIFICANCE IN HIS LIFE

The result is that he does not expect rebuke for his child-like behavior, and is not much distressed by the few occasions on which he is rebuked. A five-year-old who has not heard "Shame on you" doesn't know what grandfather is talking about. Of course, an insensitive society may teach him in time but seldom with the impact of parental attitudes and expressions. With a warmly rewarding homelife, the insults of society can be placed in proper perspective. He can more effectively cope with stress and frustration. A happy, self-confident child can accept significantly more damaging statements about himself than a less well-adjusted child (Taylor and Combs, 1952; Erikson, 1963).

When parents and older siblings speak with courtesy and respect, the preschooler achieves a more realistic concept of his worth. He does not need to look outside himself and search exhaustively for proof of personal esteem. He knows that he is valued and is not excessively preoccupied with the comments of those outside the family.

NEW LEARNING IS INTRODUCED GRADUALLY

When necessary, it is encouraged through creative games and activities planned by a patient and understanding parent. The child is not pressured into unrealistic food expectancies, new clothing, unfailingly regular naptimes, stringent health habits, lengthy separations from mother, or the giving up of highly prized security symbols. Nor is he left to flounder with no rules and no expectations.

Natural curiosity, the desire to learn about the world, and delight in developing skill are enhanced in an environment free of unnecessary rules and restrictions not directly concerned with health, safety, or welfare. Frequent parental reassurance and warm approval of his progress in work and play have stimulated pride in achievement and its resultant positive self-image. He is spoken to and encouraged to learn, in most situations, with the respect and value that only a small best friend should receive.

HE IS TREATED AS A FRIEND

Children and parents whose lives together form a partnership in growing up are friends. They share plans and aspirations, celebrate special occasions, go on excursions together, plan surprises for each other, play together, work together, and sometimes disagree together. Parental leadership is expected, although it may not always be respected. When a child's hostility or immature impulses get beyond his control, parents step in, and, more often than not, help him set limits without expressing strong counteranger of their own. His tears, rebellion, and anger are for the most part met with consideration rather than annoyance. Although the parents are sometimes disappointed, they continue to believe and trust in their child's basic desire to want to live acceptably. The child accepts his parents' faith and realistic expectations as reality and performs accordingly.

How You Can Help Your Child Develop a Positive Self-Image

Speak to him with the same courtesy you would give to an adult friend.

Offer him assistance, love, and companionship without his
having always to seek them out.

Be cheerful, even though cheerfulness may not be returned.

Give ten or more minutes of your time daily for
communication with your child.

Praise accomplishments and even partial success. No matter
how small they seem to you, they may seem big to him.

Express sympathy for what he feels are his needs (real or
imagined).

Withdraw from provocation. Respond to his cooperation.

Refrain from speaking harshly. A polite request will
accomplish more, or even a quiet, confident command.

When upset, describe *your* feelings, not *his* behavior. If you
must describe his behavior, do so objectively and without
exasperation.

Accept his opposition. Resist your need to return the hurt. He
is not your equal.

When you feel like exploding, take a long walk. It is not wise
to unload full adult verbal or physical anger upon a child.

Following a disagreement, make up immediately. Do not
allow unrelieved feelings of guilt, anger, and rejection to
burden a child's mind or yours.

Be able to apologize, even to a child, when you are wrong.

Have faith that your child wants to do the right thing whether
he does the right thing or not.

Look beneath surface behavior to understand his anger,
distress, or hostility; then help him find different outlets
and different ways to respond.

Remove him from things you don't want him to do if he
persists in doing them. Accept the fact that you cannot
force him to do that which he has set his mind to oppose.

Accept slow and wavering progress.

Tolerate mistakes in learning.

Provide opportunities for learning.

Remember his special likes and dislikes, albeit they may be temporary.

Do things *with* your child, not just *for* him.

How Negative Self-Pictures Take Shape

"The mood of a lifetime is set in the forgotten events of childhood" (Crile, 1969, p. 13). A cook can always start from scratch if an ingredient is left out of a recipe. But a parent can only hope to modify what already exists.

Described here are some ways negative self-images come into being. Knowing them can help you prevent this problem for your child.

LACK OF THE RIGHT KIND OF ATTENTION

In homes where behavior mistakes are unhesitatingly pointed out while positive accomplishments remain ignored, a favorable sense of identity fails to develop. Knowing only what is "wrong" with oneself does not identify what is "right."

Throughout youth, a child seeks answers to the questions: "Who am I?" "Where am I going?" "What can I do well already?" "What can I learn to do well?" The family that offers little praise and affection or opportunity for creative expression deprives its children of a clear self-image with which to construct answers to such questions. Without a knowledge of who and what they are, people of any age encounter difficulty in social and other roles. Meaning and structure in life are difficult to find. Such children may later become the adults who feel they are playacting in life's relationships because they do not know their real capabilities.

A child growing up in an overly restrictive and punishing home learns to ridicule and perhaps even to despise himself and thereby becomes less open and free in self-expression. Frequent negative evaluation and rejection lead him to doubt his adequacy and worth. Believing that his opinions are not worth expressing, he is reluctant to tell others his views about any situation. Expecting failure, he lacks persistence and may only passively carry out his responsibilities at home and at school. Feeling unworthy and inadequate, he may see himself incapable of making even simple decisions about himself. Thus he turns to others and their standards in search of solutions to his problems. Lacking affection and recognition, he may be dominated by his need to prove his worth or at least his power to himself and others.

Self-fulfillment is neglected when too much time is devoted to worry about weaknesses. Without energy or inspiration for maximum learning, exploring, or creating, the child is shaped more by the pressures of his surroundings than by his own natural abilities. Such a person is described as being more suggestible, more responsive to directions from others, more dependent upon others (Mehrabian, 1968). Moreover, should he choose a companion who tends to be critical, deepened feelings of inadequacy and further regression can be expected.

PARENTAL POWER

Parents have enormous power in all areas of family life. Parents have also much more freedom than does the child. They have the "right" to:

Fly into a rage at the slightest provocation.
Judge the behavior of children and others.
Dominate and use forceful behavior with children.
Withhold privileges and issue orders.
Carry through on ideas and execute decisions.
Eat what and when they wish.
Be late for dinner.
Wear what they please.
Go to bed when they please.

Come home as late as they wish without bothering to phone.
Make mistakes, change their minds.
Leave a task unfinished.
Ignore almost anyone who's talking to them.
Organize the home around adult needs.

Children, in their relatively low-status position, are almost completely dependent upon us for their survival, for the satisfaction of many needs, and for information about themselves. The extent to which we use our power has much to do with their future ability to feel capable and competent. A certain amount of "letting alone" gives them opportunities to learn. Let them make decisions on insignificant matters, even when they sometimes inconvenience us. If Billy wants to leave his unfinished puzzle on the kitchen table, have a picnic dinner in the living room for one night. Though you may not agree, respect his opinions. Acknowledge his feelings. A truly meaningful and effective relationship with other adults could not be maintained without such arrangements, yet we seldom provide them in the home environment.

NEGATIVE PARENTAL EXPECTANCIES

Much of what a child becomes rests upon a foundation of parental expectancy. A child tends to confirm expectations that he will do well or that he will fail. We give him the labels he uses to learn about himself. Behavior is strengthened by recognition. If reminded of his shortcomings often enough, the unusual laugh, shyness, whining, odd-ball clowning, hostility, or other irritating behaviors become part of his self-image and, thereafter, are resistant to change. Without parental faith and acceptance as he is, a child is not free to fulfill his real personality.

Through "always" and "never" we show our negative expectations. You may have noticed in yourself a tendency to use "always" and "never" in describing certain of your child's behaviors, especially unwanted behaviors. Although behavior is usually relatively consistent, it's seldom invariable. Fixed, vivid descriptions of a child's personal habits encourage him to continue acting out those habits as pictured. The descriptions, of course, are practically never true.

You are *always* grabbing things.
You are *always* making a mess.
You are *always* picking on your sister.
You are *always* making trouble.
You'll *never* learn to keep your distance.
You *never* listen to me.
You *never* make your bed.
You *never* let me finish what I am saying.

Why not try instructions? They do not give a child labels to act out, and they clarify one's positive, affirmative expectations.

Tell me what you want and I will try to get it for you.
Put your glass here and it won't be knocked over so easily.
Tell your sister what it is that you don't like.
Out with you for now if you are going to do that.
Come here and watch TV beside me. Then Paul's feet won't bother you.
Repeat the instructions I gave you. . . . Good, you have it all right.
You can't leave until your bed is made.
Excuse me. Both of us can't talk at the same time.

Comments about future behavior show our expectancies. Have you noticed your child's anger and resentment when you describe what he is likely to do wrong? Negative expectations damage his feelings of self-worth, triggering anger. He feels ashamed when he cannot measure up. The persistence of his behavior is not so obvious to him as to you.

Sometimes our surface statements are all right, but beneath

the surface is a damaging negative expectation (shown in italics in the examples below):

> Let me help you wrap that present. *You'll just get angry and tear up more paper.*
> Put the package on the table *before you make a mess of the ribbon again.*
> OK, we'll buy the guitar. *Of course you probably won't practice after we've spent all that money.*
> I'm glad we were able to get your new bicycle. *Don't get mad now about having to wear a safety helmet.*
> OK, I'll fix your hair. *Don't start screaming at me again.*
> All right, you may wear the dress. *I suppose you'll get it dirty as usual.*
> OK, you may go shopping with me. *But don't yell for something in every store we go into.*
> You do it this way. *How many times do I have to tell you?*
> See, you did all right on your test. *All that moping around wasn't necessary.*
> I'm glad to see you doing your homework. *It took you long enough to get started.*

Although it's difficult not to mention the troublesome behavior we resent, such expressions do not stop the behavior. They seem to make it more probable. "Children do not like to hear that their behavior has caused a problem for parents" (Gordon, 1970, b, p. 119). The feelings of reduced self-esteem they stimulate add anger to the problem, creating a circular hostility between parent and child. While most of us accept the fact that it is best not to describe another adult's behavior to him, experience has not taught us similar caution where children are concerned. Our own rearing "to be polite" guides much of our contact with other adults but is often forgotten in our conduct at home. Unaware of how much resentment we have, we may even be puzzled when a child returns the hostility.

What, then, can we do about behavior we do not like? For one thing, we can have patience. The expected unpleasant thing does not always happen. Arrange matters so that it is as unlikely to happen as possible. When it does occur, correct the problem then. Finally, if you must comment, it is usually better to describe your feelings than to describe his behavior, and better to give positive suggestions rather than negative ones. Say in a quiet voice, "That makes me uncomfortable" rather than "Stop whining like a baby."

Warnings and dares show our negative expectations. They dramatically point out our lack of confidence in a child's desire to be cooperative. Pride and resistance are aroused in the strong-willed child. You might just as well draw a line and dare him to step over it. Few parents carry out such threats as the following, but many find themselves making them. As Rousseau suggested as early as 1762, "It is enough to prevent him from wrongdoing without forbidding him to do wrong" (1967, p. 369). Don't say:

> If you can't use good manners, don't come to the table.
> If you do that once more, I'll have to punish you.
> I'm warning you. If you pull up any more flowers, it will be the last time.
> Don't you dare slam that door.
> Stop that crying this instant, or else.
> Don't you dare ride your bicycle in the street again.

Behavior is more easily shaped by a statement of the kind of conduct we would prefer him to use. Do say:

> I'd like it better if you closed your mouth while you eat.
> This is the way you are supposed to sit in a chair.
> I don't want you to pull up the flowers. Let's talk about why it's better to leave them in the ground.
> I'd appreciate your shutting the door more gently.
> Tell me what the problem is in a quiet voice.

> Our rule is final. Under no conditions can you ride your
>   bike in the street. It is too dangerous. You are very
>   important to us. We only have one you.

Thus he is not judged before he can show control over his own behavior and impulses. He's more self-directed to improvement without warnings and dares which notify him that we expect more trouble. Removal is always a final recourse if stronger emphasis is necessary. Where health and safety are concerned, the withdrawal of a privilege is also sensible.

Protect your child's feeling of self-worth. Trust that thoughtfully worded suggestions, helpful experiences, and your own example ultimately will influence him to effective behavior.

When delivering your child to the home of a friend listen to what you usually say. Comments at such times may appear to be mere formality to parents endeavoring to give notice of their good intentions to the host. To the child, they may be a source of embarrassment:

> Be a good girl.
> Behave yourself while I am away.
> I'm going to ask Mrs. Allen if you were good.
> Remember your manners.
> Don't be naughty.
> Mind Mrs. Jones and do exactly as she tells you.

You may not really doubt the persistence of your child's good behavior, but wouldn't it be better to say, "Have a good time. I'll be back soon"?

NEGATIVE SIBLING EXPECTANCIES

Older brothers and sisters find great sport, and sometimes relief from jealousy, in expressing resentful expectancies to younger family members:

> He's always interrupting.
> All she does is cry like a baby.
> She doesn't know how to sing.

She can't carry that cake.
He will cut himself.
He won't share anything.
She can't help it. She's stupid.

By setting an appropriate example and giving encouragement along positive lines, you can avoid labeling or raising doubts about the capabilities of a child. For example:

Wait until I'm finished talking and then I'll listen to what you
    have to say.
Tell me why you feel sad.
I like the way you make up your own songs.
Let me help you carry your birthday cake.
I'll show you how to cut it.
I know it's yours, but you loaned it to Dave. Give him
    another ten minutes.
That's quite a mess, isn't it? I'll help you clean it up.

NEGATIVE VOICE TONES

Most people are aware of the words they speak but not of the messages their voice tones send out. Such signals often relay a story different from the words. The child hears not only what we say but the way we say it, and much about our deeper feelings comes through to him. He is quite difficult to deceive. Being less sensitive, parents sometimes claim ignorance when a child reacts with tears or anger to the negative inflection he observes. "What are you crying about?" we ask. While most parents recognize that tone, inflection, and emphasis can be more punishing than words, we nevertheless seem unaware of the indifference, hostility, and resentment we express to children. With a simple question we may suggest a child's incompetence: "What's *wrong* with you?" or "What are you doing *that* for?" The tone of a single "no" can express respect or a whole battery of resentments. Words of approval may not convey approval: "My, but you're a cheerful one today" or "You're a sweet little devil." With a lukewarm response, we can squelch his enthusiasm.

The contradictory messages in our voice tones are a more frequent cause of everyday family conflict than is realized. It's not the limits we are setting for children that turn them away. It's the ways in which we verbally humiliate them.

Each parent's effect is somewhat different. A friendly parent may rant and rave without there being any real rejection, and without any rejection seeming to come through, while the disparaging or demeaning inflections in the quiet tones of a more autocratic parent may cut deeply.

In early childhood, angry voice tones from a familiar mother are sometimes better tolerated than from the less familiar father. Mother has a built-up reserve of goodwill upon which she can trade, and more time to rebuild lost rapport.

Even before a child understands the meanings of words, he responds to the messages of our voice tones. Soft, friendly tones of the human voice have produced signs of pleasure from earliest infancy. The sound of mother's voice is sufficient to quiet a baby's cries. Tough, harsh tones are responded to with observable displeasure.

As a child becomes more self-sufficient, parents become less concerned about how they respond. They may not guard against undertones of retaliation and revenge. What does a young child learn and feel when spoken to in a domineering way?

See what you made me do!
You can't speak to me that way!
Don't you dare interrupt me!
Don't talk to me in that tone of voice!

How can we teach politeness when we are being impolite ourselves? Most of us do not usually communicate with other adults in this manner. Why not apply similar standards of politeness to children?

That's all right. It was an accident. Let's clean it up.
I'd like it better if you asked me kindly.
When you want to tell me something while I'm busy with
guests, give me a signal.
You sound a bit angry. What's the problem?

NEGATIVE FACIAL EXPRESSIONS AND BODY MOVEMENTS

Children attach meaning to all kinds of nonverbal cues. From earliest infancy they look to parents' eyes and facial expressions for clues about the meanings of their experiences. A single glance can quiet doubts, fears, and insecurities. Not only are love and security visible there, but so too are resentments. The frown of disapproval, the cold look, the forced smile, the taut expression—these are a few of the ways we communicate negative feeling.

Body movements and gestures also communicate negative messages: the angry walk, the turned back, the shrug, snapping the fingers, shaking your head, and threatening hand movements are among the more obvious. Even the posture one takes when communicating affects another's response. Remaining relaxed when a child defies you may gain cooperation; whereas a tense, defensive posture may increase conflict. Negative feelings, discouragement, exasperation, disappointment, resentment, rage, lack of interest, indignation, or merely toleration can be expressed without a word being spoken. Unspoken abuse is difficult to understand and put into words. It makes a child more insecure than openly verbalized anger.

It's not easy to see ourselves objectively. We often are unaware of the hidden messages coming through or of the consistency of our acts from day to day. Surprisingly little is known about how people really communicate—about the signs and signals received as we observe the gestures, facial expressions, body movements, and speech of others. There is much yet to learn, if, as Mehrabian (1968) suggests, less than 10 percent of our messages come through in words.

PARENTS' BODY ATTITUDES

Long before a child can speak the names of specific body parts, he learns from slaps and warnings that some parts are off limits. When he's older, he learns that he can only investigate in secret and at the risk of punishment or shaming.

By school age, a child has numerous perceptions about his physical appearance. He may see his ears as big, his feet flat, or his body too skinny. He may see his nose as straight and handsome, his hair attractive. Seldom are his conclusions self-constructed. He hears various aspects of himself being described in family conversation before he constructs such concepts of his own. This is a matter that requires our attention.

A healthy body image cannot easily develop without planning and attention. The following help the child develop healthy views about his body:

Provide early athletic training, formal or informal. It improves opportunities for more accurate perceptions about his body and its capabilities.

Use the correct names for all parts of the body. When bathing, wash all parts of the infant's body without more attention, concern, or hesitation toward one part than toward another.

Don't express aversion to the sight or smell of body waste. Your repulsion may reflect on the body that involuntarily produced it.

When a child comments about his less attractive features, help him see beyond the limits of his own perspective. Tell him:

> You have many attractive features. I haven't really noticed whether your ears are big or not. It really doesn't matter. I like you because you are you. I wouldn't want to change one part of you.

Some children grow tall faster than others. When you are
grown, many of your friends will have caught up with
you. Some people grow taller than others. There's no
reason we should all be alike. *Or,* I think it is great we
are not all alike.

I think big feet are nice. They give a lot more support for
running and walking.

You are handsome from the top of your head to the tip of
your toes.

Let preschool children learn about their physical differences
from each other, as they go about their daily activities of
bathing and using the bathroom.

Should you find several children engaged in undressing
games, give them something else to do without excessive
comment. Such behavior is merely normal curiosity.

Don't express concern about masturbation. When not
excessive, it is a sign of maturation. Tell him, "Children
enjoy that at times, but it's something you do in private."

Don't regularly remind your preschool daughter to keep her
dress down. Put well-fitting underclothing on her and
ignore her "unladylike" behavior. When she's older, show
her how a lady sits.

Don't be overconcerned when your very young preschooler
takes off down the street without his clothes. Retrieve
him and explain, "Clothing protects you from hurts and
scratches. It helps to keep you warm."

When children want to take baths with their parents, simply
say, "Adults take baths by themselves." Children and
parents do not look alike. Body hair and the size alone of
the penis or breast in the adult can be frightening and
difficult to forget.

CRITICAL COMPARISONS

Inferiority feelings rest upon unfavorable comparisons that
start in childhood. Most children accept and even respect their

siblings' obvious strengths and weaknesses to the extent that they are accepted by parents and others. It's when disparaging comparisons are drawn in the presence of children that they are apt to adopt similar prejudices. They are likely to react to each other not from the basis of childlike standards but in accord with the views of the parent. For example, such comments as the following may brand a child:

See how nice Johnny behaves.
You don't see Patricia acting that way.
Why can't you keep your hair as neat as your brother?
Dorothy knows how to dress better than you do.
Mrs. Brown doesn't have this trouble with Tom.
Your sister has her lessons done. Why don't you?
Bob knows how to get good grades. He has the brains in the
    family.
Tom isn't shy the way you are.
You're acting just like that brat, Roger.
Billy is more athletic than you.

Children want to be loved for themselves alone, not because of their similarity to someone else. They have a right to be different, to be as they are, without having to be better than another in order to feel acceptable.

Love must not depend upon how handsome, well-groomed, scholastically successful, responsible, industrious, polite, popular, or well-behaved he may be, nor upon any other single quality. The ability to accept your child as he is depends to a degree upon your ability to accept yourself as you are. An established principle of behavior asserts that persons have difficulty tolerating in others traits they find unacceptable in themselves.

Faced with frequent disapproval and comparison, a child grows up believing that others are more adequate, more competent, and more effective than himself. Should he excel, he may fail to recognize his own achievements as such.

PRAISE AND APPROVAL

IT'S NEGLECTED

Parents react more frequently to oppositional behavior than to good behavior. Stolz (1967) asked parents to describe interaction with their children. Although not completely unresponsive to good behavior, three-fourths of their recollections dealt with behavior they would like to change. Punishments were noted four or five times as often as were love, praise, and attention. Parents relied heavily on control and obedience. Little emphasis was placed on the use of affection, verbal reward, or parental example to encourage desirable behavior. Good behavior was taken for granted. When a child behaved "properly," parents often perceived it as obedience rather than the result of specific learning.

THE VALUES OF PRAISE

These values appear largely unknown to parents. Many have not learned the importance of minimizing undesirable behavior by concentrating on appreciating good behavior. Praise has numerous advantages:

Praise strengthens learning. When praise follows the completion of a performance, it increases chances that similar behavior will be repeated. Research has frequently shown that mere repetition is not automatically strengthening. Practice alone does not necessarily make perfect. Children especially need frequent verbal approval until a habit is well-established. Once a response has been developed, the learned behavior often becomes self-rewarding.

Praise shapes and clarifies reality. Accurately assessing one's own traits poses a problem. Judgment, intellect, physical attractiveness, personality, femininity, and masculinity need the feedback of information from others. When parents realistically impart this information, the child's view of himself is clarified and enriched. In addition, their confidence fosters the child's confidence.

Praise adds meaning to what a child is doing. Tasks take on new values when his competencies in accomplishing them are pointed out. Writing the letters of the alphabet is mere routine until mother points out how nice and round his circles are or how well he makes the letter *b*. Cleaning the bathroom is more fun when dad expresses his satisfaction in the faucets, which shine like new.

Learning becomes pleasant and satisfying when the pleasure and the pride of the parent are easily observable. Pleasing the significant people in the child's life increases his interest in learning and possibly his later enjoyment in an accomplishment for its own sake. Research on achievement indicates that mothers who reward achievement efforts and anticipate success have children who display a high degree of achievement motivation. Skill and performance are enhanced when correct responses are rewarded by social approval (Rosen and D'Andrade, 1959; Crandall, Preston, and Rabson, 1960; Stevenson, 1965; Bower, 1966).

Children are not alone in their need for reinforcement. Parents also are motivated by a need for approval from others. We buy new clothes, clean house, redecorate, entertain friends, go to college, and seek prestige jobs not merely for our own pleasure but for social approval as well.

Praise encourages esteem for oneself. Before a child can feel free to give love, he must first feel love for himself. Your expressions of love and approval give him feelings of "all rightness" about himself. Being loved, he can give love in return.

Praise need not be reserved for a perfect performance. Psychologists have demonstrated the effectiveness of rewarding even approximations of a correct act. Progress as well as achievement should be recognized. Mistakes, on the other hand, can stand a great deal more ignoring than most parents realize.

Praise that is deserved never spoils anyone. Earlier generations believed that praise would make children conceited or self-centered. They did not know that conceit or self-centeredness is more the result of insecurity and lack of confidence. The happy, self-confident child does not need to toot his own horn. He reacts naturally, considerately, and warmly to others.

Parents usually don't have the time to give too much praise. The average child would benefit from substantially more parental approval than is ordinarily available to him. He needs to be frequently told that he has done well. It's our approval that helps him learn to measure his worth as an individual. How much he needs that attention may be observed in the frequency of his requests for attention. Lee says that a child is not showing off or demanding attention when he behaves this way, but that he is intoxicated with the excitement of his new-found skill: "He wants to show us all the time what he can do. 'Hear me read this,' 'Look, I've got down to here now,' 'Watch me do this. . . .' We must not snub him now—when he needs our praise, admiration, and encouragement" (1969, p. 119). He wants to share his pleasure with us. Our joy gives him joy. Our praise and admiration give him the courage to keep trying.

Parents sometimes report a reluctance to praise one child for fear that another will feel rivalry. Concern of this sort is unnecessary if each receives his own reward when it is due. When parents easily and freely acknowledge learning and accomplishment, each child knows his turn will come. If it is difficult to find things to praise, make a list of the things he can do well.

CONDITIONS THAT LIMIT THE EFFECTIVENESS OF PRAISE

Seldom is praise unsuccessful as a means of guiding behavior. When its efficiency is reduced or a parent is rebuffed, one of the following may be responsible:

Lack of democracy. Dictatorial and demeaning child-rearing methods diminish the usefulness of praise. Cooperation is most encouraged by a companionable and trusting relationship. A child works hard for the praise of a parent who is his friend.

Judgmental praise. Praise that describes his character—"You are a good boy"—is fine occasionally. However, it is less effective than praise that tells him what it is you like about that which he has just accomplished. For example: "Your setting the table was a big help. Now I can have dinner ready on time."

Public praise. Many children are reluctant to be put on display. They may feel self-conscious if praised in front of guests or in public. The child may feel too that the parent is trying to impress the visitors with what a good parent he is, how kind and understanding he is, or in some other way trying to make points with the guests rather than trying to encourage and support the child. This is especially apt to happen if the child is seldom praised in private or only praised in public.

Excessive praise. Frequent and repetitive praise that dwells always on the same subject may make a child self-conscious. It becomes uncomfortable rather than rewarding. While too little reward slows learning, intermittently rewarded behavior often persists longer than behavior that receives continuous reinforcement.

Your feelings of the moment. Half-hearted praise is apt to be experienced as rejection rather than regard. And praise given in such a way as to imply that a child's behavior is astounding, unexpected, or unusual can seem more like reproof than regard.

Inappropriate focus. For example, a child has been in a recital; afterward, the parent bubbles on about how pretty her dress is and says nothing about her singing. Frequently praising for little things and seldom or never commenting on the big accomplishments confuses children.

Manipulative praise. The effectiveness of praise is diminished when parents use it to get something out of the person or child rather than to express appreciation or delight. Praise, like love, should be a gift.

Insincere praise. There is a difference between flattery and compliments. Children are very sensitive to hypocrisy. They can also sense when praise is cold and grudgingly offered, lacking in warmth and delight.

A child's other problems. Praise given to a "problem child" who seldom receives it or to a child who momentarily is feeling unworthy may have a discouraging rather than a rewarding effect. The child may misbehave to prove your mistake. For instance, praise for kindness toward a brother or sister he ordinarily resents may be met with hostility. He may refrain from further kindness in order to prevent what he feels is unwarranted praise.

YOU CAN LEARN TO GIVE PRAISE

Express love and tenderness when a child deserves your appreciation. Communication of such feelings while a child is small makes learning less difficult and more enjoyable. Speak as you would to a friend. Let him know that you like it and are happy when he displays consideration for others, when he carries out a task or does good work. Be aware that he often feels rewarded with a response as simple as a warm smile.

If, as a result of your own rearing, you feel reluctant to praise, take courage from the fact that expressing approval and delight becomes easier as your own perspectives enlarge and you begin to "discover" your child. The positive images he accumulates from your approval build in him an expectancy that future experiences will be pleasant and productive. His resulting sense of personal worth, combined with a realistic acceptance of his lack of perfection, contributes to the confidence with which he will seek enjoyment in the realization of his potentialities.

It is not difficult to find things to praise when you are looking for them. The everyday activities of a preschooler are filled with attempts to learn. Don't fail to compliment him just because you think he should have been doing something long ago. As a way of guiding interest and creativity, words of encouragement prove far superior to saying nothing. The following examples may guide you in what to say when encouraging your child to repeat certain behaviors, to go on trying, or merely to build his self-confidence.

WHAT TO SAY:

Encouraging self-reliance.

> How well you cleaned your room all by yourself! Doesn't it look pretty?
> It makes me feel good to know that you can fix your own lunch.
> You walked to Andy's house all alone today!
> What a fine job you did tying your shoes!
> It was hard to get those pieces to fit together, but you did it!
> You got dressed all by yourself this morning. That's really grown up!
> You read that story very well!

Rewarding control of aggression.

> That was very polite and kind the way you gave Larry some blocks when he tried to take yours away.
> Thank you for your directness in telling me how you felt. I did not realize I had spoken so abruptly.

I like the way you explained to Leonard that he must wait
until you are finished with the scooter.
How patient you were with little sister when she was
unhappy.
When Billy was angry, you were right to remind him that you
didn't step on his toe on purpose.
I was pleased at how politely you explained to Davy that you
didn't like his writing in your book.
Your explanation helps Bill learn how his behavior looks to
others.

Appreciating helpfulness and responsibility.

You saved my day! Without your help, I would not have been
ready when the company arrived.
It's a big help when you run errands for me.
How well you made your bed! You're learning all sorts of
new skills!
Your toy shelf looks perfect! The whole room looks better
when things are put away neatly!
I like the neat way you hung up your towel and washcloth.
You worked hard on that book review. You are learning some
important things.
Your helpfulness makes getting dinner very pleasant.
I'm proud of the way you keep right on trying. It shows real
initiative and perseverance.
That was a man-sized job. You worked hard.
How attractively you arranged the flowers. It's a beautiful
bouquet and makes the whole room prettier.
I'm pleased at all the interesting plans you've made for your
party.

Rewarding thoughtfulness and generosity.

It made Tommy feel better when you helped him fix his boat.
It was polite to serve your friend his dessert first.

I liked the courteous way you asked Patty for the wagon.

You were very kind and thoughtful the way you made
grandmother feel comfortable.

You took turns with George very well.

It was good of you to help Sally to the school nurse when she
was hurt.

Thank you for remembering to spend some time with auntie.
She was happy.

It's nice to have your help putting the dishes away.

Rewarding self-expression and sociability.

You explained the problem to Janie very well, so clearly and
simply.

I was pleased at how well you introduced the guests when
they arrived.

That's quite a grown-up word you used. You're developing
an excellent vocabulary.

I like to hear about the things that happen at school. Thank
you for telling me about them.

I agree. That was a funny story.

Sing me that cute song again.

That was a nice smile you gave grandmother. It made her
feel warm and loved.

Dad and I enjoyed hearing your speech. It was interesting
and clearly presented.

Bob would be interested in hearing about your experience
this afternoon.

How well you entertain your little friends when they come to
play! You make them feel very welcome and happy.

Letting him know he looks good.

How elegant you look in your blue shirt.

I'm proud of my handsome young man.

How beautiful and shiny your hair looks when you brush it
    well.
How handsome you look in your new suit.
Red is just your color.
You look good even with mustard on your chin.
Where did you get that beautiful smile?
Did you know—you are quite a distinguished-looking young
    man!
I enjoy those bright shining eyes.
That's a good-looking set of muscles you are developing.

Letting him know you like him.

Son, you're quite a guy! I feel so lucky to have you in my
    world.
How's my good friend?
Hi, glad to see you back.
Sorry to hear you aren't feeling well.
It's nice to have dinner out with my son.
I'm glad you had a good time at the party.
Come let me cuddle you while we watch TV.
It's a pleasure to have your company while I'm fixing dinner.
I enjoyed seeing all the things you've been doing at school.
Come along. I enjoy having you ride to the store with me.
I'm glad you're my girl.
We're going to have a lot of fun growing up together.

IN CONCLUSION

We have to be careful to not overdo phrases such as "I'm
pleased that . . ." For one thing, our pleasure should be apparent from our voices and expression as we commend him. The
words "I'm pleased" may only distract him from noticing the
really important dimensions of the situation, while he focuses
on the relatively trivial aspects of our pleasedness, likingness,
etc. We may even be encouraging him to conclude that there is

no point in the behavior unless others know about it. The most important aspect of the child's behavior in these instances is that he has made the world a neater, kinder, prettier, more courteous place in which to live and is getting the knack of new skills. This is what our words should indicate and stress. Not merely that we like it. The fact that "I like it" or "I am pleased" is an added dividend, not the real point of the behavior, and the most crucial dimension.

The idea here, in part, is to make exceedingly clear precisely what children are doing so well. In addition, there is an equally important, though more subtle, point. The idea is to cast them for a truly worthy role, a role that will use their best potentials, and to help them develop a clear self-concept that includes these valuable and valued dimensions. In the same way that adverse labels and derogatory descriptions can cause the child (or adult) to develop a debased self-image and regard himself as forever incompetent, so also can favorable labels and gracious descriptions cause the child (or adult) to develop a self-image that includes vividly his best capacities and abilities to grow and learn. He sees himself as a person who already has many assets and can develop lots more of them. This greatly facilitates his doing so (Voeks, 1973).

FREEDOM

For the development of his most civilized, friendliest, and most creative potentialities, a child needs the security of a democratic home—a place where he's free to express himself without fear of belittlement or loss of love. He needs the freedom to try out emerging independence as he feels ready, not necessarily when parents or others say he should be ready. If not pressured into change, he enjoys feelings of independence. His progress can be managed successfully by respect and consideration, but seldom by domination.

The problem lies in knowing when a child is mature enough to shape some areas of his life by himself. When should he receive assistance, how much, what kind? Discussed here are some noninterfering ways that parents can assist his striving for independence to move forward. They are worth a try.

To Speak for Himself

LET HIM BE SHY

Shyness often occurs in children. When parents and others refrain from emphasizing it, a child is not permanently labeled. Avenues for new learning remain open when "shy" does not become a part of his self-picture. He reacts naturally and is not limited by what we have said about him. He is not ashamed of being shy or hesitant if others are not.

You may find it difficult not to answer immediately for the hesitant child when others speak to him and he fails to answer. Shyness bothers many parents because they don't understand it. As did their own parents, they may feel their child was born that way and that there is little hope. They are distressed and embarrassed by it.

Verbal self-confidence grows slowly. You can help it grow, but it takes time. Self-confidence grows out of the pleasure parents display when they are with their child, and out of the opportunities for self-expression they provide. Shyness ceases to be a problem for the child who has learned that:

He has ideas and opinions worth listening to.

His ability to solve problems and make decisions, right or
wrong, is respected.

His understanding of the environment is in many ways
reliable and predictable.

He can correct his mistakes and that his blunders aren't
irreparable.

To learn to speak for himself, a child needs to be accepted as
he is. A study by Giffin and Heider showed adult fears of
speaking before public gatherings to be directly related to low
self-concepts and submissiveness of personality. Fear of forgetting, of being laughed at, and of being evaluated by others—
resulting from self-appraisals learned primarily in childhood—
were characteristic of the high-anxiety adult speakers. In contrast, "The low stage-fright groups were eager to voice their
opinions whether others liked it or not" (1967, p. 317).

ALLOW HIM TO CRY

Many of the sounds made by the infant and later the preschooler are attempts at communication, even his crying and
whining. If we are frequently angered, first by his crying, then
later by his ceaseless chatter, more mature forms of communication are discouraged. "Don't be a crybaby," "Don't talk so
much," and "Don't ask silly questions" stifle learning.

When he's unhappy, be sympathetic. He may have more to
cry about than we know. He would not seek sympathy if he did
not need it. Since we cannot really know what goes on in a
child's mind, we must accept his communication even though
we may not understand it. Becoming a socially responsive and
communicative adult requires an early environment in which
primitive efforts to communicate receive recognition.

FIRST ATTEMPTS AT SELF-EXPRESSION
SHOULD RECEIVE RECOGNITION

Let a child's remarks about immediate objects and events
stand, though they may be less accurate than your own. He

lacks experience and knowledge upon which to base his views. The adjective that doesn't fit may be a new and appropriate way to describe a situation. The joke that isn't funny or the poem that doesn't rhyme at least can be interesting. They may even be superior accomplishments at his age level. When he awkwardly mimics his favorite TV star, enjoy it. Let him add words to the song he doesn't quite remember. Our acceptance of these first stumbling efforts gives him the courage to try again. If he frequently fails to capture our interest, he may stop trying to communicate.

LET HIM CRITICIZE

As Briggs suggests, "The child convinced that father knows best is hardly full of self-confidence" (1970, p. 238). When your child begins to criticize your point of view, let him have the satisfaction of challenging you in a more grown-up way. We can express our views without insisting that he accept all of them. It's difficult to immediately convince him anyway, even with reasoning, that we may be right. Being able to agreeably disagree lets him grow to feel confident about self-expression. When the ideas he creates are valued by others, he has the courage to make renewed efforts to express himself.

Compliment a good idea. Don't hurry to terminate a conversation. On unimportant issues, listen without correcting much of what he says. If you don't quite agree, tell him:

I don't quite agree, but you may be right.
You have a point.
You may be right. Try it and see.
That is an interesting observation.
I don't mind if you don't like my idea, as long as you listen to it.
I agree with some of what you say, but I don't think this part is quite right.

Incidentally, the last item above can get some really lovely conversations going even with very young people. Also it communicates that there is more to the world than total agreement or total disagreement—a detail handy to learn early, the earlier the better. It is also an exceedingly handy habit and attitude to have when the child becomes a teen-ager.

Ultimately a child *must* challenge our viewpoint. He cannot rely on himself as an adult with the power to stand alone until he grows beyond his vision of his parents as "all superior." This awakening usually comes as he approaches adolescence and we are met with: "Don't you know anything, Mom?"

To Think for Himself

A child learns to think for himself when thoughts, feelings, and actions are respected, though they may seem impractical by adult standards. A child learns best if the imposing of parental will is reserved for occasions when health, safety, or welfare is in jeopardy or when the needs and rights of others are being ignored or misunderstood. A child needs:

FREEDOM FROM CONTINUOUS PARENTAL JUDGMENT

An excess of our control communicates to a child that he is being rejected because he does not feel as we feel. We must be willing to relinquish some of our feelings if he is to accept his. We cannot expect him to like everything we like, be as neat as we are, be in a hurry when we are in a hurry, be happy because we are happy. We need to remind ourselves that his interests are as important to him at his level of comprehension as ours are at our adult level. When we can accept our child this way, we are less likely to make judgments such as the following:

You don't know what's good.
Such a filthy outfit to wear to school.
What are you doing *that* for?

What's wrong with your blue shirt?
Why are you doing it *that* way?
Why are you taking so much time?
What do you want with *that* thing?
Can't you sit still?
Why don't you speak up?
Why can't you be more careful?
Oh, is *that* all you have to say?
That's no way to talk.

The child who receives much comment and direction of this kind cannot learn to trust his own decisions nor does he feel accepted and understood. Where conformity is not really essential, our tolerance of his immaturity helps him build trust in himself:

These sandwiches are delicious. I wish you'd try one.
You might want to change that outfit because of those spots.
I'm curious about what you are doing there.
You may wear that one if you like, but your blue shirt has all
    its buttons and isn't so faded.
May I make a suggestion?
I have some things I must do soon. Do you mind hurrying a
    little?
Looks as though you have something interesting in mind.
You seem restless. Want to walk for a while?
I can't hear what you are saying. Would you speak a little
    louder?
May I give you some assistance there? This seems to be going
    wrong. (Then tell him what he is doing that is fine.)
Could you explain that to me again with a little more detail?
Ask her nicely, Don.

Klein expresses this approach in a helpful way:

I can only provide my son with a real and consistent explanation of what I consider to be the best way. Where I don't know, I owe him the admission that I have doubts. Where I am sure I know what is best for me, I tell him. Where I think I know what is best for him, I try to sell him. But finally, he is the one to decide. [1968, p. 270.]

FREEDOM TO MAKE DECISIONS IN HIS OWN BEHALF

On matters that concern only the child, allow him to do things in his own way and make his own decisions. How he builds his blocks, how he catches bugs in a jar, how he sings, and how he plays in general and what he plays can be left largely up to the child and should be. Similarly, what he wears indoors, how fast or slowly he talks, what school clubs he joins, and much else can be left up to him. For instance, there are possibilities such as these:

> We are having leftovers for dinner tonight. Which would you
>   rather have, the string beans or the creamed peas?
> Which would you rather wear to school today, your pink dress
>   or this yellow one?
> What would you like to have me read to you tonight, this
>   story or something else?
> Daddy and I are going over to grandmother's this afternoon.
>   Which would you like better, to go with us or to stay here
>   with your older sister, Sue? (Assuming this is OK with
>   Sue.)

On things that do not matter, let a child make choices and decisions not at the same level of maturity as your own. Self-confidence cannot grow if he perceives others as knowing all the answers. As you would your adult friends, let him accept or refuse some of your suggestions. If he does not wish to know of a better way to fix his bicycle, polish his shoes, or arrange his room, let him learn on his own. Our resentment will not help him. It only makes him feel guilty while he keeps on opposing us. On more important matters, we can think it over cooperatively.

Let's see how things go before we decide definitely.

I don't agree, but I'll go along with the idea if you are still
interested next year.

Let's think about that for a while.

That certainly has possibilities. Get more information on the
subject and we'll talk about it soon.

Examine everyday situations in which children sometimes
attempt to make decisions in their own behalf and decide
whether doing it your way is so important. Here are some.

Carol (age seven) knows a better way to wrap her friend's
gift.

Mark (twelve) knows, without father's help, just how to
untangle the kite string.

Peter (ten) insists on washing the windows his way.

Danny (six) refuses to stand still while you wash the last spot
out of his shirt, which you know is there and he knows is
not.

John (five) wants to go to the park, not to Andy's house.

Your guests have arrived for dinner and everyone is seated
except Walter (five), who wants to stand.

Nancy (eight) wants a hot dog for breakfast.

After three bites of dinner, Mary (four) is too full for more.

Billy (five) would rather water-paint than use crayons.

David (nine) wants to empty the wastebaskets after his TV
show, not before.

Five-year-old Harold's soup is too hot. He wants an ice cube
in it.

Sam (seven) wants to sit in the row in front of you at the
theater.

Nina (six) doesn't want to wear the ribbon that matches her
dress. She likes another color better.

Tommy (ten) doesn't like butter, mayonnaise, or lettuce on
his sandwiches.

Warren (eleven) wants to pick out his own new desk.

Sally (six) knows that her way to write her name is best.

OPPORTUNITIES TO THINK, RATHER THAN TOO MANY "DON'TS"

What feelings are engendered by negative orders such as "Don't step on that paper," "Don't write on my book," "Don't use my towel," "Don't put your hands on the window," "Don't shout," "Don't put your feet on my chair"? Depending upon the emphasis in the parent's voice and facial expression, they may generate more concern about parental resentment than about the behavior they are meant to change. When mother explains more fully that a certain behavior should be stopped because she can't concentrate with all the racket, the youngster has something to consider. Learning with understanding is encouraged. He has an opportunity to increase his information, to reflect, and to form concepts. For example:

Let's pick up these homework papers before they get stepped on.

I'd rather you write on this piece of paper. I want to read my book.

This is my towel. Here is yours.

See how your fingers make spots on the clean window.

Dad and I can hear you much better if you speak quietly.

I'm afraid your shoes will damage the chair.

ACCEPTANCE OF THE CHILD'S INDECISION

Little brother announces that he wants to set the table, which is usually big brother's responsibility. Let him try. He puts the plates on the table and leaves. When mother calls big brother to finish the job, little brother runs back to insist it is his work. Instead of berating him for indecisiveness, let him resume the task.

Be patient with the little one who occasionally can't decide what to wear. We all have that problem sometimes. If this really is occasional, let him make numerous clothing changes if necessary in making up his mind. On some occasions your suggestions may help him solve his problem. At other times distraction to other interests works best. If the problem is a common one, narrow the choices to two or three alternatives, giving the child an opportunity to practice decision-making in a less complex situation.

Billy can't make up his mind about riding on the pony at the carnival. After begging dad to purchase tickets, Billy decides he doesn't want to ride after all. He's too frightened. He tries again later only to find that his courage fails him a second time. Be patient. His lack of immediate courage won't bother him if it doesn't bother you, and he will have a better chance to overcome it. If his lack of courage does bother you, he may well develop the habit of simply instantly announcing he does not want to do something, definitely and finally, whenever he feels the least bit afraid.

Let children take their time about making up their minds. Given time to ponder, they have greater opportunity to weigh the merits of a situation, to increase their information, to overcome fears, and to make a better decision.

ACCEPTANCE OF THE CHILD'S FORGETFULNESS

Let him be a scatterbrain, at least part of the time. Affording him the right to forget builds confidence and lets him know he needn't be ashamed of being wrong. The forgotten lunch money, the sweater that disappeared at school, the overlooked books—these are unplanned and unanticipated. His own distress with himself is sufficient punishment. Trust him. You will discover he does not wish to inconvenience himself or you. Understanding is most helpful.

It must have been distressing to discover you had no money
for lunch. I'm glad you phoned me.
Before we replace the lost gym clothes, check in your

classrooms and the lost and found department. Maybe you'll find them yet.

Don't worry. Replacing your glasses will be expensive, but you didn't lose them on purpose.

You forgot your English report? That's OK. Glad you remembered in time. We can still go home and back before school starts.

You forgot to buy milk? We'll have something else for breakfast. Toast and juice will be fine.

Forgetting your music lesson was easy to do. It's not yet one of your regular habits.

ACCEPTANCE OF THE CHILD'S MISTAKES

He has the right to make mistakes or to be wrong when he has not intentionally done so to disturb others. And he has the right to be treated with respect when his wrongs are made known. None of us can do everything perfectly all the time. Possibly none of us can do anything perfectly any of the time. The child is new at everything and everything is relatively new to him.

Parents who give youngsters this privilege raise children who are less afraid to admit to themselves or others their faults and errors, and thereby are in a better position to correct those errors. In addition, children who readily admit their faults are judged by their teachers more healthy mentally than those who admit few faults (Taylor and Combs, 1952).

To Do for Himself

ALL OF US NEED ENCOURAGEMENT

By the age of four a child who has been given opportunities to try can dress himself fairly well, care for many of his own health needs, self-start many of his own creative activities, and play without constant supervision. But he will not assume such responsibilities with unfailing regularity. Now and then he may need an extra parental nudge or boost; however, once you get him started, he will usually carry on alone. As soon as you feel he is ready, let him do the simple things himself. There are times when even for the pleading or crying child you can tactfully decline to offer your direct assistance.

I'm not sure. What do you think?

Give it a try.

I'll help you if you have trouble.

You can do it.

Have you thought of trying it this way?

Do you think it would be easier if I helped with this?

Would this help?

Which shoe fits this foot? Let's set the shoes side by side and look at them.

Which button goes here? If we start at the very bottom and do one at a time, it will go better.

Our continuing encouragement and approval stimulate him to greater self-reliance. Praise efforts even though achievement is not yet in view.

Nicely done. You came closer that time.

That was a good try.

You almost made it.

You are doing better each time.

THE FREEDOM TO RETREAT

At the same time that he grows toward being able to do more things for himself, a child also needs the security of retreating, without belittlement, to the comfort of parental assistance. No child ever really feels that he has had enough parental comfort and attention. His feelings are mixed between wanting to continue enjoying parents' helpfulness and wanting to reach out for greater independence. Even a forty-year-old wants to retreat occasionally. So also do seven-, eight-, and nine-year-olds. How frequently depends partially upon parents. If his needs distress you, he may feel rejected and demand help longer. If you continue to enjoy helping him on occasion while generally encouraging his own independent efforts, longer dependency is not likely.

A child becomes emotionally ready to do for himself and is eager to try when previous needs have been satisfied well, when pressure to change is not abusive or excessive, and when change is not abrupt. "We know from observation and our own laboratory studies that the infant who *separates himself* does so without anxiety" (Rheingold and Eckerman, 1971, p. 26). Let him decide. Losing some of mother's assistance is not so final when he knows he can get it again if he is so inclined. Aggression and overdependency are often related to repeated frustration of a child's early need to feel secure and dependent upon mother's love and care.

Dependency problems are common even in the animal world. Mother-infant separation behavior was studied in two species of monkeys, referred to as bonnets and pigtails. The two groups differed greatly in their development of independence.

In both species, it is the infant who first initiates most breaks in contact with the mother from early life onward. The essential difference between the two species is that the bonnets are more relaxed mothers. They are less likely to suddenly retrieve their separated infants. They allow their infants more freedom to depart and return to the mother, and to interact with others. The mother weans, rejects, and punishes less strictly than the pigtail mother. By the end of the first year, bonnet infants are less dependent on their mothers. Their social play is several times greater than the pigtail infants, who spend more time in exercise play. They appear to be more secure, leave mother more often to go further away, and are freer to approach other members of the group, both adults and peers. (Summarized from Kaufman and Rosenblum, 1969, pp. 41–60.)

The powerful influence of mothers' behavior is demonstrated in the different rates at which independence developed for the two species. The strength of this bond that ties the infant to his mother has been observed in many animals. Even twelve-year-old chimpanzees have been known to return periodically to visit their mothers (Lawick-Goodall, 1971).

Self-reliance can be encouraged with praise when a child shows independence, but it cannot be forced when he does not. When your preschooler insists that he cannot pour his juice, cannot reach the glass he wants, cannot spread the peanut butter, cannot turn on the bath water, cannot dry himself, cannot find his coat, his scissors, his blanket, or his shoes, you or an older sibling may have no alternative but to give the necessary assistance. As mentioned earlier, you only need to get him started. Let him do most of the work. Within reasonable limits, let him be as childish or immature as he wishes, when you know that he also does many things for himself. But remember to reinforce him with approval when he does do it alone.

EASY TASKS

Assign tasks that are sufficiently simple so that at least partial success is inevitable. Praise the achievement of any part of a task: getting one sock on, only half-dressed, one side of his hands washed, his hair partially combed, most of the silverware on the table, one wastebasket emptied. Refrain from disappointment when he does not do more. He is psychologically motivated to repeat successful, praised experiences, while he is likely to discontinue those that are unrewarded.

TOLERANCE FOR HIS IMMATURITY AND INEXPERIENCE

Let him be clumsy, forgetful, and unthinking. He has only been in this country three years or so! He is in many ways more at sea than a new immigrant. The latter has at least been somewhere on earth with some relevant skills and knowledge. Correct the child's behavior gently, and mainly only when it is important. When your child fails on important matters, show him what went awry and what to do instead; encourage him to try again, perhaps in a different way.

Expect the little one to improve; and, even then, only gradually. If we habitually want the child to get things exactly right, we establish a model of perfection he cannot achieve and make it difficult for him to have confidence or to accept himself as he is. Unable to be successful, he may not wish to continue even trying. In any event, comments such as the following get us nowhere. They also are grossly inaccurate:

All you do is make a lot of work.
You are too slow. Let me do it.
You'll break it.
You always give up.
You don't know how to read.
You can't have sunglasses. You would just lose them.
Don't you ever change your socks?
Don't you ever brush your teeth?
You can't have a dog because you wouldn't take care of him.
Nobody dresses the way you do.

Remarks about the poor quality of performance are frequently the tactics of older siblings. Wishing to enhance their own feelings of importance, they use the younger family member as an outlet for their own emotional problems. This requires the older child's self-respect be enhanced and his position in the family made more secure, so he does not need to tear others down to build himself up.

Keep faith in your child's ability to function now. Try to be as tolerant with the older child as you were during his infancy years. When parents refrain from frequent comments about inadequacies, a child is not defeated before he has an opportunity to discover his capabilities.

PROVIDE OPPORTUNITIES

Doing for himself becomes more likely when many opportunities for self-reliance and practice are provided. Furnishing numerous, safe opportunities to practice is easier than one might think.

A stool in the bathroom or kitchen makes getting drinks and washing hands more convenient. "Wash your hands" can be a signal that lunch is ready. As a regular mealtime ritual, handwashing improves rapidly.

Toothbrushes, towels, washcloths, hairbrushes, mirrors, and combs given as presents encourage earlier use of these items.

An easy-to-reach shelf with paper cups, plates, napkins, and silverware makes it convenient for him to prepare his own snacks.

A shelf in the kitchen or family room furnished with his supplies encourages earlier creativity. Stock it with such things as a ream of inexpensive typing paper, newsprint paper, colored paper, cardboard, coloring books, picture books, reading books, alphabet and number workbooks, mail order catalogs, old Christmas cards, ribbon, wrapping paper, string, shoe boxes, blunt scissors that will cut, cellophane tape, crayons, pencils, puzzles, clay, cookie cutters, design-making gadgets, balloons, elastic bands, glue, paste, insect jars, bubble soap and pipes, magnets, spools, soft wire, and beads.

Low hooks and a low closet pole ease the problem of caring for his own clothing. (It also makes more space in the closet as there is room for another rod above the child's.)

Bedroom shelves or a drawer of his very own encourages him to care for his possessions.

His own alarm clock helps the older child learn to wake himself for school.

A list of his friends and their phone numbers beside the
phone encourages your kindergartner to learn how to use
the phone.

Dimes for emergency calls home, tucked away in desk,
clothing, or billfold add to his sense of security and
self-reliance.

The ability to use a house key is convenient for occasions
when mother is delayed with shopping.

TO BE CREATIVE

THE PRESCHOOLER AND CHILD OF MIDDLE YEARS

Children are born with a marvelous curiosity, an interest in
learning, a desire to know about their world. Failure, by itself,
seldom discourages them. They will try again and again. Why
does this trait have to be spoiled by parents excessively concerned with instant success, neatness, with being careful, or
with fear of disapproval by others? Many children just a few
years old have already learned to be afraid of making a mess, of
making mistakes, of what people will think. Creativity cannot
easily flourish when they are afraid to experiment, afraid to be
wrong.

The child needs a democratic home. Creativity is most encouraged in homes where domination, criticism, and rules are
limited and where parents are tolerant of periodic mess and
disorder. Moustakas (1956, p. 4) suggests that "all criticism,
judgment, comparison, and evaluation interfere with being and
becoming." Mooney (1956) believes that every individual is a
creative person if he is free to use his potentialities.

Within reasonable limits let a child be free to relax and enjoy his home. Where freedom of expression prevails and creative materials are readily available, the average four-year-old will be busy making things and amusing himself a considerable part of each day. Let him build and construct—float toys in the bath water; paint on newspapers on the kitchen floor; make hideaways in the family room out of old bedspreads, chairs, and cardboard boxes. He especially enjoys building small enclosures in such a way that he can observe others while remaining hidden from view. These often are furnished with all manner of items from around the house. Margaret Mead (1965) finds this to be a favorite play even among primitive children, who build hideaways out of branches and leaves. The more opportunities you give him to improvise, influence, and change his environment, the more he learns.

Do not be overly concerned about messes. A child busily experimenting is not neat. He is preoccupied, working hard, and unconcerned with order. Waste of materials must be expected. It's difficult to teach conservation without restricting creative activities. Indeed, it is doubtful that the preschooler can fully understand the concept. More important than waste of materials and neatness is the self-initiative, joy in achievement, and confidence that grow out of freedom to invent, experiment, and explore. These character attributes outweigh by far the disruption, clean-up time, or waste involved. Actually the waste is negligible. Save wrapping paper, boxes, ribbons, string, cardboards, short pencils, buttons, aluminum trays, paper typed on one side, and other materials to replenish your child's supplies. Purchase at sales or in quantity.

When a child has been working hard constructing elaborate block designs, drawing pictures, or inventing, help him arrange a display of his work. Let him and the family enjoy the results of his efforts. It is worthwhile to walk a different route through the family room for a few days to escape falling over forts, block castles, or Indian villages. Pride in achievement is encouraged when his work is not dismantled immediately and put away in favor only of orderliness.

He needs companionship while he works. Don't put creative supplies in the back bedroom. Children need to be where they can feel the security that comes from the presence of parents. They want to be where others are available to give spontaneous praise and approval. Who can blame them? It's no fun to be stuck off in a room by oneself. Imaginative experimentation develops best when desks, tables, art supplies, books, blocks, and toys are near family work areas, where he need not be wholly alone to use them.

If you are careful to preserve what the child has built, he is more likely to cooperate with you in cleaning up. When he is not agreeable to assisting with cleanup, do it yourself. It takes only a few minutes compared to the many hours your child enjoyed learning to create, persevere, and accomplish. Rebellion at cleanup and the resentments that accumulate over it are discouraging to creativity.

He needs approval. Admire his work and exercise caution about criticizing it. When he brings things for evaluation, praise his progress without concern for his shortcomings. When you accept his accomplishments, you are accepting him.

Don't interpret or describe. Let him tell you about his work. Refrain from asking, "What is it?" The results are not so important as his fun in the doing. Say instead:

Would you like to tell me about it?
I like the deep red you have used.
That's a very interesting design.
Such a pleasant combination of colors!
How neatly you wrote the letters of the alphabet.
I like the cheerful smile on the little girl's face.

You worked hard, and took a lot of pains with that. That's
   great!
That's quite an imaginative picture.
How pretty!
I'm happy you enjoy working with your crayons.
I like your picture because it is yours.

Avoid comparisons between his accomplishments and those
of others. Whether the comparison is favorable or unfavorable
to him, it drives him into competition and, more damaging, into
competition with someone he probably loves. Concentrate on
the characteristics inherent in the achievement itself, as in the
examples above.

He does not need assistance. Showing a child how to make,
do, or draw interferes with creativity. His acceptance of what
he can create becomes difficult if the parent's more perfect
example is available. Unable to make his production look like
yours, he becomes dissatisfied and gives up easily.

Praise and approval rather than our examples stimulate creativity. A child enjoys what he can do by himself if his parents
enjoy his accomplishment with him. And he doesn't stop building the block fort, putting the model house together, drawing
pictures of a tree, a house, or a boat if he is not discouraged
from viewing more perfect examples of how his ought to look.

The creative child shows enthusiasm and interest in the world
around him. He enjoys excelling. He finds identity, meaning,
and direction in life. As Cobb (1967, p. 132) writes: "When the
creative urge is strong enough, it generates a power that seems
to become self-operative and self-guiding."

He can usually work out his problems. Creative play often
has a therapeutic effect. Listen to the stories that children make
up as they play house, school, or monster. Worries and uncer-
tainties are brought out into the open as they act out what is

real and unreal. Putting on a puppet show with her friends helps Nina work out stage fright. Playing house helps her get a feeling of what it might be like to be father, brother, or big sister, or to acknowledge that some day she might be a mother.

A child's wishes and needs are expressed in the drawings he makes, often before he can express them verbally. The dog that mother won't buy goes for a walk with him on paper. All kinds of pets, play houses, flower gardens, and even friends become reality on paper. Feelings about people and the world in general are expressed in the clouds that smile, in the flowers or people that look sad. He is the battleship shooting down all the planes in the sky or the engineer driving the railroad train. He can draw or paint out his wish to beat up big brother, although as yet he may be unable to verbalize or even understand his anger. He may hammer, pound, and dig his angry feelings away at the workbench and sand pile.

THE OLDER CHILD

When the creative efforts of his infancy and elementary-school years were a source of fun and satisfaction to him, your older child will continue to be active, inventive, and self-initiated. A sense of achievement satisfaction vital to successful intellectual development has been acquired in the formative years.

As his interests expand, help him obtain the equipment these require. Protect him from interruption. Aid in his search for information. Libraries continue to be the most useful source of data on any subject. The new cat, dog, turtle, guinea pig, rabbit, grasshopper, or beetle can be made more interesting with a book on that particular species.

Sometimes children pursue interests that seem like a waste of time, such as collecting bottle caps, chewing-gum wrappers, train schedules. When this happens, it's better to ignore your feelings and look for something to praise. For example, his persistence or way of going about it may be superior. Ask questions. Expanding interests to other areas may result.

Failure to maintain continuous interest in a project or hobby often distresses parents. We needlessly worry that he may never persist. Let him reach out to new areas even though old ones have not been fully explored. Each interest adds to his fund of knowledge. Childhood is a time to explore. A child whose curiosity is caught by a variety of subjects, although he may not go very far with many, has gained more than the child who never has been challenged. He more quickly discovers what his real interests are. Armed with this knowledge about himself, he can answer far better the questions arising as he enters adolescence: "What am I?" "Who am I?" "What can I do well?"

PHYSICAL SKILL AND RISK-TAKING

Physical activity comprises a large part of the preschooler's life. He is "on the go" continually—running, jumping, climbing, balancing, tumbling. He wants to use his body. Why not? There are many advantages to be gained by the early development of his physical abilities.

PERSONALITY AND LEADERSHIP ARE POSITIVELY INFLUENCED

Leaders in the field of physical education have long known about the benefits to be derived from development of physical abilities. Among these are health, self-confidence, social skills, and the ability to compete with age-mates. Children with skills to contribute more often take leadership roles in their play with others. In this connection, of particular interest is the research of Cratty. He suggests that psychological well-being is in many respects related to physical proficiency.

Programs of motor activity for children three years and younger are beneficial, with better performance elicited when the parents are not the teachers. . . . Sociability is promoted for the three-year-old who engages in active games with other children. He learns to think, plan, and control his actions. . . . Teamwork teaches him to tolerate competition, to work together with others, and relate to his peers. . . . The persistence and tolerance of discomfort which children learn in sports activities can be expected to carry over into other tasks. . . . Self-confidence is considerably affected by a child's belief in his ability to control body movement. . . . Enhanced physical maturity and performance increases the extent to which adolescents are found to be comfortable with the size and shape of their bodies. They are less self-conscious and more willing to engage in wide movement activities, such as dancing, swimming, tennis, and other sports. [1968, pp. 65, 40–41, 56, 18, 19.]

INTELLECTUAL PERFORMANCE IS IMPROVED

Are you aware that physical skill is related also to intellectual success? Ball-throwing, catching, batting, hopscotch, and jump rope develop body-eye and hand-eye coordination, important to successful scholastic performance. Physically strong, active children are likely to be better students, more apt to be well-adjusted, admired by their peers, and less fearful that the world is full of danger. That intelligence is improved by an enriched physical environment has been demonstrated by a number of researchers. Especially thought-provoking is the following study:

Two sets of experimental animals were reared, one alone in empty cages, the other set in a small playground equipped with runways, swings, ladders, and other devices. The animals reared in the enriched environment not only performed better on standardized learning tasks later in life but chemical and anatomical differences were observed in the higher centers of their brains, as compared to those raised in isolation. (Summarized from Rosenzweig, Krech, and Bennett, 1966, pp. 99–104.)

IS PLAY ENOUGH?

Elementary school offers excellent opportunity for accomplishing the physical development so clearly beneficial in shaping social and intellectual learning. Yet far too few schools make provision for physical-education programs or plan noon-hour guided-play activities in which children may participate if they wish. Physical-education specialists are well aware of the deficiencies but are limited in their ability to change long-established practices. In many instances, children merely roam the playgrounds at recesses and lunchtime, attended only by one or two adults who serve more as policemen than leaders. As the children become bored with the few perceptual motor alternatives available to them, interpersonal conflict becomes their principal "sport." As mothers well know, special cliques develop that children have difficulty moving into and out of. Having a special "buddy" is of vital importance to each child when school playtime is totally unplanned. A child will often cling to this same pal year after year because he fears nonacceptance by others, or being a "loner." Should he venture from this friend, he may not be reaccepted if his reaching out is rejected by others. His social status during lunchtime and other free-play periods may become his most important concern about school. Being without a friend is more noticeable and painful at school than at home or in the neighborhood.

A tolerant sense of community fails to develop when the social structure of the playground is left entirely to the children who happen to dominate through popularity or aggressiveness. Children are not competent judges of one another. "Playground pairs and sub-groups set values, approve of, and award status for behavior different from that approved by most pupils and teachers" (Glidewell, 1971, p. 737).

Of course, some will say that children need a respite during school hours from concentration and guided activities. Our answer is that "voluntary participation" in guided play is not restrictive. It is tension-reducing and fun, and a much needed respite from the interpersonal conflict that occurs when children are subjected day after day to playground equipment, hopscotch, and jump rope. What appears to be a busy and happy playground just may not be so for all children. Many mothers learn of their child's unhappiness at school as other children come to dominate the social environment; for example, the hopscotch marker that gets called "out" when it is mostly "in"; the ball that gets thrown most frequently to certain friends; the "turn" at jump rope that is usually last. Less aggressive children may never enjoy full participation because they are not favored by the leaders who often hold their positions throughout the elementary-school years.

Age-mate selection in the ordinary community may not change much year after year. Grade level and room assignments become invisible boundaries. Within these lines, the social structure, largely designed by the children, sometimes influenced by kindergarten and first-grade teachers, persists throughout the school years.

In addition, a kindergarten–through–third-grade child may spend two or more hours daily in afterschool play with the same buddy with whom he walks the playground before school in the morning, at noon, and at recesses. With both afterschool play and at-school free hours uninterrupted by an opportunity to learn effective social attitudes, left-out children have little opportunity to enjoy a variety of classmates or social experience. Too little communication with companionable adults in "relaxed play" is enjoyed by children today.

Others will say, and rightly, that being rejected is not the end of the world. What is so devastating about rejection? Usually it is not the rejection itself but our reaction to it: the mistaken conclusion that rejection means one is a total flop, that rejection today means rejection tomorrow, that rejection by Cindy Lou means rejection by everyone, that rejection indicates an inherent flaw such that one cannot modify his behavior in ways which will win acceptance if desired. Some might believe that all we need to do is explain this to a child. The problem is that the average child is not usually capable of such objective views until much later in life, after a pattern of attitudes and self-image has been established. If rejection occurs too regularly, the feelings it creates cannot be easily undone.

A large part of why children are so afraid of rejection by their peers may be because their parents are so afraid of rejection. Parents sometimes act as if the child's popularity were the most important thing in the world, very difficult to obtain, very apt to be lost. Actually, the problem is so universal that your child will learn fear of rejection from other children whether you have emphasized it or not.

Fear of being a loner is not something parents can easily change once it is done. They can reduce the probability of its occurring by providing their child with a secure infancy and offering him numerous contacts with friends during the pre-school years. The secure child is not so likely to be rejected or to fear it if it happens. This subject is discussed more fully in the chapter on social concerns.

SCHOOL IS A SOCIALIZING PROCESS

To a great degree, a child learns to perceive himself as popular or unpopular according to the individual and collective views of the particular group chance may have placed him with during his early elementary-school years. Although parents have first opportunity to shape self-image development, school experiences are significant where his "social" self-image is concerned. Here, often for the first time, the collective views of his age-mates affect him, helping to shape self-concepts that may last a lifetime.

Specialized equipment has become the playground "baby-sitter" in schools today. Lacking guided experience in the special social relations of the playground, children lose useful opportunities to learn effective and meaningful lessons about their age-mates and themselves.

Isolated play is not enough. The elementary-school playground is as important for learning as the classroom. A sensibly guided play program is known to:

Improve health and intellect. The more physically competent children become, the better they adjust in all areas of behavior.

Provide an outlet for excess energy that might otherwise become focused on conflict. We don't have to plan for conflict. Conflict is inevitable. We do have to plan for effective self-image development.

Provide the aggressive child with proper examples for achieving his interests through constructive behavior.

Promote socialization, working together, and leadership. It favors the inclusion of the quiet, shy child who might not otherwise participate.

High school and college students are well-suited to function as part-time recreation leaders. They are less imposing than adults and are often looked up to and admired by children.

TO GROW

Parents have great power. They are relatively free to use whatever techniques they choose in influencing a child's behavior. When, to suit their interests, they require the child to surrender his, they:

Frustrate the child's need to see a task through.
Impair his trust in his ability to make judgments.
Restrict self-expression and self-confidence.
Invade his right to be a separate individual.

We must make rules for our children, since they are so lacking in knowledge and so inexperienced. We have to offer them guidance and interrupt or terminate many of their activities in order to protect them from harm and protect the well-being of other people living with them. As our child's first teacher and companion, we must not abandon our teaching role. However, we need not interfere, interrupt, and correct as much as often is done. We can give them more freedom and more opportunities to learn independently than we perhaps realize.

The Why Not's

The "why not's" in the following pages involve areas of behavior where adults should not interfere. They illustrate the child's right to behavior that is accidental, unintentional, or immature. They allow him to grow:

> Seven-year-old Steven, overenthusiastic about the job of swatting flies, breaks a windowpane. Instead of blowing your top over a three-dollar piece of glass, why not say, "Sorry, Son. Don't be upset. You are more important than a window. I can get another window. I can't get another you."

> Henry (eight) stomps away after you have asked him to wash his hands and set the table for dinner. Because something must be upsetting him, why not let him? Catch him after dinner when he is less angry. Let him help with the removal of the dishes.

> Larry (twelve) comes home from bicycling bruised and skinned. He's already had a painful lesson. Why not give him affection and encouragement rather than a lecture?

> When Jerry (eight) shows up late for lunch or arrives at the

table with dirty hands, why not respond as you would to a friend? "We missed you. What was so interesting?" or "Hi, there! Glad to see you. You forgot to wash your hands, though. Better go do it."

Andy (thirteen) struggles to bring all the groceries in from the car in one trip. It doesn't work. Why not let him help clean up the mess? If you have exploded, apologize and let him know that he has a right to make a mistake.

When your child has trouble saying certain words, why not say the correct word in your answering comment rather than interrupting him?

Your son says it will take only a minute to run into the store. You are still waiting fifteen minutes later. Why not withhold your anger? Consider how many times he has waited that long for you to pick him up at the playground or to take him on the promised outing.

Sammy (six) wants a bowl of soup and a cup of cocoa for breakfast. Why not? Maybe he's fed up with his usual fare, and this is a fairly nourishing breakfast.

Rex (five) wants to ride in the grocery cart. Why not? Perhaps he realizes that he'll soon be too big to enjoy this privilege much longer.

Ben (six) wants a dime for the supermarket camel ride. If mother buys the latest fashion magazine, why not ten cents for him occasionally, whether he has an allowance or not?

Your preschooler refuses to wear pajamas to bed. Why not let him wear his comfortable old shirt instead?

A very mature twelve-year-old Jack wants to accept the invitation to join the local astronomical society, an adult organization. Why not let him? It can be a time for father and son togetherness.

Father wants to read his book. Alice (five) wants him to read hers. He wants to be left alone. In five years, he probably will be. Why not give the attention she wants, if she hasn't recently had some?

Don (nine) keeps "forgetting" to wear socks in spite of his parents' instructions to put them on. He says his feet are hot. Perhaps they are. If new cotton socks don't solve the problem, it's not worth a daily battle.

Tom (five) wants to set up his blocks in the recently cleaned family room. Why not let him if no other good spot is available? How much time does it take to pick up, compared to the amount of time he spends in enjoyable creative play?

Jeff (four) wants to learn to swim but doesn't want the swimming teacher to touch him. Why not let him swim as best he can from an observing position, while he stays in more shallow water? He may permit holding later.

Your baby, for his own reasons, fights his bib at feeding time. Why not put on a washable old shirt and forget the bib?

Ronnie (three) wants a taste of what is being cooked for dinner. Why not give him some in a small bowl? Helping mother test flavors may encourage new food interests.

You find daughter fixing a bowl of ice cream ten minutes before dinner. Why not say, "Sorry, dear, dinner will be on the table in a few minutes. Have one bite before I put this away"?

Kathy (three) picks the newly bloomed flowers, and, of course, without stems. Why not float them in a bowl? Take her back to the yard later and explain why it's better to let the flowers grow. Only occasionally do we pick just a few for the table.

You've set daughter's hair and are combing it. She wants it straight. You know of a better way to fix it. Why not let her express her needs her own way?

Janice (three) is building a block tower. The second block is

placed far off center. Why not let her continue? She still
has a lot of time to learn about balance.

Fred (six) says his cocoa is cold. You say it's warm. You like
your coffee just the right temperature, why not let him
have his drink the way he likes it?

Your preschooler has been reacting to recent frustrations with
a new door-slamming response. Why not give him ten
minutes of friendly attention before he gets to the door-
slamming stage?

Barbara (six) doesn't want to give up her security blanket.
Why must she? It makes for nice cuddling in front of the
TV. Sometimes a new one is acceptable to replace the
bundle of rags.

Bruce (ten) fails to arrive home for dinner as expected. Why
not keep his dinner warm as you would for an adult
friend?

Sandy (four) is reluctant to play at the homes of her friends.
Why not let them come to your home until she feels more
confident?

Stanley (five) offers to help with the vacuuming. Why not let
him? Do over his work later if necessary.

Donny (three) wants to help you set the table. Why not let
him? You can add what he forgets later.

TWO

What Parents Ought to Know About Anger

THE USEFULNESS OF ANGER

Losing one's temper, at least occasionally, is understandable. It's natural to feel anger when dominated, ridiculed, abused, rejected, or taken advantage of. "If someone pushes ahead of you in a line, it is reasonable to ask him to go back to the end of the line; it is not realistic just to swallow your anger" (Madow, 1972, p. 115). "For parents, anger is a cue which teaches us about ourselves as well as about our children. Realizing and accepting it can be an important constructive experience" (Coopersmith, 1973). Anger lets us know something is amiss. When we respond to it by trying to understand and correct the situation producing our frustration, anger can be useful.

Anger is useful when we use it to communicate our hurt feelings rather than to hurt back. Anger is useful when we see much of another's anger toward us as primarily an expression of hurt and when we make efforts to understand it. The assumption that those who are angry with us do not love us is not so likely true as the probability that those who are "never" angry with us might not love us (Hodge, 1967).

Clearly justified anger, open and natural, verbalized by a parent with whom the child feels secure and loved, not prolonged or out of proportion to the age of the recipient, not frequent or habitual, can be constructive. Expression of one's feelings without insult is not easy, but it is helpful. At times it gets the message across when other methods have failed. We may say:

95

I'm tired of the quarreling. Out you go.
If you two can't settle your problems peacefully, I'll settle
    them for you.
I don't enjoy being spoken to in that tone of voice.
It provokes me when you leave your room in a mess.

There are other interesting views of anger. Hauch (1967)
asserts that we should not say to a child "You upset me" or
"That upsets me." The disappointing behavior of the child alone
does not create our disturbance. We don't have to get angry.
When something frustrates us, we upset ourselves over the
frustration. As Stagner (1961) points out, when we are angry
we are allowing ourselves to be dominated by the stimulus.

To become more effective as parents, you will want to learn
something about this emotion of anger, which is as recurrent as
night and day. Feeling guilty and frustrated will not solve the
problem. Understanding can help you deal with it more realistically.

THE PROBLEMS OF ANGER

Where children are concerned, anger is unproductive when we
let it explosively control us. Their self-images may be hurt by it.
Our wild behavior and unkind, inaccurate comments may be
difficult for them to forget. We forget that they are also learning
their own control or the lack of it from observing our behavior.

UNPRODUCTIVE

When anger is out of proportion to its stimuli, unrestrained in
frequency, or delivered for behavior that is accidental or almost
unavoidable, it works against the type of learning recom-

mended here. The development of happy, self-confident children is best accomplished in an environment of trust and respect.

When anger controls us, it is difficult to look for "motives." "An angry parent does not decipher the messages that surface behaviors are intended to relate" (Coffman, 1969, p. 104). The child may be judged totally by his acts rather than his reasons, with the result that his reasons may become unclear even to himself. The child's needs remain unmet. We cease trying to understand his behavior and instead become involved with our own feelings and a need for power. We do and say things we do not mean and which are not true. What is a child to do if we are lying, unreliable, or irresponsible? Is he to believe us? We may neglect even the restraint and courtesy we would provide even an enemy. Some of the effects of anger:

A child cannot learn sympathy when we frequently show our anger rather than our hurt feelings, disappointment, or sadness.

Expressions of anger may stimulate parents and children to continued aggression (Trotter, 1972; McCandless, 1967).

Anger stimulates counteranger. The feelings a child experiences when faced with parental hostility seldom are transformed into better self-control. They more likely are transformed into resentment toward the parent and reduced self-worth for the child.

Anger inspires the very behavior parents do not want from their child. Research demonstrates that aggression can be stimulated by merely witnessing an aggressive model (Wheeler and Smith, 1967). Lipsitt and Reese (1969) and others call it "observational learning." The observed behavior of others may elicit similar responses in the child.

Anger may say that you do not trust your child, that you

suspect him of purposely planning to annoy you. He is
not given an opportunity to limit or check his impulses
before being judged.

Anger is disappointing. Discouraged, the child may not try to
control his behavior. He waits for parental hostility to set
his limits for him.

Anger can strengthen the behavior it is intended to eliminate.
Especially if a child gets little attention when good, he
may prefer your anger.

To withhold or minimize our anger doesn't hurt us as much
as to express it hurts the child. A child cannot damage seriously
our self-image, but we can damage his. Observe your behavior
in the ordinary home situation. Whether you explode in anger
or not, you may have forgotten the entire matter ten minutes
later. Your child is in a different position. His self-image is not
yet formed—it is being developed. He needs your emotional
support far more than you need his. His sense of self-worth
does not recover as quickly from rebuke as does an adult's.
Immediate signs of reapproval are important.

WRONG MESSAGES ARE DELIVERED

On-the-spot anger (often delivered for a first offense) appears more like revenge than concern for a child's welfare. It
suggests that we see momentarily uncooperative, unskilled, or
inept behavior as deliberately planned to offend us and that his
normally good behavior holds no weight as an indicator of the
dependability of his character. Without our trust, he cannot
learn to trust himself.

This does not mean that parents may never appropriately
become angry or disagreeable. Sometimes the child's behavior
really is abominable and we would do well to say so. Sometimes it is not the child's behavior but our own that is outra-
geous. Our own childhood experiences, lack of information, and

low frustration-tolerance levels limit our ability to avoid hostility. Nevertheless, we can work at reducing conflict. Parental love seems more real when we are not frequently angry. Communicating our love more openly, frequently, and adequately is one way to reduce our rages and outrages.

PARENTAL ANGER INTERFERES WITH IDENTIFICATION

A child does not necessarily strive to be like the parent of his own sex. He is most likely to want to resemble the parent with whom he feels most companionable. An emotionally strong and friendly parent evokes feelings of closeness that result in a child's wanting to be like him. Various elements of parents' behavior may be copied: sense of values, optimism, negativism, mannerisms, hostilities, and ambivalences. Regrettably, we cannot keep him from adopting attitudes and feelings we would rather not pass on to him.

Other adults too, such as group leaders, teachers, coaches, older siblings, and other parents fill identification roles and provide images with which our children identify.

PARENTAL ANGER INTERFERES WITH LEARNING SELF-CONTROL

Children learn to be hostile and aggressive from parents who are hostile and aggressive. Learning by imitation is a significant factor in child development. The best example for learning self-discipline is a parent who can manage his own emotions most of the time. New ways of reacting are acquired by merely observing the behavior of others. Parents continuously serve as models from the time they awake in the morning until the children are tucked in bed at night.

We cannot expect to be loud, abusive, or hostile without losing the child's love, trust, and esteem. Appeals for self-control from an impatient, explosive parent have a hollow ring. Children are more willing to accept direction from a parent who actively involves himself and with whom they feel comfortable and companionable. Parents who cause children to feel inadequate build inferiority, not self-confidence.

A CHILD FEELS REJECTED

He feels rejected and unloved when those he is fond of frequently react to him with anger. Loss of a parent's approval approximates for him a loss of the parent—a primary source of anxiety for the young child. He may feel frightened, guilt-ridden, and hostile. Tensions not relieved through mutual communication sometimes are transformed into physical symptoms or behavior and personality problems. Anger he cannot express to the parent may be turned against another child.

Son is told in an angry voice not to be so dictatorial about what he wants. Reacting to his embarrassment and lowered feelings of self-worth, he kicks over sister's playhouse, accidentally spilling her flower arrangement. She howls with indignation. He gets further reprimand. Son cleans up the mess. Upon completion, he throws the damp sponge into sister's face and the disturbance continues. Further parental anger may stop the surface behavior ultimately but not his counteranger. The problem is best met by an unemotional parent who separates the children and attempts to reestablish the lost parental rapport that was the original cause of the problem.

Rejection is especially difficult when parents alternate affection and harsh treatment. It is confusing to be loved one minute and disliked the next. Security and self-esteem are threatened if one is frequently placed on an emotional yo-yo. In such circumstances, a child not only feels rejected and angry but also experiences considerable anxiety about the incongruity of his expectations. Each time he perceives his parents as kind, loving, and considerate, recurring harsh treatment contradicts this perception. The resulting frustration and ambivalence are difficult to understand and to deal with.

The extent to which a child feels rejected, anxious, or angry because of parental anger depends upon its degree and kind, as well as its duration and frequency. The seriousness of these feelings can be reduced by the parents' follow-up and attempts to correct the problem. Tensions can also be reduced if parents permit, within limits, a display of hostility toward themselves. The child who is free to express himself is able to relieve some of the anger he feels for the offending parent. Misunderstandings can be reduced when they are talked about.

THE "WHY" OF PARENTS' ANGER

Our inability to manage our own anger deserves our concern. How can we expect children with only a few years' experience to know how to control their feelings if we frequently are ourselves unable to control ours when confronted with the disturbance caused by a small child? A child's inequality, the insignificance of his offense, and his usual good behavior all may be disregarded when we are angry. What lies behind parents' anger?

REDUCED SELF-ESTEEM

Psychologists are coming to understand more fully the role that psychological pain plays in the stimulation of anger. It is natural to defend our self-feelings. We want to return the hurt, even to children. "We are more likely to tolerate aggression on the part of children toward siblings and peers than aggression directed toward ourselves" (Cratty, 1968, p. 63).

Self-esteem is jeopardized when others attack us, injuring our pride. What occurs when our child is involved may be described as follows:

> The child's adverse behavior threatens our sense of competency, reducing our self-esteem.
> This can trigger anger and the child is punished.
> Punishment is delivered largely in response to our need to protect our self-feelings and sense of power.
> Not understanding our real motivation, we call it "teaching the child respect."
> Thus, out of lack of information about ourselves, much of what we teach (while angry) is merely a cover for our own rage and reduced self-esteem.

Disobedience reduces our self-esteem. Parents may become angry when little Billy refuses to keep quiet, play fairly, make his bed, wear a hat, go to sleep, eat his dinner, or pick up his toys. We misinterpret his lack of obedience as rejection of us rather than of our authoritarian demands. We do not see our demands for cooperation, which we believe are in the child's best interests, as domination. Domination is hard to accept at any age. Only when expressed in a congenial spirit is domination tolerated with ease.

Six-year-old Edward ignores father's request that he stop running through the house. Father is annoyed by the inconvenience of his son's behavior. His annoyance turns to anger when Edward continues. Father now perceives the lack of obedience as disrespect. The punishment and verbal anger Edward receives are due more to father's reduced self-esteem than to his sense of responsibility for Edward's proper upbringing.

The child's self-assertion reduces our self-esteem. It is difficult for adults to appreciate the sincerity of a small child's determination to do what he feels is best for himself. A child does not view the world from our point of view. As his likes and dislikes about his world accumulate, practical or not, he wants to assume control of his own behavior. He is rebellious mostly because we stand in his way. "We adults know how helpless the infant is, but the infant does not know it" (Bettelheim, 1967, p. 15).

Customarily we are less defensive during the early years of infancy. We trust the motives that animate a dependent little one. Our faith, however, seems to diminish as increasing maturity stimulates the infant to assert his independence and he comes into conflict with the standard of values we have so well assimilated in our own learning. His resistance to what we believe is important brings him his first resentments.

Informed parents are not so likely to regard this reaching out for independence as being directed against them personally. They know that with guidance and imagination a maturing child can in time usually be persuaded to conformity, if conformity is imperative. Understanding his extra sensitivity, they resist overreacting with anger, which can be especially defeating. They explain why certain forms of behavior matter. They exemplify such behavior in their own actions. They instruct and guide and listen to their child. And they let him win occasionally. To develop a child's self-confidence requires that we accept considerable defiance in a calm and reasonable manner. He must feel that he has some influence on his parents if he is later to believe in his ability to persuade others.

UNREALISTIC BELIEFS

Let's review some of the unexamined, untested beliefs about child-rearing that stimulate anger:

That the misbehavior sets a permanent pattern. Much discipline contains an element of fear that a single episode of undesirable behavior forecasts its continuation as a lifetime habit. We believe that what takes place today will be repeated tomorrow, and sometimes it is. But sometimes it is not. When we fail to look beyond the experience of the moment to evaluate whether it is episodic or part of a trend, to trust and have faith in a child's basic desire to do right, then our negative expectancies disproportionately shape our child's perception of himself.

Usually a child does not repeat behavior not frequently modeled by parents or others, nor repeatedly emphasized by parental comment. Early childhood finds him preoccupied with a desire to test out his environment, unimpeded by the restraints of socialization that will affect him throughout most of later life. He lives for the present. We adults view current happenings as related to the future. Not until the age of seven or eight does a child begin to enlarge his capacity for accepting postponement, for objectively viewing a situation, for willingly doing things for others.

Failing to think of themselves as capable of helping him learn to set desirable limits, parents may use the only methods they know: anger and punishment. "If fathers and mothers consider the fleeting moods and the temporary attitudes of their off-spring as permanent, then they will be miserable, and unhappy and tormented" (Liebman, 1966, p. 210).

That we must force the message in.

Eight-year-old Charles, who appears to regard his parents' warnings with nonchalance, receives many more spankings than ten-year-old Joseph, who breaks into tears at the first sign of their anger.

Parents seek guarantees. Without a visible sign of remorse or a child's admission of sorrow, they may not believe that their message is understood. With anger, and sometimes punishment, they attempt to reassure themselves that the message gets through. Yet, like blowing one's top when out of gas on the freeway, it gets you nowhere.

Effective discipline is largely and generally free of anger. A child can learn civilized behavior without parental loss of control. In fact, he learns it better from parents who model it for him.

There are no "instant-result" methods for influencing behavior in positive ways. Parents cannot ensure that the message they want to teach is grasped immediately. The effects of guidance are not often readily observable. We must wait for results and have faith that respect and reason will in time have desirable effects. For instance:

A friend reports that David (seven) has kicked a girl at school. Rather than expect him to serve sentence in the form of physical punishment or the removal of a future privilege, why not believe that he can learn from a simple discussion of the problem? Listen to his side of the story. When mistreatment of others is not a common occurrence, your trust encourages him to behave as you wish him to.

Mary (seven) fails to slice an orange the way she wants it. Angry, she tosses it into the wastebasket. Why not refrain from adding your own anger? She can learn from polite instruction. Say, "Please don't throw good food away. If you don't want it, put it in a bowl in the refrigerator. Let me know and I'll help you cut your oranges the way you want them."

That misbehavior will lead to delinquency. Parents worry lest disrespect, disinterest, and lack of obedience are deliberate and a sign of future delinquency. Not fully understanding the natural self-centeredness of children, they blame the child's character rather than his immaturity. Reacting in an angry manner, they incite the very rebellion they fear. Delinquency does not occur without reason. Parents who are not delinquent themselves, who have faith in their children, who guide and instruct them, and who enjoy playing and working with them most of the time are not apt to produce delinquent teen-agers. Surveys of delinquent children reveal that the parents were usually punitive or rejecting. One or more of the following conditions usually exist:

The child is subjected to heavy physical punishment, abuse, and belittlement.
One or both of the parents are lacking in warmth, sympathy, and affection.
The child is consistently neglected and uncared for.
The parents strongly prohibit aggression toward themselves but often condone it toward others.
The parents have numerous emotional problems and lack of esteem for each other.
One or both of the parents are excessively hostile.
Fathers tend to ridicule the boys when they make mistakes.
Few delinquents have close ties with their fathers (Bandura and Walters, 1959; McCord, McCord, and Howard, 1963; James, 1970).

The research of Devereux sheds light upon the role of parents in the case of the less dependable, nonachievement, gang-oriented children. In his study, it was found that the children received either too little or too much of various parental treatments: "The parents were either overly permissive (possibly perceived as neglect or rejection by their children); or parents were highly authoritarian" (1970, p. 138). Their children preferred a gang more than a single friend and were unable to hold to internalized moral standards when peers were pressing them for deviance. The children most able to resist peer-group pressure came from homes where adequate amounts of spare time were spent with parents, especially the mother. The relationship was characterized by moderate levels of child support, discipline, and control.

Devereux thus asks, "Are we releasing our children to the world of peers too soon and too completely?" (1970, p. 138).

Bronfenbrenner summarizes the situation similarly: "It would seem that the peer-oriented child is more a product of parental disregard than of the attractiveness of the peer group—that he turns to his age-mates less by choice than by default" (1970, p. 102). Too strong peer-group reference interferes with a youngster's ability to adopt mature values or learn standards for appropriate adult behavior. Such children yield more to peer pressure than do those who spend more time with adults.

That the child must be taught that the world is not always fair or consistent. Some parents believe the child must learn early that the world is not always fair or consistent. They say "nobody's perfect" and go on to conclude that the child may as well learn at home that people will sometimes disappoint him and treat him unkindly. This is a false basis for learning at home.

Conflict does not have to be planned. Disappointments and harsh treatments do not need to be concocted. More than enough occur in the ordinary events of daily living. Even though some parents believe otherwise, harsh treatment does not toughen a child. It reduces his respect for himself and others and renders him even more vulnerable to mistreatment. Too many disappointments in early life have a damaging effect upon self-image and one's view of others' worth. Strength to meet the hardships of life grows as confidence in himself grows.

That parents have the right not to be bothered. No sooner do we find a moment to relax than we are interrupted by the needs of a little one, or so it sometimes seems. Anger rises when small children intrude frequently upon privacy or the pursuit of our interests. Yet children do need attention. They cannot be expected solely to live a parallel existence with us. We do need time to ourselves and this should be arranged. However, a persistent attitude of anger, disinterest, or detachment produces much family distress. Frankly, we do not have the right *not* to be bothered by younger children if there is no one else to care for them. Family members who assume this privilege frequently assert their hostilities thus:

> That's my seat.
> I'm watching this TV program.
> Why can't you close the door?
> Get out of my way.
> Why don't you get lost?
> All you do is cry.
> You don't know what you are talking about.

A family is a team. All members have responsibility, within reasonable limits, to be helpful to one another, especially to younger members. Acceptance of this fact creates a pleasant home atmosphere. Taking five or ten minutes as needed to settle problems and care for needs saves emotional wear and tear on all. Immediate peace sometimes must be relinquished for later harmony. Consider the following problem situations:

Young son keeps turning on the light after father has turned it off. Son wants to color in his coloring book. Father wants to watch a special TV program in the dark. Why not help son organize a place for coloring away from the TV area? If son returns to turning on the light, what can you do? Consider letting him have his way on this occasion. Some situations may not merit a "battle of wills." Preferring not to force an issue does not give a child the illusion that his behavior has been approved. A child can learn to respect the rights of others even though he is allowed occasional deviations. When the parent feels that a situation demands strong measures, he must have sufficient time to initiate the removal procedures suggested later in the section "Last Resort Discipline."

Father and son are playing table tennis. Feeling left out, six-year-old sister disrupts the game. Angry comments belittle her but fail to dissuade her. Try taking a few minutes away from the game. Sympathize with her wish to partcipate, and let her know exactly when it will be her turn to receive your time and attention.

Two older brothers have set up a tent for an evening on the lawn. A dispute occurs when the boys try to remove five-year-old sister who wants to sweep out their tent. Why not save the peaceful evening and encourage the boys to give her ten minutes alone with the tent? She is happy and the boys come back to a clean tent.

IGNORANCE

Without comprehension of our child's easily wounded and vulnerable self-esteem, we do not realize how devastating are our hostile voice tones, our acting mistreated, and our use of belittlement. Uninformed about the effects of anger, we are swept up in the various forms of rejection, impatience, and annoyance directed against children; and which are, as noted earlier, often disproportionate to the offense. Anger makes it very difficult to take an objective view of ourselves and the situation.

Lundin suggests, "Perhaps there is a little bit of the sadist in all of us to the degree that we are reinforced by submission" (1969, p. 267). When a child reacts with docile obedience or some expression of hurt or injury, parental anger may be satisfied.

The child in the grocery who is slapped for not obeying his parent's command to stop whining may not be slapped for the increased crying which then follows. The parent is satisfied with an overt expression of hurt.

For the child, it is puzzling, it hurts, and it is frightening to have someone he loves and who may have expressed affection for him the moment before suddenly react with hostility. It is a sad fact that the strong feelings parents display at such times often affect the child's self-image.

How frequently one explodes in wrath is not necessarily the crucial factor. All experience leaves some impression. Many adults can recall a single humiliating experience of parental anger from their own past. An angry parent's voice and facial expression sometimes are long remembered but seldom recalled as they deal with their own children.

OUR OWN EARLY EXPERIENCE

As political, religious, and social attitudes and views are taught—consciously and unconsciously by one generation to another—so are patterns of emotional response. We relive with our own children many of the experiences of our childhood. We speak in a way not dissimilar to that of our parents. The traits we like or dislike in our children are apt to be similar to those our parents liked or disliked in us. We often punish the same behaviors our parents punished in us. Having been taught that hostility toward parents was judged disrespectful, we may react accordingly when our children show it.

EMBARRASSMENT

"What will others think?" seems to be the rationale for much discipline. In the presence of friends, a child may be ridiculed for an accidental mess, slapped in the face for being assertive, or spanked for striking a child who may have hit him first. It seems to be an attempt to prove ourselves good parents.

Parents are particularly embarrassed when their child is argumentative or defiant in the presence of others. They may lose their composure if they do not receive what they believe to be a proper degree of respect from children in public.

Interruption of conversation supplies frequent reason for parental rebuke, especially when it happens in front of guests and when the interruption is perceived by parents as disrespect. Repressing a desire to speak is as difficult for a child as the postponement of almost any other wish or need. Patience and consideration grow as he matures and receives helpful parental examples. It's relatively easy to motion him aside and let him speak to you away from the presence of others.

Any child will usually respond to prearranged plans for communicating when others are present. He only needs to know what you feel and what you want him to do. You can say:

It is embarrassing to be interrupted in front of guests.
While the guests are here, play in your room or in the yard. When you come in, please don't walk through the middle of the living room.
Wait for the conversation to stop before you interrupt. If it is urgent, tug at my sleeve and I'll excuse myself right away.

While parents resent being interrupted, they seldom hesitate to interrupt their own conversations when they feel the need to reprimand a child whose behavior seems improper. This sometimes is desirable, but it is easily overdone. Greatly concerned about the impression a child is making, they allow nothing to go unnoticed. In front of guests, they may impatiently remark:

Don't run.
Your napkin is on the floor.
Look at your face. It's a mess.
Eat your food.
Speak up. We can't hear you.
Go wash your hands.
Pick up your sweater.

The child is embarrassed. You may have noticed how children disciplined in your presence quickly glance to your face hoping that their predicament and embarrassment is unnoticed.

FRUSTRATION

Sometimes we feel helpless about our inability to communicate effectively to a child matters about which he should be concerned for his own welfare. Food, clothing, health habits, safety, and skill development may be a cause for continual conflict. We care about his well-being, though he may not.

Gaining his cooperation may seem impossible. If one is subjected to these problems over a prolonged period, tempers
probably will erupt. A child's resistance to tasks that have not
yet acquired positive value for him may be very distressing.
Helping him become interested is a time-consuming project, but
one that pays large dividends and one that parents can learn to
accomplish. We are not as helpless as we sometimes feel.

THE CHILD'S DISTRESS

Socialization requires that inappropriate desires remain unsatisfied; hence there is often no alternative—one must simply
tolerate much of the noise of a child's frustration until, through
maturation, he learns to accept our limits in a timely fashion.
Toleration for his crying protects his sense of self-worth and
emotional openness. Resentment, accompanied by references to
him as a "crybaby," may or may not produce conformity; it will
certainly reduce self-esteem. Usually he will continue to cry and
rebel even though filled with feelings of guilt for failing to
measure up to our expectations. His feelings may remain unrelieved for as long as we remain angry. It is helpful, then, to
remind ourselves occasionally that his behavior is not designed
deliberately to distress us. He does have reasons, though they
may not be obvious to himself or to us.

Crying reduces the intensity of his frustration. His parents'
patience and refraining from harsh criticism allow his ego to
grow. Regardless of how loudly he asserts his wishes, you can
teach him without shouting back that:

You have work to do after an hour of games.
Mother cannot set up the wading pool on a cold day.
Mother cannot go back to the store immediately and get him
   another balloon.
Dessert comes after he has finished his dinner.
When he's ill, he cannot go to Billy's house to play.

The dog is not his, and he cannot keep him.
He can have one piece of candy but not two.

By tolerating much of his distress, giving sympathy instead of resentment, and acknowledging his feelings, we do not subject him to guilt and counterhostility for having displeased us. We model appropriate behavior for him to follow. We keep channels of communication open.

THE CHILD'S DEPENDENCY

Clinging, fear of leaving mother, and other evidences of lack of self-sufficiency are examples of stimuli that arouse parental anger. Parents are resentful of the child who refuses to do for himself what we believe he is capable of doing.

Independence does not come easily. For the child, it's difficult to give up the comfort of having others care for you. His requests for assistance may sound like demands: "Help me get dressed." "Make me cocoa." "Help me take a bath." His obvious immaturity affords him considerable control over parents. Conditioned from earliest infancy to expect parental care and attention, he thrives from getting as much as he wants. Reversing such a comfortable state of affairs must be a gradual process.

Parents may think that his demands are deliberate attempts simply to assert and enjoy his control over them. It may be hard to see the needs that motivate his demands. He himself may be unaware of those needs. Have you noticed how often a child misinterprets his own feelings?

He will request food when in fact he seeks the comfort that mother seems too busy to give.

He looks for assistance in getting dressed for an outing away from home when he wishes relief from the fear of the unexpected.

A need for companionship or love becomes a request to "Help me take a bath."

He may cry at the slightest excuse, claim his books are
   difficult to put away, or protest that he doesn't know what
   to wear, without knowing that his real need is parental
   sympathy or companionship.
Bored or unhappy, he may turn to thumb-sucking or cuddling
   his blanket.
Cheating to win in games with friends becomes a way of
   building self-importance.
His tummy-aches, which seem real to him, may be a bid for
   parental attention or a deep need for reaffirmation of
   parental love and concern.

Continuing dependency sometimes arises from a lack of
adequate and reliable care during the critical years when it was
needed most. If his cries were frequently left unanswered by a
parent afraid of "spoiling" him, he may have come to feel helpless and to fear abandonment greatly. In his insecurity, he
clings to mother, demanding frequent support to alleviate his
fears. He pleads with mother: "I don't want to go. I'm afraid.
Don't leave me. I want to stay with you."

Similar dependency needs have been observed in other creatures. Some species of birds and animals may become *imprinted*
by some close moving object, living or mechanical, which they
see shortly after birth—the thing becomes firmly fixed in their
memory and they are deeply attached to it. Once this attachment is established, acceptance of a substitute, even if it
happens to be the real mother, is resisted.

Punishment appears to increase the strength of such attachments. The research of Hess (1959) shows how the baby duck
whose toes are stepped on during the imprinting period doesn't
run away in fear but cuddles even closer to the punishing
object. Similarly, the baby duck who is pecked as it follows its
mother or who has difficulty following her over rough ground
may become more strongly attached to the mother than do its
less threatened siblings. Monkeys mistreated by their mothers

during infancy show stronger mother-attachments than do other monkeys (Seay, Alexander, and Harlow, 1964).

In a similar way, research indicates that the human child whose needs were criticized and punished during certain early critical periods displays more dependency traits than the child who felt secure and well-cared-for during early childhood.

DISPLACED ANGER

Our better judgment is sometimes ignored in the face of child distress. When we are busy, the child in his dress-up clothes may get the popsicle or ice cream cone he begs for. Then, should an accident occur, parental anger about the mess, combined with anger at ourselves for not having resisted his pleading, is easily displaced onto the child: "That's what I thought you would do. You don't have the sense you were born with."

On a shopping trip, mother may agree in an abrupt tone and manner to purchase the toy her child is pleading for: "All right, but that's the last thing you are getting." She feels anger, directed at herself, for not being able to say no and resentment toward the child for putting her in a difficult position. The child feels guilt for having wishes that are displeasing to the parent and anger at being resented, as well as loss of pleasure in his interest.

Mary (seven) has convinced mother that she needs a new ice-skating costume. Mother begrudgingly purchases it, announcing to Mary that she could go ice skating ten times for the amount of money that it took to buy her something to look pretty in. Mary, reacting to mother's resentment, displaces her reduced self-esteem to her friend whose enthusiasm over the fun of the afternoon is dampened with: "You can't skate."

Carol (eight) wants to try the special new TV dinner she picked out at the grocery, not for lunch on Saturday, but now. Mother, seeing no real reason for interfering with her right to be different, goes along with the idea, although she doesn't quite approve. Mother's resentment at the interference with her own dinner plans takes the edge off Carol's wish to experiment. Comments from curious siblings at dinner further reduce her pleasure in trying out an idea of her own.

Parents often try to solve children's conflicts by telling rather than doing. Becoming actively involved poses a problem when one is settled comfortably for the evening. When our requests for cooperation go unheeded, anger at our own ineffectiveness can result in an explosive reaction toward children.

Distress over business or social affairs may be displaced unconsciously upon the child whose behavior of the moment offers a convenient excuse for the release of hostility: "Shut up!" "Beat it!" "Get out of here!" A father subjected to authoritarian superiors and with little autonomy in his work is more likely to behave in this way toward his sons (McKinley, 1963).

"Anger is sometimes used as a cover for fear or sadness, especially in boys and men. In our culture, where fear and sadness are regarded as weak, rage is often used to camouflage them. They need to hide them from themselves and others" (Voeks, 1973).

Having tried on numerous dresses only to discover that none suits her particular requirements, mother may become angry over minor disturbances that in a less complicated situation would go unnoticed.

Upset over a quarrel with one's spouse or other person, a parent deals less effectively with children's problems, finding it especially difficult to tolerate noisy activity. Children, rather than the spouse or other person responsible, may become the target.

Frustrated over our own awkwardness or error, parents often model anger which the child observes. Such anger appears to be self-administered belittlement:

The swearing over the broken dish.
The cupboard door that gets slammed because of the knot on father's head.

The fist that is pounded on the table because of an overturned
coffeepot.

The tricycle wheel that is smashed when fixing it becomes
overly difficult.

The rake that gets pounded to pieces after father steps on it.

As noted earlier, children imitate all kinds of behavior. Just as
they learn how to walk, talk, dress, hold a spoon, brush their
teeth, and comb their hair by observing and imitating parents,
they copy parental expressions of anger.

ILLNESS AND FATIGUE

A lowered state of physical energy from illness or fatigue
reduces a parent's self-control and causes his anger to be more
easily provoked. Under the stress of the moment even parents
who clearly understand child behavior may disregard their
standards and resort to undesirable techniques of punishment.

CHILDREN'S MESSES

The quickest and often the angriest parental outbursts occur
over the messes children make. Something spilled at dinner can
arouse sufficient anger to eliminate for the remainder of a meal
any opportunity for pleasurable family conversation.

Daren (ten) upsets a serving bowl of vegetables onto the floor. Angry
parental comments follow. Daren reacts to his parent's anger with
counteranger. He stalks off and refuses to clean up the mess. Why
not clean it up yourself? Next time, offer to help without expressing
dismay, anger, or resentment at behavior that was not intentional.
Note the change in the child's response.

Mothers seldom have a day that does not require a cleanup.
Accepting this as an inevitable part of parenthood makes the
job easier.

Infants don't mind messes. In time, however, from their
parents, they learn abundant resentment of such mishaps; and

as adults, they pass this attitude on to their own children. One can note how universal is such learning by observing the child in a nursery-school group who bursts into tears over a spilled cup of juice. How did he come to be afraid? Certainly a mess is uncomfortable, for some even more than for others. But surely children deserve the same treatment parents accord a guest who accidentally spills or breaks something in their home: "That's all right. It won't be any trouble. We'll take care of it."

CHILDREN'S CARELESSNESS

We often lash out in anger when children accidentally injure us—when they shut a door on our fingers, step on our toes, bump into us. Of course it hurts, and we probably yell loud enough to make that clear. It hurts, too, if your best friend shouts at you when you think he should know that you didn't do it on purpose. Imagine the child's feelings in this situation:

Father and son are walking. Son unthinkingly walks in front of father. In maneuvering to keep from falling, father hurts his foot. His anger and reprimands are loud and clear. "Why can't you watch what you are doing? Don't you know any better?" Son reacts with counteranger. Father is insulted, feeling that he should have received an apology rather than returned hostility.

Perhaps he should, but if an adult friend had been involved in the accident, father would have said instead, "Oh, it didn't hurt much." Blame for injury not purposely planned is disappointing. Why, at least, can we not say, "Yes, it did hurt, but you didn't do it on purpose."

INSENSITIVITY

Although normally we may be quite aware of our position of authority, of our greater experience and wisdom, in moments of anger we may react to our children as though they were our equals. The closeness of the family reduces sensitivity to age differences even for parents. We feel hurt when a child spurns us, talks back, or disobeys. His hostile words ("I hate you!" "I won't do it!") may threaten our self-esteem. The punishment we deal out when he slams a door in our face may sometimes be more accurately described as hurting him back. We call it discipline; and we call his reaction, when he strikes back at us, disrespect.

In a similar way, brothers and sisters of varying ages and abilities tend to react emotionally to each other as equals. Older children find it hard to refrain from criticizing the immature behavior of their younger siblings, who seem in many ways so equal to them. Younger children feel slighted if they do not receive the same privileges as their older brothers and sisters.

SOME THINGS TO DO ABOUT OUR ANGER

INVEST A FEW MINUTES' TIME

Get up and out of your easy chair. Many parents raise their voices in anger and threat of punishment without budging one inch from comfort. We can't solve problems from behind a magazine. Sooner or later we must actively involve ourselves in order to redirect behavior that has gone beyond the limit of endurance. Quite often, however, this happens only after parental anger has reached the exploding point because of the loss of peace and the frustration of having commands ignored. Then physical and verbal punishment is administered that would have been unnecessary had time been given to restructuring the situation at the outset.

A few minutes invested at an early moment can pay substantial dividends. We spend considerable time and effort on aspects of a child's social life. What about his emotional life? There is no need for punishment when an explanation will work as well, but be sure to explain both "why" and "how." Being too quick to judge, blame, or punish is more like revenge than discipline. A court often accords more leniency. The child so punished might feel:

My parents must believe that I will do this thing again that they are so unhappy about. They are wiser than I. If they believe so, it must be true. If my parents do not trust my behavior, it is probably true that I am not trustable.

Avoid reading into expressions of indifference motives that are not there. Seldom is a child deliberately trying to disobey or annoy us. Despite his behavior of the moment, trust that he ultimately can be persuaded, by reason and example, to more acceptable behavior. If you believe that he has this capacity and your actions verify this belief, he learns to believe so too and tries to be worthy of your faith.

Be willing to stop what you are doing. When not emotionally involved, you are not so easily upset by interruptions. Being more objective, you'll find it easier to discover the real reasons for his behavior.

Susan (six) has been quietly entertaining herself for over an hour. Suddenly she becomes irritable, throwing her equipment and materials on the floor. Investigation discloses that the puppet she is trying to construct is beyond her ability. With parental sympathy and distraction, she is helped to understand that her distress is the result of a complicated task that up until now she was mastering very satisfactorily. Had the parent reacted adversely to her objectionable behavior, her intense self-anger would have been complicated with hostility toward the parent, plus shame and disappointment with herself at having displeased the parent.

Sally (seven), who has invited a friend to dinner, is making a fuss at the table, talking loudly, interrupting and disturbing others. Talking with her away from the table, mother discovers that her earlier remark, "Gulping your food is impolite; see how ladylike Polly eats," disturbed Sally. Sally says, "You never tell me that I'm a lady." Discovering that reduced self-esteem triggered Sally's hostility and aggression, mother is able to supply the reassurance necessary to encourage her return to cooperation.

Upon arrival home from school, Gloria (six) seems angry with the world. You become the object of her anger as she lashes out with fists and feet. When questioned about events before her arrival home, she reveals that two little friends had decided to "run away from Gloria." In this situation, parental anger would only have increased Gloria's reduced self-esteem, the original cause of her distress.

THINK BEFORE YOU SPEAK

Ask yourself, "Is this the way I would talk to an adult friend?" If we pause, we give ourselves time to find out why the child is misbehaving. Insight helps us control anger. It often prevents a child from being wrongly judged. The same behavior that aroused our anger on one occasion may not arouse it on the next if, in the meantime, we have achieved insight into the motives behind our child's behavior. We respond differently when we see behavior as accidental rather than deliberate—when we try to understand the feelings that cause a child to behave in disturbing ways. No matter how great the apparent provocation, try to restrain explosive anger. Cooperative behavior is a set of highly complex interactions, and learning cooperative behavior requires a gradual process lasting most of childhood. Anger cannot speed it. To lose your temper only gives your child a model of how to be angry.

A healthy emotional relationship with others, adults or children, requires that insight be continually striven for. We must learn to restrain some of our first automatic reactions to behavior. Ask yourself, "What would make me act as my child is behaving?" Look to the moments just past. There you may find the stimulus that prompted the improper behavior. As you develop skill in understanding how children really think, feel, and grow emotionally, many of your hostilities will evaporate or be reduced greatly. A desire to protect your child's developing self-confidence will silence many of your quick-tempered outbursts. Emotions become more pleasant and easier to control when we learn to view ourselves and others objectively.

FOLLOW A DEFINITE PLAN

Don't overreact. Good discipline takes longer than a few seconds. Wait until strong feelings have subsided. It's difficult to be fair when angry. Quick anger, punishment, and threats are unlikely to settle problems and usually cause some loss of rapport. Our adult friends are seldom treated that way. With friends we usually try to suppress annoyance and let deeper feelings of empathy come through.

Be sensitive to how things seem to a child. Find out how the problem looks from his frame of reference. What needs is he attempting to cope with? "To see the person as he sees himself is the deepest way to know and respect him" (Moustakas, 1956, p. 4).

Behind the obstinate behavior of the moment is a basically sensitive human being who prefers happy people and approval. Give him a chance to demonstrate this longing. A little distraction is often all that's necessary to help a child reorient his behavior. Even a brief hand signal may be sufficient to let him know when he's off limits. If more is needed, consider these suggestions for helping him behave more pleasingly:

Identify the behavior you want changed. Tell him what you prefer to have him do. Be polite whether he is or not.

Lend a hand to solve the problem in which he is enmeshed.

Role play. What we expect is more clearly understood when we show him how we would behave in similar circumstances.

Explain the consequences of his behavior and why the behavior you are recommending is superior. Let him know how his behavior makes you or others feel. As Gordon suggests "Send an 'I' message rather than a 'You' message" (1970, *b*, p. 117).

If the above do not work, gently but firmly remove him or the disturbing object he is using. There may be increased anger and resentment at the frustration caused by the removal. Let it be his alone. Often he is relieved that the episode is over.

When parents signal or explain their preferences, the child has an opportunity to test his ability to change. When we rage and threaten, he does not think of compliance as being something of his own doing but rather as something resulting from the imposed will of his parents.

In some situations, giving your child time to refuse and resist may be useful. He will often accept our ideas if he's had an opportunity to temporarily rebel. Changing his behavior is easier when we do not return his anger:

Henry (seven) is angry. He doesn't want to go with the family on a planned outing. Father lets him know that he is expected to go along. Nothing more is said. Although Henry continues to imply that he's not going, he does later join the family. Thus, compliance is experienced as his own doing rather than something forced upon him. Had father interrupted his acting out too soon, Henry might have continued to refuse out of defiance or complied out of fear.

Jean (eight) climbs into the front seat of the car between father and big brother. She insists that it is her turn to ride up front. As big brother is map-reader for the trip, Jean is ordered to the back seat. She refuses to move. Father pulls to the side of the road and storms until Jean is frightened into moving and the whole family is upset. Rapport with father is disturbed when he uses fear rather than reason and patience to gain his ends.

Father announces that neighbors are dropping in. He suggests that Billy (three) put on his shoes and join them. Billy storms off, saying that he doesn't want company and he's going to stay in his room when they arrive. Billy cools off and joins the guests when they arrive. He knows that the decision is his own. It was not forced upon him by an ultimatum that he join the family or else.

DON'T PROLONG ANGER IN SILENCE

Silent reproach is more threatening than words. Children sense the resentment it carries and feel as insecure as do adults when they receive it. They too prefer to know where they stand in the affections of the significant people in their lives. They have no one else to turn to.

When an initial explosion is over, communication and affectionate regard should be promptly reestablished. Angry feelings should be talked about. Silence may leave parents and children with inaccurate interpretations of each other's feelings of fairness. When angry, discuss your feelings in an open and honest way, preferably after you have allowed them to cool slightly.

I don't like it when you leave your art supplies all over the room after you are finished with them.
It's not fair to make us all uncomfortable. Let's hear what you are angry about. Is there something you want to change? Is there something you are not satisfied with?

Of course a disagreement is unpleasant, but it is less unpleasant when it is brought out into the open than when angry feelings remain unrelieved. It is also more honest and more helpful. Talking it over without blaming the child indicates your concern. It says, "You are important enough for me to tell you without trying to hurt you."

Redl (1966) writes that not showing anger because we don't feel like communicating is as wrong as not giving the affection a child needs because we happen to be distracted or worried. Depending upon the circumstances, a mild display of anger may be needed even if we don't feel like giving it. When behavior is designed to test our reaction, the person needs to know its effect on us. Even a child understands that when someone you care about has been abusive to you it should hurt. Without overreacting we can let him know our feelings in an open, honest way:

That hurts. I don't like being called names.

You don't have to agree with me, but I'd like you to hear my side of the story. Maybe you can help me understand. I don't want to continue feeling angry with you.

If you are angry because you lost your notebook, why do you yell at me? I'm not responsible, and I don't like being treated that way.

Misperceptions are crucial in the development of conflicts between parents and children, especially when feelings are not talked about. When a child feels hurt, angry, or unhappy, he may believe that his behavior adequately conveys his feelings. A parent, perceiving his child's behavior as "exaggerated" or "put on," may hope that ignoring or minimizing it will help it go away. Neither parent nor child may realize that the other is not getting an accurate message. The child, believing his distress obvious, may feel that he does not matter much to an impassive parent. It is wise to accept most behavior as the child believes it to be. Tell him, "You feel sad [or angry]. Sit here with me and let's talk about it."

DON'T WALK OUT

Parents who walk out on disagreements, who remain distant, aloof, and nonspeaking, are unknowingly playing the game of being abused. On the grounds that they don't have to tolerate mistreatment, they get back at the offending child. The child is placed in the position of an offender, of having wronged the parent. He has practically no alternative but to believe that the superior parent is right. The unrelieved feelings of guilt, hostility, and rejection through which the child must suffer are difficult to understand. He does not have the words to communicate the strong feelings that distress him. It's even difficult for him to understand just what in his parent's behavior arouses the uncomfortable feelings within. Unpleasant feelings persist and interfere with his ability to function effectively. Temporary regression of behavior may occur: crying, whining, and tantrums. Distress persists in some degree until a sign of reacceptance is received or the child decides he does not care about the parent. A situation such as the following describes some effects of unrelieved feelings of rejection:

Father is taking photos of a departing friend. Mary (five) wants her picture taken, but father is out of film and in a hurry. Mary does not perceive the significance of father's problems and seems unreasonably demanding. Father departs for the office visibly angry at having been subjected to Mary's tears and demands. Her last image of father shows his anger with her and her behavior. He leaves and may soon forget the incident. Meanwhile, Mary's feelings of rejection are unrelieved, and an hour of problem behavior ensues. The telephone receiver is banged up and down until Mary is removed from it. She then sits down at the piano and pounds away. The depth of her rejection is unreduced until mother takes time out to reorient her with reading and other activities. Cuddling and companionship do much to bring her back to more cooperative behavior.

The unpleasant episode following father's departure might have been avoided had father known about unrelieved feelings of rejection. Although the child often seems determined to annoy or distress us, he has no enjoyment in the loss of affection he undergoes for having displeased the person he loves and depends on. He does not even understand the counterhostility he feels when parents are angry with him. Strong anger toward an available parent can be worked through and dissipated during the interaction in home activities with that parent. An angry parent who must depart for work or who isolates himself in the home leaves the child with unrelieved feelings of anger and rejection.

Situations similar in some degree arise when childhood friends disappoint one another. Strong feelings are difficult to work through when opportunities for continued interaction are not available. Your child may be difficult to live with for a while after he has fallen out with a valued friend.

Much of a child's hostility, like that of a parent, is triggered by reduced self-esteem. Hostility is a natural reaction to pain, emotional as well as physical pain. When parents understand this more fully, they will react more often with sympathy rather than anger. They will relieve feelings of rejection and reduced self-esteem by sending signals of reacceptance quickly. Reasoning will replace authoritarian control. Limits will be set without anger. They will not walk out on disagreements without leaving behind a few pleasant words, even for children who appear not to respond:

I still love you.
I'll talk with you about this problem as soon as I return.
Let's read that new book you have when I get home.

Children are more tuned-in than parents may realize. In some ways, they have greater sensitivity than adults who rely on words more than empathy. They observe our inner struggle to control anger; they see how we suppress or release it, how we recover from it. The example we set in not prolonging anger encourages them to behave accordingly. Even in situations where it is the child who walks out on a disagreement, don't wait for him to make the first sign of reconciliation.

Martin (ten) is sent way from the family for creating a disturbance. After he has had time to cool down, seek him out. Whether he returns your greeting or not, make a friendly comment. Let him know that you want him to rejoin you, that you do not carry a grudge.

Return of parental support is necessary immediately, or as soon as anger has dissipated. If he wishes to be unhappy, the decision should be his alone. Your behavior should let him know that you no longer wish to be angry. Offer warmth and cheerfulness:

Dinner is ready.

There's a good movie on TV tonight.

We aren't leaving until you get your coat and come along.

Do you have any suggestions for what to fix for dinner tonight?

Would you remind me to take these books back to the library?

HAVE THE COURAGE TO ADMIT YOUR ANGER

It is a normal emotion. Most of us, in moments of anger, occasionally impose unjust or unwise treatment. After a parent, beyond his limit of endurance, has resorted to unfair physical or verbal abuse, he should correct the situation. He should apologize. Our willingness to admit our mistakes, to make a change in direction, brings a lot of respect from children.

The child's sense of reality is at stake. When we deny or try to hide our stupidities and our shortcomings, the child may not be deceived entirely, but he will be confused. Without our apology, he remains emotionally in the unjustified position of having wronged his parents. Frequent failure of the parent to admit displeasure and anger interferes with the child's ability to accurately perceive reality. Although he may have doubts about the fairness of his parents' treatment, the authority of the parental position and his own immaturity leave him virtually no choice but to rely upon our opinions and behavior as his guide.

When his feelings tell him that we are angry or resentful, but we deny it, the incongruity produces conflict. Subjected to repeated contradictory messages (a contributing factor in schizophrenia), he learns to be anxious about his world and the validity of his own perceptions. Parental words should not contradict what he can sense from observing our behavior. He doesn't know how to establish a reliable frame of reference wholly by himself. Such things as these are very confusing to him:

When in anger we say things we do not mean and which are not true, but we do not retract them.

Parents regularly leave the fulfillment of his requests until last while indicating that this is not true when he expresses concern.

Mother is upset over a disagreement with father and doesn't explain that it's not the child with whom she is displeased.

He is reprimanded for failing to answer the phone and nothing is said when he explains that he didn't hear it ring.

He is accused of causing trouble when his parents, planning to be away, give him the house key only to find themselves locked out when their plans change and they arrive home earlier than expected.

Father claims to be his friend but rages at him over an accidentally spilled cup of milk.

He is told to ask for what he wants and then told that he is overly demanding.

He is disciplined for tuning out the radio to which dad is listening and nothing is said when he explains that he was trying to adjust the reception.

He is told to say what he feels and then reprimanded for doing so.

The family is on their way out to dinner, and he says, "I don't want to go to the sandwich shop." Father growls, "OK, you

don't want sandwiches; we'll go home!" When asked why
    he is angry, father says, "I'm not angry!"
He is blamed for starting a fight that turns out to have been
    instigated by someone else and nobody apologizes.
He says, "You don't want me along" and the parent says, "OK,
    stay home if you want to be difficult."
He is blamed for losing mother's pen, and nothing is said
    when mother finds it right where she left it.

Perfection is not possible, but wise and dedicated parents can
do much toward improving their ability to help a child develop
an adequate frame of reference. Mistakes will occur, but recognizing and admitting them is a significant step ahead.

Sorry, that is not quite true. I wanted to hurt you back.
Yes, I do seem to have been postponing my promises to you
    until I get everything I want done completed. I'll stop right
    now and read to you.
You'll have to excuse me, dear. I've just had a disagreement
    with your father. I'll be in a better mood soon.
I'm sorry I lost my temper. I felt that you heard the phone. I
    thought you were being indifferent.
Sorry, I was angry about being locked out. It was not really
    your fault. You did not expect us home so soon.
You are not clumsy. I'm sorry. I cannot always control my
    anger about messes. Sometimes I say things that were said
    to me when I was a child.
That was unkind. I did tell you to ask for what you want. I
    just didn't expect that you wanted so much.
I'm sorry I misjudged you. I didn't need to speak so abruptly.
I'm sorry I lost my temper. My feelings were hurt when you
    spoke so sharply.
Sorry, I was angry. You have just as much right to want
    chicken for dinner as I do to want sandwiches.

That was unkind. I should have looked into the situation more carefully rather than blaming you. Sometimes we say things without thinking because we are angry about being disturbed.

That's not correct. We do want you along. I was angry and tired, but I shouldn't have been unkind.

GET FATHER INVOLVED

The whole family, but especially its boys, are less susceptible to emotional problems when they have a companionable, fair, and respected father. Father's experience with his own father may cause him to want to appear strict and businesslike. Earlier generations often believed that gentleness was a feminine trait and that in a man it meant lack of masculinity. Unaware that boys and girls of any age are encouraged by a father's fond hug and expressions of sympathy and tenderness, many a male parent has missed some of the joy of loving a youngster.

A meaningful relationship with father is also important to mother's emotional security. Father is needed by mother as well as the children in the infancy years. The quality of the husband-wife relationship greatly influences the care and affection mother can give to the children. Mother has a tremendous influence upon personality development. Her emotional adjustment is reflected in the children. She cannot give the great amount of love and attention vital to each child's emotional development if concerned and worried about her relationship with her husband, for whom she now has less time and energy than before the children arrived. An unhappy mother withdraws from her children.

Mother's feelings toward father are extremely important to the way in which the children will relate to him. Children take their cues from mother in responding to father, especially when he is absent much of the time (Nash, 1965).

If father feels like an outsider, it may help if he understands that the bond of mutual love and affection between mother and child is a natural development, designed by nature to insure the survival of the infant. Recent observations and studies indicate that certain sensitive periods exist immediately after birth, when mothers become strongly attached to their infants. "Infant crying, babbling, eye-to-eye contact, smiling, alertness, and interaction have a powerful effect upon mother" (Ambrose, *et al.*, 1969, pp. 196–201). Freud asserted that ". . . the love of the mother for her infant whom she nourishes and cares for is something far deeper-reaching than her later affection for the growing child" (1964, p. 67). As danger that the infant will not survive lessens, so does the intensity of the bond between them, except for the child in those situations where the security of his relationship with mother has been threatened. For instance, by prolonged separations from mother, arrival of a sibling, or intense conflicts over health needs. When these occur, attachment needs may be retained longer.

As mother becomes less crucial to the growing child's daily survival, father's companionship, affection, and guidance assume increasing importance. His participation, although important in the infancy years, appears even more necessary from middle childhood on. Deutsch (1944) contends that the maturing child turns gradually away from mother and the dependencies of childhood in favor of active adjustment to the outside world, represented for both boys and girls by father.

A child's dependency upon mother in the early years should not be allowed to cause father to become more of a spectator than a participant in the child's life. Regardless of mother's seeming efficiency and the child's love for her, father should share child-care responsibilities. Starting in earliest infancy, he should:

> Give physical and emotional care, leaving no aspect wholly to mother.

Play with his children.

Read books to them.

Take them on outings.

Offer encouragement and indirect assistance with schoolwork.

Treat adolescents like young adults. For example, let them
learn to take public transportation and meet dad at work
for lunch. They need to see where dad works, too.

Be interested in their special interests.

Attend recreational and club affairs when his companionship
can make a significant contribution.

Fathers provide a model of masculinity. A boy who feels comfortable with father will adopt many of his ways of reacting to life situations. For girls, father's companionship, love, and approval provide confidence in being feminine and later in her ability to adjust to the male in society. Both boys and girls imitate father in various ways:

Boys:

Pride in being male.

Showing respect and courtesy for femininity.

Regard for the role of father and husband.

His aspirations and achievements.

Boys and girls:

Self-discipline to control anger and hostility.

Being companionable, affectionate, and considerate.

Being helpful to mother, sharing household duties.

The way he deals with insults and failures.

Being interested in games, reading, or sports.

His curiosity and eagerness to learn about the world.

His skill in handling money and making decisions.

His interest in friends and community affairs.

In matters of discipline, father in some ways is less free than mother to be authoritarian, harsh, unrestrained in anger, or rejecting. Fathers do not have the fund of familiarity that mothers have acquired. Although results may be achieved more quickly, harsh words from a father, whose return home from work has been anticipated all day, may hurt deeply. Disagreements are likely to be more intense between father and child than between mother and child. Mother is viewed as more friendly and less threatening (Kagan, 1956). Father has less time to restore lost rapport than does mother. Children rebel, lose confidence, and withdraw from an overly strict father. Or, in case of deep insecurity, they may overidentify in order to quiet frightening hostility.

Both boys and girls need reassurance of their acceptance and attractiveness to the parent of the opposite sex. Similarly, relationships between parents—the respect, consideration, and affection parents show for each other—determine a child's first expectations as to what marriage for him will be like. A healthy relationship between parents is reflected in the personalities of their children.

GET OLDER CHILDREN INVOLVED

Older children have a significant effect upon the emotional adjustment of younger brothers and sisters. The domination, name-calling, hitting, and belittlement delivered to bothersome siblings must have limits. Self-images are hurt by it. Younger children imitate and often attempt to return rough treatment. Since to do this to their elders is not ordinarily possible, a weaker age-mate or a younger playmate may receive the punishment.

Children come to understand much about the psychology of getting along with others if it is simply explained. They benefit from insights that encourage cooperation. For example, we can tell them:

It's better to use reasoning and a polite request rather than a punch to retrieve your ball from little brother.

When helping younger brother with his work, he will work
harder if we praise what is right and ignore what is wrong.
If this is not possible, we should not make a big issue out
of what is wrong.

Little brother stops working when you get angry with him
because he fears he will receive more criticism.

Patience for little brother's crying when he cannot have what
he wants helps him learn to accept our limits sooner.

Ignoring sister's name-calling is the best way to discourage it.

Baby sister is not old enough to understand our feelings yet.
She will take turns, share, and play more fairly when she is
more grown up.

Sometimes it is better to tell brother how his behavior makes
you feel than to describe his behavior to him.

People get angry when you tease them, partly because their
feelings are hurt.

Family members don't have the right "never" to be bothered.
Younger children cannot grow well without our help.

When we keep dislikes and fears to ourselves, younger family
members have a better chance to grow up without them.
For example:

> Fears of snakes, bugs, and animals.
> Not liking certain foods.
> Not liking certain school subjects.
> Fear of the dark.
> Dislikes about people.

In front of younger children, we should discuss certain
subjects only with great caution. When they hear talk about
wars, tornadoes, lightning, floods, fires, death, burglars,
volcanic eruptions, earthquakes, their active imaginations
can invent fears difficult to cope with. Some children even
fear that just having unpleasant thoughts can make them
happen.

THE SCHOOL CAN HELP

The whole child goes to school. It does not make sense for the school to take responsibility for only a part of him. In personality development, school is second in importance only to the home. Its program should display some concern for his psychological growth. Numerous long-lasting self-perceptions are shaped at school. Often, for the first time, a child is subjected to the collective views of his age-mates. His personality is strongly affected. Grouped with children who respond affirmatively to him, he learns to feel self-confident. Grouped with children who give little social approval, he tends to withdraw.

Numerous self-image concepts are shaped by the ways in which teachers respond to him. Their attitudes and ways of behaving are models for him to copy. Perhaps more important, their concepts about his intellectual abilities may determine for the rest of his life what he will think about his capacity to learn. He comes to perceive himself as a fast or slow reader, good or poor at math, an efficient or inefficient worker, a slow or quick thinker. Glidewell summarizes the situation thus: "The teacher holds great power in the classroom and by contracting or extending his power and acceptance he can influence pupil-to-pupil interaction, reduce interpersonal conflict and anxieties, increase the mutual esteem and self-esteem of pupils, and effect wider dispersion and flexibility of peer power" (1971, p. 736).

Children's learning the psychology of "getting along with others" can be greatly facilitated when taught in the elementary-school classroom, which has an atmosphere more objective and less biased than that of most homes. We can educate our children, but we cannot persuade all parents to inform themselves. At-home, do-it-yourself counseling occurs most often in the aftermath of a crisis. At such a time, a parent may not be able to model the self-control he preaches about.

A knowledge of psychology at an elementary level can be

beneficial to children, parents, and teachers, as demonstrated by the following situation:

Anne (seven), getting ready for a roller-skating birthday party, finds gift-wrapping an ordeal. The ribbon won't tie right. The colorful papers do not meet her requirements. She starts over with a new piece every few minutes. Mother's attempts to help only increase her irritability. She becomes undecided about whether she wants to go.

She responds to mother's request to sit and talk about it. First mother explains that the way people feel about something is often related to one's experiences the last time they were in a similar situation. Can Anne remember what happened to her at the last roller-skating party? She remembers falling and being afraid to join the "grand march."

Mother decides to try "closure" (discussed on page 243). She explains that it sometimes helps if one can anticipate what is going to happen in the new experience. They talk about what might take place at the party. The children will meet at Dave's. Two cars will take them to the rink. Her friends Margaret, Joan, and Nancy will be there. Not all the children can skate well. Dave's mother, who has planned the party, is pretty and she likes to work with children.

Anne interrupts the conversation with eagerness to get dressed. When asked later what finally convinced her to go, she said that she felt much better when it was mentioned that Dave's mother was a very nice person who likes to work with children.

THREE

Understanding Children's Emotional Problems

CRYING

Why Does He Cry?

HE FEELS SORRY FOR HIMSELF

And why shouldn't he? Don't tell him "There's nothing to cry about." Something is troubling him or he wouldn't be crying. Crying is his first means of communication. Studies show that he may need to feel secure that crying is acceptable before he is capable of more mature communication.

Our preschooler doesn't plan to be miserable just to complicate our lives. He cries because he is not yet mature enough to use words to communicate the intensity of his needs or the complexity of his feelings. Not possessing adult techniques of concealment or transformation, he releases his tension directly.

CHILDHOOD IS SOMETIMES FRUSTRATING

As an almost totally self-interested, self-motivated creature, a child finds parental control frustrating. Roadblocks keep getting in his way as he strives to meet his self-needs. Parents continually confront him with demands and expectations to do it their way, expecting him either to postpone what he wants or to substitute something else for it. He must:

Save his candy for after dinner.
Eat breakfast whether he wants to or not.
Keep his hands off many interesting objects around the home.

141

Keep his hands off many interesting things in the department
stores.

Keep his hands off many interesting things everywhere.

Stay at home with a sitter when he prefers to go with mother.

Take an afternoon nap whether he's sleepy or not.

Let his friends play with his wagon when he wants it himself.

Not hit the kid who is provoking him.

Share mother with brother when he would like all of her time.

Listen to mother's refusals about the toys advertised on TV.

Put on his clothes when it's more comfortable without them.

Lastly, he must put up with the frustration of his own
inabilities.

HE IS BORED

Boredom may be more significant than we know. The human
infant needs stimulation. Much of his time is spent looking for
new stimulation. He wants variety in what he sees, feels, hears,
and experiences. He will fret, fuss, and climb on mother if his
environment lacks interest. Rheingold and Samuels demonstrate
how quickly ten-month-old infants begin to fuss in an unchanging environment with almost no objects to manipulate.

Two groups of eleven infants were placed with their mothers in a
simple environment consisting of a plain room without furniture. All
the infants were fretful and agitated.

Through the introduction of toys, a change of setting was brought
about one group of infants. Thereupon, fussing and climbing on
mother sharply decreased. These children did not seek the mother
out again.

In contrast, the infants in the control group did not receive a change
in environment through toys. They spent most of their time fussing
and clinging to mother, manipulating her and whatever objects they
could find: a doorstop, baseboard heater, drapes, walls, floors, their
own clothing. Toward the end of the experiment, these infants also
received toys. They ceased fussing in less than five seconds and did
not display such distress again. (Summarized from 1970, pp. 1–18.)

HE WANTS ATTENTION

This is the most frequent explanation given for child distress. He may want it for his self-respect, or to feel that he belongs, or for some biological reason. Crying often gets him attention not otherwise available. Although the parental response he arouses may not be what he most desires, it seems better to him than none at all. This circumstance is emphasized if the child observes that when he is happy his parents are likely to pay little attention. Crying is his best way to capture their notice when they are busy with their own affairs. While it is probably true that he cries to gain comfort, sympathy, and relief from boredom, it's doubtful that he cries in order to dominate those around him. Parents who fear spoiling, shoo the attention-seeking child away with "There's nothing wrong with you." Disappointed, he increases the unwanted behavior, his needs now being greater than before.

MOTHER'S HOBBIES SOMETIMES ARE FRUSTRATING

When mother adds to her established routine a new project such as sewing, reading, planning a dinner party, a PTA activity, or major house-cleaning, almost certainly the degree of child distress increases. He notices the reduced amount of attention available to him. Punishment occurs more frequently as mother becomes more easily irritable and more impatient at being interrupted. Needs previously cared for without hesitation now aggravate her. Her unavailability for accustomed support and approval increases dependency behavior similar to that displayed when mother has been on an extended trip away from home. Typical reactions are increased crying, irritability, and a more vigorous search for contact-comfort, assistance, and approval.

Disputes even between older children seem more frequent when mother's daily routine changes. It's not easy to plan work and play schedules that satisfactorily meet the needs of both children and adults. Now and then reliable assistance should be obtained to give mother relief. Father sometimes can take over in the evening. Junior-high-school girls often make good playmates during the late afternoon, minimizing awareness of mother's reduced availability and providing her an opportunity for uninterrupted work while, at the same time, she is nearby to supervise.

If the children are old enough to tell time, another aid for reducing turmoil is to tell them exactly when mother will be finished with her new task. Children sometimes have the feeling that the adult is going to be engrossed forever and never again have time for little ones. This system communicates swiftly that their fear is groundless, and children then find it fun to watch the time go by. They also feel grown up, being able to "tell time" and to carry on "all by themselves" for half an hour or so during mother's shorter projects.

A MULTITUDE OF REASONS

As mothers can testify, identifying the problem may not be easy. The possibilities are numerous. The child's distress from single or multiple unsatisfied needs frequently becomes generalized and affects much of his behavior. Research shows that crying commonly arises from:

A need in infancy to be warm and securely wrapped.
A need for contact-comfort and companionship.
An upset in daily routine.
Fear of strange places, faces, or things.
Alarm, illness, fatigue, hunger, pain, boredom.
Too much hurrying, interference, or frustration.
A game or activity beyond his level of ability.
Rejection from a parent, playmate, or sibling.

Too much blame, belittlement, or too many "don'ts."
A difficult day with a play companion.
Difficulties over sharing.
Desire for the possessions of another.
Thwarted efforts to join the activities of others.
The need for a congenial play companion.
Anxiety over recent removal of security symbols, such as
    bottle, blanket, pacifier, thumb.
Recent separation from mother and fear of future separation.
Conflict with adults over toilet training, bathing, eating,
    dressing, sleeping.
Postponement of a goal, wish, or need-fulfillment.
Impulses that he finds difficult to hold in check.
Lack of exercise to assimilate his high level of activity.
Fears about anticipated new experiences.
Jealousy of a brother or sister.
Prolonged use of medication, such as a decongestant or
    antibiotic, with its side effects for some children.

Obviously some of these examples overlap, but they serve to illustrate the wide range of conditions or occurrences. Such frustrations are often reacted to in ways other than simple crying or irritability. Anger, aggression, apathy, regression, and withdrawal are some that are discussed elsewhere.

Finding a Solution

ACCEPT HIS UNHAPPINESS

It isn't easy, but try to accept without resentment his disappointment noise when fulfillment of wishes and needs appears impossible. Offer him love, sympathy, and (on occasion) a comfortable shoulder to cry on. Let him know you understand how strong and overwhelming feelings may be:

Tommy (five) stomps and cries when he can't have a second candy bar while his friends are having their first. Mother explains that he has already completed his. Reasoning does not relieve the painful reality of his feelings. Why not give him something else to do while the others are eating and thus help reduce his disappointment.

There are times when we can't do much about the crying and whining connected with hair-combing, dressing, bathing, misplacement of possessions and home responsibilities. This is frustration noise. Experiencing and expressing a certain amount of it is a necessary part of growing up. If he thinks it helps to cry, let him express his feelings. If you avoid becoming frustrated yourself, perhaps even excusing yourself briefly if his behavior becomes too uncomfortable, you do not cause him to take special note of crying. Without the attention of parental resentment, it's not likely to acquire special significance, and he's not made ashamed of feelings that are difficult to control.

Of course, the crying that accompanies hair-combing, bathing, or dressing may stem from our being rougher than we think. We may tug, jerk, and scrub harder than we realize. The little one's skin and scalp and joints are far more sensitive than ours, so we need to take special care. Their cries can be warning signals alerting us to the need for easing up and proceeding more gently.

TRY FIRST TO QUIET HIM BEFORE MEETING HIS REQUESTS

Frequently responding to a situation while he still cries may reinforce this method of getting attention. Encourage more mature behavior by requesting that he describe his needs as best he can in a voice that is quiet and clear:

Ask me in a quiet way.
When you are quiet, I can understand better what you say.
As soon as you are quiet, I'll bring your lunch.
As soon as you are quiet, I'll help you find your slippers.

RESPOND WITH WARMTH AND INCREASED ATTENTION WHEN
YOUR CHILD IS HAPPY

Give less notice to his crying behavior. A child receiving sufficient attention when he is happy will not frequently use distress as an attention-getting mechanism.

SUGGEST ALTERNATIVES FOR WHAT HE CANNOT HAVE

When his unhappiness over the postponement of wishes continues to the point that you are uncomfortable, it's better to stop him than to resent him. Don't reward unrealistic demands for attention. Instead, suggest alternatives:

I'm sorry, dear, I just sat down to read. I've already read several books to you. Please come play with your dolls here next to me.

If you need to continue being sad, please do that in the other room so that I can concentrate.

Rather than be unhappy about not knowing, call Mrs. Johnson to find out whether the girls are wearing hiking clothes or their Brownie outfits today.

It's not time to go yet. Please be patient. When the clock hands are here, it will be time to leave. Come help me put these things away so that we can be ready to go on time.

It's difficult to give up the comfort of having mother do some things for you, but you don't have to start all at once. I'll still be helping you with many things for a long time.

I know how difficult it must seem not to buy the doll you want, but there are other things you need more. Come sit on my lap while we talk about it.

Varying degrees of annoyance, irritability, and aggression are normal reactions to the limits we must set. Letting him face a certain amount of frustration is necessary to his effective growth.

DON'T LET HIM CRY TOO LONG

Ten minutes is long enough for a child to cry without attention. Depending on the circumstances, even that may be too long. Although crying may have begun as an attention-getting mechanism, when a child has cried to exhaustion, hours may be required for him to recuperate and regain composure. In addition, he may feel a sense of shame and abandonment when both he and his cries are ignored too long by a parent who seems not to hear or care. Your lack of interest when he has been crying indefinitely may seem like rejection to him. Helping him feel more secure before he cries for attention is an art, but it solves many problems.

SPOILING

What Is Spoiling?

As science and technology make "luxury" more commonplace, we tend to view each new generation as more indulged and pampered than the preceding one. It may be inevitable that grandparents will see grandchildren as "spoiled." Yet, if possessions alone spoil, then most adults can correctly consider themselves more spoiled than their children.

A child who cries is sometimes called spoiled. But for him to learn that vocalized distress gets him what he wants does not necessarily indicate "spoiling." It merely confirms the effectiveness of his technique for getting certain wishes satisfied. How it affects the total child depends upon his adjustment in other areas of his personality.

A child who is selfish or shows off is sometimes accused of

being spoiled. But these traits are normal in childhood. When excessive, they may show insecurity rather than spoiling.

To give a great deal of attention is often called spoiling. But good handling, love, comfort, and respect do not spoil babies, children, or adults and are overwhelmingly important for building self-confidence and self-esteem. The disturbances of early childhood usually arise from too little warm attention rather than from too much. Few mothers can be accused of providing attention neither requested nor even needed by a child. Seldom does a mother have sufficient time to give too much of herself to her children. She has too many other competing responsibilities: father, housework, shopping, community activities, grandparents, guests, and perhaps outside employment. In addition, some attention must be given to her own health, emotional needs, and interests. Most children must learn to wait for meals, attention, and companionship. "Just a minute" is one of the most frequently heard parental comments. Rather than fear that children will be spoiled, is it not possible that parents' real concern is the loss of more of their own personal freedom?

Could This Be Spoiling?

When we fail to help a child control exaggerated wishes, which appear unrealistic even to him, damage may be done. Some parents submit to very impractical requests. For instance, they may:

Supply money to a school boy for cigarettes.
Furnish a personal TV to a child who ignores his lessons.
Give permission to go to the movies when a child should be
    studying for an exam.
Give permission to play with a fragile toy, the personal
    possession of a brother or sister.
Oversupply food or even sweets to an overweight child.

When all demands are unfailingly gratified, feelings of insecurity arise from the loss of support a child experiences at knowing he can completely control his parents and that there is no one to help him control himself. If parents regularly do for him what he is intellectually and physically capable of doing for himself, he is poorly equipped to face later obstacles and frustrations. There are parents who grant demands such as the following to a fully capable child: "Make my bed." "Get me a sandwich now." "Bring me my book." "Pick up my clothes." "Get me dressed."

Oversubmission to a child's wishes (perhaps perceived by the parents as an abundant expression of love) is often to some extent an appeasement—the parents feel neglectful of their responsibilities and are attempting to compensate for their lack of attention. Unable or unwilling to tolerate distress, or preoccupied with their own interests, they keep him quiet by "giving him what he wants."

What Does It Really Mean?

It's difficult to state precisely how indulgent or submissive a parent may be without the child's being adversely affected. A measure of indulgence is characteristic of parents who raise children with high achievement levels, creative abilities, self-confidence, and leadership. Even in matters that the child can handle for himself, a certain amount of helpfulness by the parent may be advisable because it shows respect for the child. When a parent is within reach of the TV, a request for channel change need not be refused. While a parent is shining his own shoes, it may be a kindness to meet the child's request to have his shined, too. If a parent is fixing a sandwich for himself, it isn't that much more work to fix one for the child.

Children like to have sensible limits designed for their own best interests and those of the family. They feel insecure without them. Their absence evidences a lack of parental strength. Parents concerned about their child's welfare do not permit him to have his own way in everything. Nor do they deny his failures when he is obviously wrong. They tolerate, within reason, his distress when he experiences the frustration of having to accept parental limits.

REBELLION

With little apparent difficulty, a preschooler can out-wait, out-starve, out-yell, or out-soil any parent. He spends considerable time and energy demonstrating his developing sense of independence. No longer completely helpless, he wants to assert his own wishes. Eating, naptime, dressing, toilet training, bathing—all may become daily scenes of civil war and distress if we are either too determined or too vacillating.

What Parents Should Know

REBELLION CAN BECOME NEGATIVISM

Negative attitudes frequently have their beginnings in prolonged parent-child conflicts over health needs. Keeping home-life calm and tension-free at a time when independence and personality are emerging is no easy task. We must accept compromise and learn to retreat from conflict. A relationship with a healthy, spirited youngster is challenging. Our understanding can keep it from becoming even more demanding than it inevitably is. In matters not vital to health, safety, or others' basic welfare, to minimize pressure on the child reduces the possibility that negative habits and feelings will become fixed and lasting.

The permanence of early learning—its resistance to change—is well-known to psychologists. A great deal of evidence supports a "critical-period" theory. Experiences during certain ages of infancy appear to become established to form patterns for the remainder of his life. This permanence is noted in a study of the behavior of a female lamb taken from its mother at birth and raised by humans during its first ten days. When returned to the flock, the lamb remained independent of the other animals. Three years later her behavior remained unchanged, and she was judged an indifferent mother to her own offspring (Scott, 1962).

CHILDREN REBEL DIFFERENTLY

They vary greatly in the ease with which they find themselves in conflict with parents and others. Some youngsters are not very definite in their wants and needs and are quite susceptible to persuasion. Others are strong-willed and positive about what they want or do not want. Parental understanding helps make management of these children an easier task. Patience for emerging independence lessens rebellion; resentment increases it. Children often resist the attempts of others to control them all their lives and, to counteract being controlled, may themselves make attempts to control others (Symonds, 1949). Rebellion is natural in child development. As observers have noted, a child feels the need to protect his growing sense of "self."

SELDOM IS REBELLION REALLY PLANNED

The no's of his today are not necessarily the no's of his tomorrow. The situations in which a child chooses to assert independence are usually fortuitous. They may arise out of emotional significance that results from your insistence. Unless a clear confrontation between parent and child develops, thereby focusing special attention upon an event, a child may not even remember what it was he previously resisted.

The child seeks parental love, but not parental control. He needs to develop independence. But he doesn't always go about it in ways pleasing to parents. One common situation may be described as follows:

The child rebels because he "knows what he wants." The parent is angered because he sees the child's lack of cooperation as directed against him personally. Both are reacting to their own views rather than to reality. The child, however, may find himself punished for having interests different from his parents'. If his behavior repeatedly conflicts, he comes to feel guilty. Guilt and its accompanying lowered feelings of self-worth stimulate further resentment and resistance. These anger the parent more, and the circular process continues.

What Parents Can Do

ESTABLISH A DAILY ROUTINE EARLY IN YOUR CHILD'S LIFE

Familiar routine builds security and reduces rebellion. A regular time for breakfast, lunch, dinner, bathing, bedtime, and for meeting other major daily needs makes home a comfortable place to be.

Allow for occasional breaks to add variety to the routine and to keep it from becoming restrictive. Children sometimes feel trapped when they must always comply without fail. A certain amount of flexibility is needed in any organization. As children grow beyond infancy, demonstrate your respect and consideration with occasional schedule changes to fit their plans.

DON'T GIVE EXPLANATIONS TO THE YOUNGSTER
WHO FREQUENTLY REBELS

The mere mention of a resisted activity may trigger increased resistance. Lead or carry him, without saying a word, to naptime, dinner, and bathing. It then becomes more like an event that just happens inevitably rather than something into which he is forced. After you get him there, conversation will help keep him distracted.

When bathing, talk about the bubbles that can be made with the soap and water. Make a game with objects that you may collect from around the house, "Guess what is under the washcloth?" "What floats?" "What sinks?" When seating him at mealtime, describe things around him: the pictures on the plates; the colors of various objects on the table, their shapes and designs. Keep a box of noninjurious household gadgets handy for talking about and playing with while he eats.

Sometimes being a bit indirect can help when a child is rebelling. For example:

> You are getting ready to go to the grocery and your four-year-old says, "I'm not going." Pretending not to hear may be more successful than challenging him with "Oh, yes you are."

> You have made noodle soup and your child says, "I wanted vegetable soup." Try ignoring the remark. Or say, "Oh, really!" If he repeats himself, say, "I heard you" and let it go at that. He may eat it if he gets little attention and you seem otherwise occupied.

> You've prepared lunch and your child says, "I don't want a sandwich." Simply request that he leave it on the side of his plate. He may decide to try it.

REFRAIN FROM THREATS AND BRIBERY

They undermine discipline and evidence lack of confidence. Seeing that you doubt your ability to influence him with reason, a child is quick to adopt these same tactics for gaining control over you and others:

The parents say:

> Santa won't come if you don't behave.
> If you promise to be good at Aunt Mary's, I'll get you that doll you wanted.

If you eat your lunch, you can have a piece of cake.

If you don't wear this dress, I won't buy you any more.

Dad's going to be very upset if you don't get the yard work done.

If you don't bring up your grades, no more allowance!

If you'll sit quietly in the shopping cart, I'll get some candy for you.

The child later says to mother:

I won't be good if you don't get me the toy I want.

If you don't get me a new doll, I won't go to Aunt Mary's.

If you don't give me my dessert now, I won't eat dinner.

I won't do my lessons if I can't go to Susie's.

If you don't get me some candy, I won't go to the store with you.

The child says to his friends:

I'm going home if you won't let me play with your doll.

If you don't jump rope with me, I won't be your friend.

If you don't let me be first, I won't play with you anymore.

If you don't give me a bite of your ice cream cone, I won't like you.

REFRAIN FROM FORCING

At the same time that routine is helpful, it is not worth the cost of a power struggle and disrupted rapport between you and your child. Routine becomes ineffective when it must be forced. The child who is forced to eat, dress, bathe, and pick up playthings learns to perceive these activities as unpleasant. Regular health habits can be learned at any time in life, while learning that the world is a pleasant place *must* be acquired in the formative years.

A lively, energetic youngster cannot be expected to be meekly obedient. It's natural for him to resist being controlled. There are times when he may displace resistance from other areas in which you are controlling him. You may make him go to school, but you can't make him eat or sleep. Cooperation must be won, not ordered. When you speak to him as you would to an adult friend, your suggestions are likely to be accepted. Rebellion is not a significant problem with the child who is accustomed to respect and consideration.

SOME REBELLION IS REDUCED BY PERMITTING IT

We can tell children how we feel about a situation without always expecting them to comply or affirm their agreement with us. Our views may be accepted at a later time:

You'll like swimming lessons once you try them. Mrs. Smith is a very friendly teacher.
You look handsome in blue. You may do what you like, but I like best the way you look in this shirt.
This salad is delicious. You ought to try it. It's OK if you don't want to. You'll like more things when you are more grown up.

Rebellion often loses its impact and is discontinued more readily if permitted to occur. Only when it becomes a special issue between parents and children (as many food problems do) is it apt to be prolonged.

Children do not feel the need to dress, eat, sleep, or bathe merely because we want them to do it. To accept their resistance as a fact we cannot and need not change helps us become more imaginative in our methods for gaining necessary conformity. Almost any activity can be made an interesting game if we are willing to take the time.

When a child says, "No, I don't want to," try asking him, "Why?" He's often more cooperative after having an opportunity to express his opposition. You may even thank him for openly stating his objections. (Some of his "reasons," incidentally, are exceedingly interesting and sometimes enlightening.)

If the situation still doesn't go the way you want, don't lose your sense of perspective. Is the matter really so terribly important? Much of what we expect of children is important chiefly as it affects our own convenience and is not necessarily of any real benefit to the child.

LET HIM THINK ABOUT IT FIRST

Announce activities in which a child's cooperation is expected without allowing yourself to be drawn into a discussion of his reluctance to participate. Tell him, "Get your clothes ready for the party this afternoon." If he argues that he isn't going, say, "I hear you" or "I'll talk to you about it later." After thinking about it for a while, he may be more agreeable.

LET HIM SAVE FACE

It may be appropriate to relax and let a child have the last word. If rebellion is needed to save face, he may not give in no matter what the consequences. When disagreements have reached the point where they no longer are useful learning experiences, they should be discontinued. Who has the last word is far less important than the message imparted. Whether we "win" all the way or not, he has heard our expectations. He will think about them.

EXPECT CONFORMITY SOMETIMES

In situations where a child's lack of judgment is a threat to the health, safety, and welfare of himself or others, there are no alternatives. No "ifs" about it—he must cooperate. If he has had ample opportunities to manage less important decisions on his own, he's likely to comply. We can tell him:

Yes, dear, I see what you would like to do, but it cannot be.
   You are not old enough for scissors with sharp points. These
   are for you.
It's perfectly all right for you not to want to listen to our
   conversation, but you must be quiet so that others can hear.

I know how you feel, but you don't have to like everything
   you do. Some things are just necessary.
That's the way things are for now. Maybe later we can talk
   about it again.

What do you do with the child who refuses to go on a family
outing? For one thing, whether he wants to go or not, he needs
to know that you want him. Sometimes the need for this reassurance is the only reason for his announcement that he's
staying home. Almost always it is at least part of the reason.
Your conversation might go as follows:

THE CHILD:	THE PARENT:
I'm not going.	I'd like to have you come along.
I don't have to.	Yes, you do. Here are your shoes, socks, and coat. Put them on in the car.
Why should I?	Because I think it will be an interesting trip, and we want you with us. Let's go.

SHARING

What Parents Can Do

Although children do not share easily until eight or nine years
of age, reinforcing the appearance of generosity toward others
with praise and affection may encourage its development
sooner. Sharing also is learned as he observes the sharing behavior of parents and other family members.

LET CERTAIN POSSESSIONS REMAIN SOLELY HIS

He doesn't need to part with something new—a fragile toy, a
prized Teddy bear. Having certain things that are his alone

helps develop a sense of property and a greater appreciation for the strong feelings other people show for their belongings.

Mothers who insist on children having equal property, equal shares, and equal turns have to supervise constantly. Too frequent concern about equality causes a child to focus increasing and unwarranted importance on possessions and allotments. He may complain, "My turn was shorter," "His toy is nicer," "My piece of cake is not as big." He can become obsessed with getting his share, always, and no matter what.

Play activities are disturbed less frequently when children are permitted within reason to use a particular toy, swing, or tricycle until finished. Let each child claim possession for as long as he is interested. The preschooler's short attention span permits this to work out to almost everyone's satisfaction. Mother is not interrupted so frequently then with demands that "It's my turn now."

In nursery-school situations, where many children must use the same equipment, available adult supervision permits more easily the timing of popular playthings.

What Parents Can Say

This is a very special toy of Polly's. She doesn't want to share it now. You may choose from one of these.

I know it's hard to wait, but you can do it. I'll call you when John is finished.

Anne wants her bottle of bubble fluid. Make two more bubbles and return it to her.

Jane knows the doll is yours. She will give it back when you want it.

Let's look at your toys and decide which ones you will share when Scotty arrives.

How do you think Mark will feel if you give his brother a turn on the swing but not him?

You would like to play with the red truck? Let's see if we can trade something for it. If Mike doesn't want to trade, I'm sure he will let you know as soon as he is done with the truck.

Both of you cannot have the skate board at the same time. One of you can use the scooter first, or play in the sandbox.

You both seemed to reach the trike at the same time. Can you settle the problem of who will be first yourselves, or should we draw straws to see who will be first?

Here's something you might like to play with until Dave is through with the toy you want.

That's a big fight you're having over a little ball. Now, let's settle it sensibly.

Dick doesn't want to keep your toy. He picked it up because you were not using it. He'll give it back in just a minute.

We'll set the alarm clock for ten minutes. Then it will be your turn.

Grace has been waiting a long time. Can you get off the swing by yourself or do you want me to help you?

WINNING AND LOSING

Similar to the problem of sharing is the problem of winning and losing. As mothers know well, the young child often begs to join in games he sees older children and parents enjoying. The efforts of family members to teach him to follow rules and be a good loser can cause a great deal of frustration. Many a game board gets overturned as younger brother walks off in a huff. Self-esteem does not appear strong enough in the early years to cope with this kind of test. Sensibly change the rules for young children. Make it easier to win more frequently than to lose. The child seems to understand that you are modifying the rules for him. As he matures, around eight or nine, he accepts progress to the more rigid rules of the game and will accept losses more cooperatively.

JEALOUSY

Hostility toward brothers and sisters with whom a child must share his parents' time and affection is inevitable. It hurts to share loved ones. Even an only child may feel rivalry for the parent with whom he must share the favored other. An adult may himself find it difficult to really believe that his parents belong just as much to other members of his family as they do to him.

Most of us do not fully comprehend the strength of jealousy. Its effects can range from mild irritation to intense inferiority feelings and fury. Not easily recognizable in behavior, jealousy may be unnoticed by parents. It may be hard to distinguish from normal everyday distress. Although not erasable, jealousy may be overcome to some extent if its causes are understood.

How Parents Contribute

Families differ in what they consider important for the boy and for the girl. Their preferences affect the rivalry for status that exists between siblings as well as the development of each child's attitudes and personality.

Girls receive less discipline and more protection.
Boys may be punished more and protected less.
Girls are picked up and comforted when they are hurt.
Boys are taught early to be brave and take the bumps.
Aggression for a girl may not be acceptable.
Boys may be taught to fight back.
Daughters may not be considered important to family status.
High values may be placed on being a son.
Being small and attractive is prized for girls.
Boys should be tall, strong, and athletic.
Girls may remain dependent and attached to mother indefinitely.
Boys must become self-reliant and independent from mother early.
Girls may not be pressured to excel.
Boys are encouraged to be successful in intellectual as well as athletic skills.
Sexual freedom is discouraged for girls.
Parents appear to be less concerned about boys.
Girls may be interested in dolls and babies.
Boys are not supposed to be interested until they are fathers.
Many girls are still expected to be happy and efficient with home responsibilities.
Being capable in similar ways is not stressed for boys.

Parents do not have identical feelings for each child. You may have caught yourself pointing out differences:

Mary gets all A's. Sally doesn't even try.
George is such a good boy. He is never any trouble.
I can't do a thing with Bill.
Dave is into everything.

Discussions in which a child hears himself thus described, or omitted, influence his concept of himself and may create hostility toward the "good" boy.

Parents change over the years. The differences among children growing up in the same home with the same parents should not be surprising. At any given age the environment for one child is not the same as that for another of that age. Parents' personalities change, their interests, skills, and knowledge change, and the home environment changes as the years go by. We do not provide each child exactly the same experiences. The mother with one child is different from the mother with two. Each additional child means additional emotional demands on her and lessens the time she can devote to any one member of her brood. Her first child is the only child to have mother all to himself during the critical formative years of infancy. He receives more handling than later-born children, who must share the parents. Children who arrive later have the advantage of their parents' experience. They are exposed to different parental attitudes about children and child-rearing. The child who is an infant while mother is emotionally or physically ill has an environment different from that of the one who arrives when mother is well. Young parents may be anxious, worried, or financially pressed. Older parents may feel more secure. Their discipline may be more democratic and less authoritarian.

Jealousy exists in virtually every family. The extent to which children feel secure or insecure has much to do with the intensity of the jealousy they feel.

How the First Child Is Involved

A first child usually resents having to share with a new baby the affection and attention that formerly belonged all to him. He may feel as threatened as one parent would feel if the other were to bring home a new spouse with whom to share affection.

It is the sharing rather than the newcomer that is resented. "Rivals" often play together without problems when mother's immediate presence is not a stimulus for competition.

Mixed feelings of love and hate are difficult to understand, but are common. At the same time that a child loves his mother, he may feel betrayed and angry at her fondness for the baby. Being older, he cannot compete with the infant, whose baby ways get him more cuddling and attention. Formerly he had mother all to himself. Now he must tolerate the continuous presence of a newcomer who is never far from mother's side—at home or away. For him the hostility he feels may be frightening and guilt-producing.

Nevertheless, self-esteem usually appears higher in a first or only child than in other children. (During the critical years, of course, the oldest child is often an only child.) The increased handling, attention, and social approval he experiences in infancy seem to increase more or less permanently his feeling of security in the world.

The Middle Child

A middle child's position is less ideal than many assume. He may never experience the center of the stage alone. Ahead of him in most things is an older sibling, with the acknowledged prestige from being older. He is bigger and stronger and enjoys privileges sooner. He is first to go to school, first to get a new bike, first to get new clothes, first in many things. And behind the middle child is younger brother, upon whom he sees love and special affection lavished. Younger brother may be a source of intense conflict—he is most protected, and everything he does is "cute."

If the younger sibling is a girl, the middle child's problems, if a boy, may be even more complicated. The identification that mother and daughter may feel for each other is something that brother cannot share, and he may not be willing yet to transfer his companionship from mother to a father who is not readily available. Mother has been for him, as now she is for sister, his closest friend, primary protector, teacher, and source of affection. But as he grows beyond infancy, society encourages him to search for masculine companionship, interests, and activities. Sister is not faced with this problem. Mother is more available to her than father is to the son. She often is free to pursue both masculine and feminine interests indefinitely.

No matter how well the middle child matures, he is still in the middle. His problems remain about the same throughout childhood. He never can reach the status of the oldest nor enjoy the extra love and protection that younger brother or sister enjoys.

The Youngest Child

The youngest child, because he is the baby, is apt to be overindulged and overprotected. His parents are more experienced and may be able to give him material and cultural advantages not possible to the other children. Sometimes he may be wholly ignored, the parents being worn out, too busy, and even fed up. He has other problems, too. While older siblings may provide extra companionship and personal care, they also resent his bothersome enthusiasm. His frequent distress over unfulfilled needs and his more active play continually interrupt their more quiet endeavors. When older children want to watch adult TV, he wants children's programs. When they want to play a game with their friends, he wants to join in. When they want to read quietly, he wants to play noisily. Thus he may receive more belittlement than any of the older children experienced. Self-image development may suffer if parents are also critical.

Other Factors

The sexes of the children, of course, drastically influence their attitudes and relationships within the family. A brother and a sister may assume certain close relationships but not certain others. Acceptance, or the lack of it, in the surrounding community may shape needs and rivalry for status. The possession of skills and abilities affects a child's self-confidence. Teachers and playmates add to his different experiences and outlook on life. The age-spacing between siblings and the size of the family may affect the degree to which a child feels threatened by the presence of siblings. Research on dependency behavior suggests that boys between the ages of two and three who come from large families may seek more contact with a female teacher than boys from smaller families (Waldrop and Bell, 1964). Mothers with more than the average number of children may not have time to give needed contact-comfort, praise, and approval.

Guides for Reducing Jealousy

Jealousy exists whether children are one or ten years apart. Resentment of the rival may be strong. An older child may ridicule and intimidate a more protected younger member. Proving his sibling's shortcomings helps elevate his own self-esteem. Although jealousy cannot be eliminated entirely, rivalry can be reduced. Help him recognize the various advantages that go along with being older.

> You can talk to me. It's nice to have a big boy to talk to.
> You are stronger and can do many things that sister cannot do.
> You have certain privileges brother doesn't have.
> You can play games without being angry when you lose.
> You can ride a two-wheel bike, climb, play games, read and write, take care of your own money, and go to the city on the train with dad.
> You had mother all to yourself when you were a baby. Sister must share me with you.
> You get to go to nursery school.

You can reach things you want. Little brother must ask for
   help.
You can use words. Sister can only cry to let us know she has a
   problem.
You have learned to share and take turns. Brother is often
   upset when things are not all his.
You get to have a weekly allowance.

Accepting and recognizing jealousy can improve the situation.
Letting him know you understand helps him feel less guilty
about his strong feelings.

I know it's hard for you to accept that mother belongs just as
   much to others as she does to you.
We all enjoy cuddling and taking care of baby sister. We
   enjoyed doing the same for you when you were small. Now
   we not only enjoy cuddling you, but we can talk to you and
   do things with you.
You are angry because I give attention to sister. She needs me
   now. I will be glad to take care of you when I am finished.
You feel that brother gets more attention than you. When
   you feel that way, come tell me about it.
I picked up your things too when you were little. When
   brother is older, he will do more for himself the way you do.
You feel that sister is a lot of trouble. She interrupts, cries,
   and wants things that are yours. Aren't you glad to be older?
   She will grow out of this age as you did.
Little brother seems a nuisance because he needs so much
   attention. He even prefers your angry attention to none at
   all.
It's difficult to feel that brother is five years younger than you
   are and needs more attention. It may help if you think
   about how young his friends seem.
Mother likes you just the way you are. She doesn't want you
   to be like anyone else.

You don't believe that sister is hurt badly enough to make all
the noise she is making. Maybe her feelings hurt more than
her pinched arm.

You want to go with me alone. We can have a good time even
with little sister along. She is too little to leave at home.

You are annoyed at brother's childish behavior. We must
wait for him to become as grown up as you have become.

Verbal communication is not all that is needed. There are also
various things we can do in the background to keep jealousy
under control.

Reserve some time each day or so for each child by himself.
Let him be the center of your attention. Be his special
friend for a short time. One child may like to go for walks,
another may enjoy shopping or going to the library. Don't
talk then about others. Let that child be your only child for
that time.

Help a strongly competitive child develop added status
through interests outside the home.

Let each child have friends that he's not asked to share.

Don't expect older children to take a great deal of
responsibility for younger ones. Their resentments will be
expressed to the child.

Don't expect children to work on tasks together if they do
not get along.

Each child has some possessions that are truly his alone. He
should have a place to keep them where others cannot go
without permission.

Recognize that older children may need expressions of
affection as much as younger ones. Individual reassurance
is more impressive than collective.

When a child needs special help, don't be fearful of
neglecting others. They know they'll receive the same
attention if they need it.

Try to keep promises. If you must be reminded frequently, a
  child loses faith that you are interested.
Tell older children interesting stories about when they were
  younger. They sometimes forget that they received the same
  fond attention being bestowed upon younger members.
  They love this and it makes a very helpful continuity to
  their life.

ANGER, HOSTILITY, AND AGGRESSION

When we analyze these strong emotions that can be so disturbing to the pleasure of a family, we find a number of differences.

Anger: Is usually episodic and transitory. It's over and gone.
It occurs when goals are blocked, when behavior is restrained,
when a possession is removed, when property is in danger.

It is aroused by physical and emotional pain, as when physical punishment is experienced or self-esteem is threatened or
reduced. It occurs when security is in jeopardy, as when parents
leave the infant with others to go on an extended vacation.
Fatigue, fear, sorrow, frustration, and embarrassment also stimulate anger.

Hostility: Is deeper and more enduring than anger. It is often
an unconscious and persistent feeling of rage or hatred toward
others, having its beginnings in the unpleasant experiences of
childhood. Fear, guilt, and love for others inhibit its full expression.

Aggression: Takes place when anger and hostility are acted out, usually through hitting or fighting. It is an attempt to protect or extend property, status, or self-esteem. It can be learned by observing the aggressive behavior of others. It can exist without the presence of anger or hostility. One can observe this in the infant's struggle to overcome helplessness, and in the persistence with which adults strive for success.

These emotions are often irrational and destructive, but they are also normal. "It is healthy for a child to become angry or at least to feel angry when someone abuses him, takes advantage of him, or violates his integrity. It is healthy for him to react with anger when people whom he loves are under attack, or when someone tries to demean his loyalties, or when someone tries to abuse a weaker person for whom he feels responsible" (Jersild, 1968, p. 376).

As a child matures, he learns from our example what to do with these emotions. By helping him recognize and admit his anger, we sometimes help him improve a troublesome situation. Seven-year-old Jerry, who borrows pencils without returning them, can be informed how it makes one feel, and how it is apt to affect his chances of being allowed to borrow pencils in the future. Eight-year-old Janice, who can't tolerate losing, may play more fairly if her friends protest.

Anger, hostility, and aggression are triggered by a variety of stimuli. Which emotion is expressed depends upon the child and the strength of the stimuli. The conditions that seem to most frequently arouse such feelings in the home are our next subject.

Common Causes of These Emotions in Children

REDUCED SELF-ESTEEM

"Whereas the young child becomes angry when his immediate wants or needs are not met, the child in the middle school years is angered by teasing, ridicule, criticism, or long 'lectures' about his behavior" (Landau, Epstein, and Stone, 1972, p. 154). Anger is frequently a child's reaction when parents or others are critical, thoughtless, rude, or rejecting. When mother says in a sharp tone, "What did you do *that* for?" or "Can't you watch what you are doing?" some children may behave destructively. It's natural to feel anger when one's self-esteem is attacked.

Look beneath the surface for clues to what has caused reduced self-esteem. No child feels angry without reason, although the reason may not be fully apparent, particularly to himself.

When Steven (ten) explodes in anger shortly after arriving home from school, it may not be what it appears to be. He may say that he doesn't like what is being prepared for dinner, that you forgot to buy his notebook, or that he doesn't like music lessons. Only later do you discover that he was really upset about having to pick up all the scrap paper on the school play yard after splashing another boy in a mud puddle who had splashed him first.

Mary (six) has phoned her friend several times only to discover that she has made arrangements other than those previously planned. Mary is disappointed. The forgetfulness or indifference of a friend is hard to accept. The depth of Mary's disappointment may be observed in the way anger is expressed toward whatever and whoever happens to be convenient. The walls of her dollhouse come tumbling down. Tears and anger are released over the ice cream she cannot have, the doll she cannot find, the father who is too busy to read to her. Everything seems to become a reason for being unhappy. Unaware of her reduced self-esteem, parents may overreact with strong discipline. Affection is most needed to overcome feelings of rejection. By failing to look for reasons, we may add to a small child's problems.

FRUSTRATION

Anger occurs when the young child cannot adequately handle the frustration of unfulfilled wishes and expectations, such as the candy that mother won't buy, the truck that big brother won't share, the game that daddy won't play. These also may be viewed as forms of love withdrawal that cause him to feel reduced self-worth. We adults experience the same feelings, the major differences being that our preferences have changed and delay is more tolerable for us.

A NEED FOR INDEPENDENCE

Aggression increases as maturation leads a child to strive for independence and self-fulfillment. He wants to explore his environment as he chooses, to sleep and eat as he feels ready. Those who stand in his way, parents or friends, may be attacked. To rebel at parental wishes is one way of asserting separateness, of proving he knows what is best for himself. To grab another's toy, to hit or destroy is his way of testing his powers, as well as to get what he wants. We should recognize such behavior as steps in his development—not "mean streaks" that somehow must be punished out of existence. Understanding this, we are less likely to complicate matters by adding our own anger to his problems. Where else can he discharge his feelings if not to the persons with whom he feels safe?

Talking Back

A child who talks back is dealing with his anger realistically. He is recognizing and admitting anger, and he is letting us know that something is wrong. His ability to camouflage or bottle up angry feelings is not a measure of his respect, nor is respect something due us. Even should he wish to be polite, he may not always have sufficient control over his immature impulses to guarantee it. Let him explode without shouting back. It does not mean that he honors us less. Resist the impulse to return the hurt. Self-assertion may be hard to cope with; but, if respected, it can lead to healthy self-confidence and social acceptance. As

Liebman observes: "Much of the seeming enmity on the part of youth toward their parents is pure illusion; it just does not mean what it appears to mean; it is a step in the direction of liberation" (1966, p. 208).

A permissive attitude toward self-expression undoubtedly results in an increase of overt aggression, but it is of a healthy nature. It will not produce reports that your child has been a problem at school or elsewhere. Rather, psychological research gives evidence that children whose parents frequently punish in the home are those who more often express hostilities outside the home.

TALKING BACK MAY REDUCE INFANTILE DEPENDENCY

Some aggression toward parents can help reduce infant dependency, an important step in anyone's development. This step is accomplished with ease only by the child who feels unafraid and sufficiently certain of his parents' affection to occasionally challenge their authority without guilt.

TALKING BACK REDUCES ANGER

Admitting anger lessens it and encourages healthier communication. Seldom can we feel that we really deeply understand the behavior of another individual. When we deprive each other of insight into our feelings, we decrease our already limited ability to understand and communicate fully. Talking and listening are imperative. Words provide an outlet and reduce strong emotion when they are accepted without counterattack. Words also are a way of reaching out, of making contact with each other. We can tell our child:

> You are being very direct and frank. I will try to explain my
> reasons as clearly.
> It's all right for you to show me how angry you are if you
> also are willing to talk about it.

I can see how angry you are. You'll feel less distressed if you
tell me what you think the problem is.
You'll have to let me know how you feel in some other way.
I can't let you break my plate. You can talk, but you cannot
break things.
When you let others know about the ways in which they hurt
your feelings, it helps them change their disturbing ways.

Weinberg (1969) suggests that restating the other person's
objections is a good way to let him know that we understand
and have noted his feelings: "You don't like the food I have
prepared for dinner?" "You don't like having to go shopping
with me?" When we listen as he angrily confronts us, we permit
him to grow in his ability to handle hostility. Even if nothing is
settled, the release of pent-up emotions without parents yelling
back reduces anger and resentment.

TALKING BACK CAN TEST WRONG CONCLUSIONS

If the child feels free to express feelings to an understanding
parent, he gets anger out where it can be recognized and tested
for authenticity and appropriateness. Unfair treatment is acknowledged and corrected. Wrong conclusions about the attitudes of others are tested in the light of reality. Otherwise they
remain undercover, insidiously undermining the parent-child
relationship. Or they may be expressed in increased thumb-
sucking, negativism, bed-wetting, withdrawal, or aggression
toward age-mates.

TALKING BACK MAKES THE RELATIONSHIP MORE HONEST

A certain honesty is involved when we talk about the dis-
pleasures we feel. As parents are well aware, children are most
apt to be honest about their feelings. The repression of unpleasantness is learned from parents who dispel problems with the
comment "I don't wish to talk about it." It's more appropriate to
get disturbing feelings out in the open. It is "fair" as long as we

do not "hurt and run." We must be willing to try to understand others' feelings, to discuss reasonably, and to look for solutions. If we practice these arrangements and the other person continues to feel mistreated, then it becomes more his problem. Changing an attitude may not be within our immediate control. Whether in adults or children, sometimes many months are required to undo inaccurate beliefs and attitudes.

TALKING BACK CAN BE ABUSED

Freedom to report feelings does not imply the right to express anger at the slightest provocation. Accidental anger is acceptable. Anger used as a tool to control or abuse others is unfair. Anger continuing out of proportion to the degree of frustration is intimidation. When a child regularly misuses anger to insult, injure, or overcontrol us, we must help him set limits:

> Out with you. Come back when you feel like talking more
>   politely.
> Stop now. You may tell me what the problem is without
>   name-calling, yelling, or screaming.
> I can tell by the way you slammed the door that you are
>   angry. I think you should come out with it now rather than
>   let unpleasant feelings make us both uncomfortable.

Hitting the Parent

DON'T LET IT BOTHER YOU

Does being struck by a small child really upset you? After all, he's only half your size, or less. If he gets a strong reaction from you after hitting you, he may be astonished or frightened, or both, by his power. For you to return the attack and strike him implies that you see him as a considerable threat, that you disapprove of his hitting but not of your doing it. It lets him know of your anger but not of the hurt that triggered your anger.

The family environment repeatedly puts to test the hostilities that arise toward those we love. Our deep emotional investment in each other causes us to be easily hurt and stimulated to anger.

IGNORE THE FIRST BLOW

You can't do much about it anyway. Restrain later attack if it comes. You might say to him, "Sorry. I know how you feel, but I can't let you hit me. Tell me what you are angry about. Maybe we can do something about it."

Children are most easily taught self-discipline by parents who practice it. Restrained by a calm parent, the child can more easily see that he is the one creating most of the fuss. When parents do not overreact, he's also not so likely to feel guilty or frightened by the force of his anger. Strong feelings come to be viewed more realistically.

From his studies with animals, Harlow tells us:

It should be comforting to know that mother love, once formed, apparently remains. Mothers should be cheered when their babies are kicking them on the shins, telling them they do not love them, or stating that they wish they were dead, to know that the infant is hopelessly trapped. No matter what he does or says and no matter how little he understands it, the infant belongs to the mother forever, insofar as the primary affectional bonds are concerned. [1960, pp. 682–683.]

REALIZE THAT YOU MAY NOT BE HIS REAL TARGET

As mentioned earlier, parents are often the objects of displaced anger. A child embarrassed at being disciplined for talking at school, snubbed by a valued friend, omitted from a birthday party list, or made the brunt of name-calling may make mother or father his target at the first opportunity. Returning his anger only increases his feelings of rejection and adds you to his list of rejectors. He is more likely to tell his problems to a calm and understanding parent. We might say, "Right now you seem very angry with mother. Is it something that mother did? Did you have a difficult time at school today? If you want to tell me about it, maybe I can help."

Rejecting the Parent

The very young child often appears unable to tolerate closeness with more than one parent at a time. When parents simultaneously try to give attention, the child is likely to say, "I want Daddy. Go away, Mommy" or father is rebuffed with "I want Mommy to put my shoes on" or "I want Mommy to give me a bath."

As mother is the child's principal source of security, father is more frequently rejected. If he does not give up in the face of these rather obvious expressions of preference, he will come to know the pleasure of being needed by his little ones. He must realize that it takes a while to build up the kind of acceptance that mother has accomplished by her continuing presence since birth. If he retreats and waits to be asked to help, he puts himself farther into the background. He must continue to offer assistance whether he is sought out or not. For example, father would do well to have certain tasks with which he customarily helps—read to the children, give evening baths, tuck them in bed at night.

Mistreating Other Children

RESTRAIN HIS IMPULSES TO HIT

There are no limits with the preschooler. If he's really angry, he can leave some pretty big dents in a friend. If mother can't supervise, it is wise to put away sand shovels, ball bats, or any toy convenient as a weapon. As mothers well know, the young child needs direction, protection, and sometimes separation in his play with other children. The youngster who finds aggression successful may well enjoy repeating it toward the same victim.

DISTRACT HIM TO OTHER THINGS

Remove one child to the other side of the sandbox. Supply other toys. Suggest a different activity.

> Did you think of building a garage for your truck? Maybe this box will help.
> If we stack up these blocks, we can build a ramp for your little cars to run down.
> Would you like to make a playhouse with these big boxes I brought from the grocery?

In the case of the child who regularly attacks, rather than giving him the attention of removal, it may be wise to direct your attention to the child receiving the abuse. Recondition the aggressive child by giving him more of your time, affection, and attention when he is good.

LOOK FOR REASONS

A child's need to strike out at others cannot always be determined from observing his behavior.

> He may hit, destroy, or have a tantrum out of resentment over a brother's or sister's recent special attention from a parent.
> He may start a fight at home with brother to relieve feelings of hostility aroused when teacher took his crayons away at school.
> The retaliation he can't deliver to an older sibling or parent who hit him first may be delivered to a younger brother or sister.
> A child he wants to play with may be abused for showing lack of interest in playing with him.

Hitting may be a quick way for getting mother's attention.
A child blocking his way to the use of a certain toy may be
    attacked.
He may lash out at those whose belittlement has made him
    feel small and insignificant.
He may be overstimulated by too many playmates, too much
    play, or too much noise.
It may be too close to naptime, lunchtime, or bedtime. Or he
    may not be feeling well.

CHANGE PLAYMATES OCCASIONALLY

Some children are more of a source of frustration than others.
Your youngster may be seeing too much of one particular child.

Temper Tantrums

HIS WORLD IS AT FIRST DEPENDABLE

Much of a child's mental development depends upon the sub-
stance, order, and permanence of the objects in the world
around him. He learns about displacement and impermanence
when he discovers that a lost toy may be sought somewhere
other than where it was last seen (Piaget, 1952). He learns a
great deal about structure as he sees, feels, pulls, drops, rolls,
shakes, tastes the objects that he plays with. Most of the objects
in his life, including people, come to seem fairly dependable in
the first year of infancy. For love, comfort, and nourishment, his
parents are recognized as reliable sources. His blanket and
bottle are useful substitutes when they are not available. The
infant's world is thus secure and predictable.

DEPENDABILITY DOES NOT LAST

What happens when these things he values most highly suddenly are not so permanent or reliable as he had originally come
to expect? The abrupt disappearance of one or several of his

security symbols may shake his trust. For example, the child may cling excessively for months to mother after she returns from a two-week absence. This kind of anxiety is obvious. Other forms of insecurity may not be easily distinguished from everyday distress.

Loss of trust may result from a number of painful experiences. Various disappointments can cause him to perceive parents and their interest and concern for his welfare as unreliable—for example, removal of his bottle or a favored blanket, loss of a familiar home, an extended separation from parents, loss of a parent, loss of a pet, hospitalization, arrival of a new sibling, reduced attention, increased parent-child battles over toilet training, food, or sleep. Usually not one but a combination of such events is necessary to cause a child to react violently.

Viewed as a child sees it, the logic of a tantrum becomes more understandable. It's the small child's way of asserting himself with regard to what he considers unsatisfactory care for his well-being. Feeling a loss of confidence in his parents' dependability, he attempts to force them to care for his needs.

OTHER REASONS

Of course, trauma is but one explanation. It's relatively simple for a child to learn techniques for getting what he wants. If regularly given what he wants because of our inability to tolerate upset, he will create more upset. Parents may not have the patience or ability to cope effectively with stress. In addition, it often takes time and imagination to persuade a child to do what is best for his own interests.

HOW SERIOUS IS IT?

The resistance to change in emotional attitudes is familiar. Fears, worries, insecurity, negativism, hostility often appear permanently established. Positive and negative feelings about parents become fixed in the first three or four years of life. All experiences thereafter are viewed in the light of these early experiences. For a positive outlook on life, a child's early years must seem fairly pleasant and secure.

Sanford pictures the process whereby the extreme strains of early childhood are incorporated into the personality in this way: "The early primitive adaptations remain like wounds in the trunk of a tree; though they may be to some extent encapsulated, all future growth must go around them. More than this, as old wounds, they are susceptible to reopening or disease" (1970, p. 73).

HOSTILE BEHAVIOR OF
LONG STANDING

Studies show hostility to be the emotional problem most frequently related to feelings of being rejected and unloved. A child who believes himself unloved is unhappy and insecure. Although his perception of his family's feelings may be far from accurate, his views are what we must deal with. "He is responding to his world, not to our world" (Stagner, 1961, p. 9).

However he frames his conclusions, they cannot be easily undone. For the child who is only momentarily feeling unloved, a little affection goes a long way. If the hostile child's feelings of rejection are deeply rooted, he may need the services of a professional counselor. At the same time, he also needs our involvement. His problems are related to his experiences with us. We may have to change before he can change. A point that we tend to overlook is that it is relationships with other people that cause most of the emotional problems in life.

What's Beneath His Hostility?

HE FEELS UNLOVED

Supporting his hostility is an inability to believe or accept the affection bestowed upon him. As his parents try to reassure him, he suspects their love to be mere pretense, while continuing to test his environment for proof that his unlovability is, in fact, true. He believes that he has nothing to gain by accommodating those he feels cannot love him, hence his lack of response to suggestion or discipline. As he searches for trouble, collecting "evidence" for his unlovability, he readily becomes angry over:

The piece of cake mother forgot to save him.
The book dad is too busy to read.
The special soup mother forgot to buy.
The bike brother got for his birthday.
The sandwich mother is too busy to make immediately.
The shopping appointment mother can't make with him.

Satisfactions not immediately gratified arouse anger. For him, they are convincing evidence of the misery of his situation. Each time his irritable, defensive behavior succeeds in arousing even our mildest rebuke, he believes he has further reason for feelings of hurt and anger. Although he may in part provoke the anger directed to him, he does not see his own hostility as such. He suspects others of feeling toward him the anger he has for them. He perceives his own aggression as self-defense.

HE FEELS BETRAYED

He believes himself unable to gain our affection and high regard. He does not trust us to care for his needs. Consequently, he strikes back verbally and sometimes physically at the parents who have hurt him, who do not love him as he wishes to be loved. Total hostility and alienation are unusual, as those would interfere with satisfaction of his dependency needs, so we usually become only his part-time enemy. As the need arises, he puts on the armor of hostility in an attempt to protect himself from further hurt.

RESENTMENT FEEDS HIS HOSTILITY

With belittlement, defiance, discontent, and rejection of proffered friendliness, he shows his resentment of the world he cannot trust. He may attempt to feel more secure by making excessive demands that parents and others submit to his wishes. His anger may be directed toward a single rival; or he may turn from all in the family; or he may trust only a brother, a sister, or a pet.

FEELINGS OF GUILT AROUSE HIS HOSTILITY

Feelings of guilt may be difficult to detect, as children do not necessarily cry when they feel guilty, ashamed, or humiliated. Their behavior is very likely to be that of anger. Loss of parental love, esteem, and status, which a child needs and wishes his parents to feel for him, often triggers anger followed by feelings of shame and lack of worth if he is punished frequently. He fears loss of regard for himself as he fails to measure up to parental expectations. He may come finally to feel guilty for merely having angry thoughts toward others. The strength of such feelings depends on how frequently we react to his behavior with rage, rejection, or deprecation and on how much these reactions are offset by the warmth and nurturance that we also provide.

HE FEELS OVERWHELMED

Insecurity that seems overpowering may be expressed in coughs, allergies, sniffles (without illness as a basis), skin reactions, headaches, enuresis, teeth-grinding, thumb-sucking, sleeplessness, resistance to food, apathy, or withdrawal. (These things may be found at times, though usually only to a limited extent, in most children, whether hostile or not.)

Any one or a combination of these behaviors may be evident in a hostile child. When symptoms subside, it often is assumed that he has grown out of his problem, when in fact parental pressure may have merely reshaped it into some other problem without in any way altering his basic insecurity. Whether or not such symptoms signify a conflict needing professional attention may be determined in part by the extent to which parents feel pressured and uncomfortable because of his behavior.

How Did It Happen?

Hyperactivity may lead to hostility. Aggression may arise out of frequent difficulties flowing from his active inquisitiveness. If a child receives more parental reprimands than less active brothers and sisters, he may conclude that he is less favored.

Behind arrogant behavior is an uncertain, deeply insecure child—one who often, perhaps too often, has been corrected, threatened, and scolded. His behavior, both good and bad, may have been so frequently explained that he has come to feel smothered. He sees other children enjoyed, himself disciplined. The "good" example set by brothers and sisters, whom he believes he cannot emulate, and the seemingly endless admonitions of his parents lead him to give up trying to please. He concludes that, since he cannot be like his approved, more passive siblings, he has little to gain from trying to change his life-style. His behavior persists, and he may become more hostile.

The child who has been labeled "hostile" acts out his label. Parents may have become so sensitive to the problems he creates that they remind him of his behavior even when expressing affection.

> *You're a devil when it comes to teasing your sister,* but we
> love you.
> I'm glad you are my boy, *even if you do give me a hard time
> occasionally.*
> *Even if we do have our differences,* I wouldn't trade you for
> anything.

What Can We Do About It?

There is no quick, easy way to help the hostile child. The problem is complicated by the fact that he needs the parent more than the parent needs him. A great deal of love, concern, emotional maturity, and understanding is required of any parent wishing to resist the child's provocation and break the self-reinforcing pattern of his hostility. It takes longer to reassure him of his value and importance as a member of the family than it did to help him establish his antagonistic beliefs.

The most hostile, belligerent child wants to be loved, although he may reject it. He may experience considerable difficulty believing that any love he receives is anything more than a deception. To help him believe it takes time, persistence, and new techniques. "Hostility is a very variable and unstable mode of behavior. If the child can be convinced of the adult's loyalty and reliability as a source of affection, it may collapse and be replaced by anxiety for acceptance" (Stott, 1966, p. 164).

MAKE A FAMILY DIAGNOSIS

In their search for what produced the hostility, parents should reflect particularly upon how and what they have been communicating to the child. Hostility seldom results from a single cause or incident. Numerous experiences can be factors in precipitating the problem.

Check your attitudes. You may be expressing frequent resentment about a behavior that is quite normal. Accepting him as he is may reduce his tension and bothersome behavior.

Listen to your tone of voice. Does dissatisfaction, annoyance, or despair frequently show through? Your child may feel overwhelmed that again, for the millionth time, he has annoyed this person by whom he wants to be loved. He may give up trying to please.

Notice when problem symptoms diminish or increase. When mother or father gives more time to family matters, does hostility usually subside? Does adding or changing a playmate make a difference?

Are you frequently correcting, teaching, and explaining? Keep a brief record of daily events. You may discover a familiar thread in the situations that precede an episode of hostility.

Is his disturbing behavior a way of asking for limits that he can believe? Case histories of aggressive children often indicate that they have experienced a home environment obviously lacking in discipline and order, or one that is extremely punishing.

Does he know what effect his behavior has on you? Do you really feel angry or hurt when he's disruptive or abusive. Is that all you feel? Is he trying to see if you really care?

Do you provide him the affectionate glances and fond embraces given other family members? The hostile child may have had a warm, close relationship with you in infancy. It may be heartbreaking for him to observe your enjoyment of his younger brothers and sisters. You feel that he gets his fair share. He may want more than just a share. He also may need more than most children.

Was he abruptly separated for an indefinite time or permanently from a number of things he loved most: his mother, father, a beloved pet, his blanket, bottle, home, or friends? His sense of trust is established very early in life.

Was toilet training, thumb-sucking, eating, sleeping, bathing, or behavior a constant battle during the formative years? Negativism often has its beginning in the frequent battles over early health needs. No matter how peaceful homelife subsequently becomes, changing early learning is difficult.

What kind of relationship exists between parents? The hostility with which parents undermine the opinions and actions of each other influences children. They adopt parents' behavior and feelings. They may mimic parents' bickering, complaining, and dissatisfaction with life. They also are apprehensive and even terror-stricken when the two most loved, most powerful persons in their world are at loggerheads with each other. In fantasy, they may take the blame for parents' difficulties and feel guilty. Son may fear that he possesses characteristics mother resents in father. Daughter may experience doubts about her qualities that father resents in mother.

Is one parent overly permissive? If so, the other's discipline may seem more unjustified. In any case, their world has a basic chaos.

GIVE DEPENDABLE LOVE

To undo long-standing feelings of hostility and distrust takes time. It may require greater self-discipline and persistence than parents feel easily able to give. It's not easy to persist with unconditional love and care when a child's ordinary behavior brings daily upset, distress, and tension. But love must be dependable regardless of his behavior. He would rather stay hostile than accept affection from a parent who is a loving companion at one time and a hostile enemy at another. It is less painful to him to retain a distant or negative attitude. It is also less risky.

As Redl (1966) suggests, we cannot afford to show much

anger to the hostile child since anger, restraint, and punishment were what produced the panic or aggression that made him what he is.

BE OPEN TO CHANGE

Children who have received an abundance of punishment and correction need a change. To the limits that you can tolerate, you must become more permissive of his uncooperative behavior. Your patience and understanding will encourage him to reassess his belief that you are unfair, unkind, or unfriendly. Tolerance is therapeutic. It allows room for positive feelings to grow and sets an example for him to follow. It must be combined with increased parental attention and commendation for his good behavior. Otherwise he will be receiving less recognition than when you responded to misbehavior.

Of course, one cannot be patient all the time. We do blow our stacks occasionally. It's how frequently we do it and what we do about it afterward that count. We must let him know when we are no longer angry, whether he responds or not. He's had enough practice in prolonging hostility.

While a child's hostility occasionally should be allowed expression, if unlimited it could become harmful and habitual. When abuse from him is unacceptable, limit its expression in a firm but friendly way: "We understand how you feel; but you must either calm down now or leave until you find your good humor again" or "I'll answer you when you speak to me kindly."

We must expect that even with improved parental understanding and treatment the child will continue to react not solely to the events of the present, but also to the persistent emotions of his past. A child who has learned to feel threatened does not accept the pleasant experiences of the present as likely to be permanent. Help him increase his ability to retain the memory of pleasant experiences by recalling them in family conversation. Reawaken memories of activities and accomplishments in which he has done well.

GAIN HIS CONFIDENCE

Take a few minutes regularly to give undivided attention as your child works or plays. Within a short time, you will begin to notice a difference in attitude. Although his confidence is not gained quickly, it can be won gradually. It is more likely to be given when your attention is being fully focused on him. If he is young enough for physical comfort (and even an eight- or nine-year-old is not too old) opportunities for being cuddled and held close daily while watching TV or reading can be soothing and warmly communicative of affection.

Bedtime offers an opportunity for companionship, particularly if you refrain from the teaching that often characterizes much of your daytime conversation. Let him talk to you, or make small talk until he feels like contributing to the conversation. As your pleasure in his company reaches his awareness, he will respond. If by your attention you transmit interest in hearing about his simple, everyday experiences, he will begin to communicate with ease. He learns a great deal from just hearing himself talk. Conversation helps him put personal experiences and feelings into words so that they can be viewed more objectively.

DENY ACCUSATIONS THAT ARE UNTRUE

Answer his doubts—quietly but unambiguously. Lack of attention to his comments will be considered by him to be substantiation of his belief that he has a right to feel hostile. Convincing him of his acceptability requires that you protest inaccurate accusations that you have knowingly tried to make him angry, that you are uninterested in his company or do not love him. Continuing reassurance, verified by your respect, affection, and interest, helps him develop faith. Walking out, silence, anger, or showing that you regard his concern as silly will signify to him that his feelings of being unlovable are really true.

CHILD'S COMMENT	PARENT'S RESPONSE
You are all going into the kitchen to get away from me.	No, we are not. We want you to come too. I'm waiting until you do.
You take sister's part more than mine.	I was only afraid she might get hurt. I would protect you also.
Daddy talks to the boys more than me.	They are older. He reads to you, and he likes to go for walks and to the park with you.
You don't laugh at my jokes.	Sometimes I do. I think you tell some very funny stories.
My kitty is my best friend.	We are your best friends, too.
You never want to go where I want to go.	I can think of a number of places that we have gone at your suggestion. I would not want to ignore your interests.
Why do you always bring her along when you pick me up?	She is too little to leave home alone. Sometimes I pick you up by myself when she is at a friend's home.
You gave her more turns.	I did not intend to let her get more than you. You may have another turn.
You didn't save me any chocolate pudding?	Yes, I did. Daddy must have eaten it when he came in last night. Next time I'll label it so he'll know it is yours.
Quit laughing at me.	I was not trying to be critical. I was laughing at myself for not knowing how to answer you.
You aren't trying to catch the ball.	I didn't want to miss it. I would like to be a better catcher, too.
You spoiled the game.	I didn't do it on purpose.
Why does she get the last apple?	I didn't notice that they were all gone. She asked for it first.
I asked you to help me first.	I'll be with you in a minute. I must make sister a sandwich or she'll be off to school without lunch.

Don't expect your words to have an obvious impact. Even if he doesn't answer, you are getting through. He may not wish to give you the satisfaction of a reply, or he may answer in his more familiar negative way. Nevertheless, your understanding and your own reduced hostility will in time make him less sure of his need to be angry. As conflict subsides, hostility becomes noticeably less frequent rather than disappearing completely.

TRY A CASUAL APPROACH TO HOSTILITY

Answering your child in a casual way encourages him to cool down. If you can accept his hostility without overreacting, you offer him a model to follow in doing the same with his feelings.

CHILD'S COMMENT	PARENT'S RESPONSE
I don't care what you say.	You sound angry.
I hate you.	OK, so you feel that way sometimes.
You're a jerk.	Cut out the tough talk. I happen to know there's a sweet, lovable young man beneath that anger.
See what you made me do.	Don't yell at me, dear. I was trying to help.
Shut your face.	I don't like being spoken to that way when I haven't been unkind to you.
	Or, don't answer the next time he talks to you. Say instead: I'd love to talk but you told me to shut up.
Get my dinner.	I would be glad to fix it even if you asked me nicely.
Don't talk to me.	Hey, I'm not angry with you.
Stupid idiot.	You're losing your cool, pal.
I'm not going if that bratty, idiot sister is along.	That's enough. It's time to put your anger back in your pocket.
Dumbbell!	What's your beef?

On occasions when it is obvious that any answer will add fuel to his fire, you may be better advised to refrain from communication. Brendtro suggests that it may be wise to think twice before responding to challenges to fight such as "I don't care what you say," "You can't make me," "I'll do what I feel like." Being silent, walking away, or telling him "We'll settle it later" is not admitting defeat; the child is left wondering what you plan for later. Thus, his hostility is not escalated into a deteriorating conflict between parent and child (Trieschman, *et al.,* 1969, p. 92).

TRY SETTING A LIMIT

Depending upon the conditions, particularly the intensity of the child's feelings, setting a limit may be effective. If he's only mildly irritated, the limit may check behavior before it deteriorates.

> You have been doing your utmost to make me angry. Stop it now. I don't want to be angry with you.
>
> That's enough. You are disturbing us all and making yourself more and more unhappy. We cannot have a pleasant evening if you are going to be unhappy.
>
> If you are angry with Louise, tell her what's distressing you. No hitting.

He cannot indefinitely continue to be hostile when others do not give him an excuse. If the parent's tone of voice and manner do not reflect resentment, the responsibility for his anger is his alone.

HOLDING OR REMOVAL IS SOMETIMES NECESSARY

One family member cannot be permitted continually to make all others uncomfortable. A happy home requires that everyone must assume some responsibility for being helpful, polite, and considerate. Getting this message across to the hostile child is less of a problem when parents learn to intervene without returning his anger. Although he may resist with great determination, he benefits from the same procedures used to help any child learn to cooperate. Refusing to let him go beyond himself shows that you're interested enough to do something. He feels protected and will in time accept your limits as part of a reasonable world and part of his own self-control. When holding or removal is necessary, tell him why.

> The way you are talking is making us uncomfortable. You can play here until you feel more friendly.
>
> I must remove you until you stop bothering Virginia. It hurts her to be pinched. You can play here.
>
> I need to hold you because you are kicking the furniture. You can tell me what you are angry about, but I can't let you damage our chair.

ENCOURAGE HIM TO THINK OF OTHERS' FEELINGS

Let him know how adverse behavior makes you and others feel.

> That hurts my feelings. If you are going to be angry, I have a right to know why you are angry with me.
>
> That makes me unhappy. I'd rather not play checkers until you feel in a better mood.
>
> Bill is puzzled as to why you are angry with him. Is it because he didn't want you to use his notebook a few minutes ago?
>
> You are very important to me, but not your angry behavior.
>
> That's not fair. You are acting as though we are being unkind, when we are only trying to be helpful.
>
> How do you think Alice feels when you call her names?
>
> I see that you are threatening to break my pencil. How do you think that makes me feel?

Let him know also when he manages to do something right or makes someone happy. He may not realize he has any abilities along these lines.

Keep in mind that even useful guidance techniques can be

overworked. The parent with an abundance of comments, explanations, or corrections for every piece of off-behavior can be a nuisance. And, of course, the parent who never loses his temper may seem unreal. If you find yourself sounding like a broken record, try ignoring him for a while.

LET HIM SAVE FACE

Upon recovery from an angry episode, give no special attention to his reentry into the family. Speak as though nothing has happened. Refrain from greetings with undertones of criticism: "Well, it's good to see you in a friendly mood again," "It's about time you were over being mad," or "Aren't you glad you decided to come along?"

Friendly greetings can be profoundly reassuring: "Hi, there. Want to come sit by me and watch this program? It's pretty good." "This will be a fun trip. We are happy you came with us." Such greetings are a way of communicating quickly that you are not angry and not holding a grudge. These are facts he needs to know. They also are a way of swiftly reestablishing contact and making him a part of warmth and happiness.

THEFT

As Anna Freud (1965) points out, the concepts of "mine" and "yours" develop slowly, applying first to the child's own body, next to his parents, then to transitional objects. "Mine" is the first concept to be understood. He begins to understand "yours" as associations with others help him learn respect for property rights and as he observes the strong feelings others invest in their possessions.

The Why of It

UNFULFILLED NEEDS

Respect for the property of others may be influenced by the degree to which certain of a child's needs are fulfilled. If he enjoys certain possessions that are his alone, he is less envious of others. If self-confident, he has less need for the possessions of others as a measure of his self-worth. With the tender companionship of interested parents, possessions usually are not sought out as a substitute for affection.

CHILDHOOD FEELINGS ARE INTENSE

The intensity of childhood emotions drives many a youngster to take what he wants when he believes it might be denied him. What mother has not returned from a shopping trip surprised to find a "purchase" of which she was unaware? In such situations, help your child understand without overreacting. You can say:

How did this get here? We'll have to take it back. I didn't pay for it. Did you really want it so much? (Don't oblige him to answer. Adults aren't the only ones who do "impulse" shopping.)

We don't have the money for this now. I'll put it away so that it doesn't get damaged. We must not bring things home from the store unless they are paid for. I'll take it back tomorrow.

If his act remains unrewarded, he's less likely to repeat it. Returning a child to the scene of the "crime," including a confrontation with the store manager, is not the wisest way to deal with what may be a complicated personality issue or may be a simple "testing." It is better that he learn about ownership from family conversation and example, just as he learns about all other social demands of life. Don't either cover up or over-react. When he "takes" without permission from a friend, say:

We would all like to have things that belong to others. This is
Billy's. He will be unhappy when he discovers it is missing. We'll take it back.

This is Ellen's doll. She'll be glad it is safe.

What can you do when he takes without permission from his
parents? In addition to giving more love and companionship, a
need for which may have motivated his need to steal, we might
say:

I'm disappointed that you didn't tell me you needed money.
When you want something so badly that you feel like
taking it without permission, come tell me. Maybe we
can work something out.

UNTRUTHFULNESS

Almost every child tells a fib on some occasion or another. A bit
of untruthfulness is nothing to be concerned about. For parents
having more than the average share of this problem, the following explanations may be helpful.

FANTASY

The small child's world is filled with games and stories having
to do with make-believe, which seem almost real to him. Add a
vivid imagination to this make-believe world and you have the
ingredients for fantasy. Lack of truthfulness in the small child is
often merely a matter of experimenting with fantasy. He is
testing to see how others react to his interpretation of what is
real or unreal. Or sometimes he is attempting to remake reality
into something more desirable to him: to fulfill wishes, gain
attention, gain prestige, or improve his self-confidence.

Such unrealistic inventions are less to be concerned about than your overreaction. Too much talk about his honesty can create permanent doubts about himself. A simple answer is often all that is necessary to let a child know that you are aware of the difference between his make-believe and the real world and that you figure he is, too. Parents' failure to go along with his stories brings him back to reality.

> Don't you think it happened more like this?
> You're fooling. I distinctly heard her say four o'clock.
> Better count those again.
> You wish you could have gotten a new doll, too.
> Tell me more.
> That's not how it seemed to me.
> That looks like chocolate on your face to me.
> I hear you talking.

FEAR OF PUNISHMENT

A child may be untruthful for fear of punishment or criticism. Rather than face his fears, he justifies his behavior by denial or rationalization. The real or true reasons are then disguised from others and possibly even from himself. You will not have this problem if your child does not fear punishment for reporting the truth. When your child spills grape juice on the rug, tell him:

> I understand that you are saying you didn't do it. Nevertheless, when something like this happens, let me know immediately. The rug will not get stained if I know it is there and can wash it out right away.

REDUCED SELF-WORTH

A child may wish that the tale he's telling were true. Lack of attention and too much belittlement are stimuli for trying to get recognition through boasting about things that never have happened. With assistance he can find ways to honestly excel, thereby eliminating the need for unrealistic schemes to increase his feelings of importance. If sufficiently praised and rewarded, a child develops the confidence to find satisfaction in real achievements.

PARENTAL EXAMPLE

Parents themselves may set a poor example. Children are far more observant than most of us realize. We underestimate how much they learn when we:

Exaggerate a story in our favor.
Fib to escape an appointment.
Deny a mistake we have made.
Joke about shortchanging the salesman.
Express words of warm welcome to the neighbor we privately berated.
Give instructions to inform a caller that we are not at home.
Tell them that we are going to be home when we are not.

A real problem exists when parents deny the truth along with their child. When it is clear that Junior did shoot the neighbor's cat with his beebee gun, that he did break the window in the school auditorium, we must not be too embarrassed to help him assume responsibility. Without parental assistance, he has difficulty learning to accurately interpret reality.

TATTLING

Betty (six) hears a friend using improper language on the playground and reports it to Miss Phillips, her teacher. Miss Phillips chides Betty with "Don't be a tattletale," disregarding the fact that getting others into trouble is not one of Betty's habits.

The child who reports the behavior of others is often belittled by adults. But calling him a "tattletale" should be regarded as more offensive than his reporting an incident he has observed.

Most children want to compare their observations with others. How else can they learn to understand feelings? Reporting what he sees and feels to teacher or parent helps him find out about its authenticity. He wants to know, "Do others feel as I do about this?" By accepting his information without criticism and interpreting it, we offer him an opportunity to look at a situation from another point of view, one that may be more objective than his own.

The persistent tattler may be letting us know of his reduced self-esteem. Announcing the faults of others, he seeks to reassure himself of his own values. Sensitive to his lack of confidence, we can search for ways to help him raise self-esteem.

DESTRUCTION

The valued oil painting of great-grandfather has been damaged. From various living-room walls, he has looked down on many generations of children. No matter where you stand in the living room his eyes appear to stare down at you. Now he has a neat nail hole in his forehead. Restoration will be costly.

Who put the nail hole in the painting? Who broke the vase? Who tramped on the flowers? Can you find out? You usually won't get a confession unless your child is willing to talk or you are a good guesser.

Destruction is usually an acting out of momentary feelings. Hurt that a child dare not return to his parent or others is imposed upon the property of that person or a convenient substitute.

A child whose parents regularly use reasoning rather than harsh discipline is more likely to own up to mistakes. He may feel considerable guilt without further discipline. He will admit wrongdoing if past experience has shown that parents try to be fair, if admissions of guilt are not usually followed by ridicule or harsh chastisement. Children are basically good. They aren't likely to develop into criminals if not treated as such.

When a child has faith enough to confide in you, keep that confidence. Do something to help him rather than punish him. Assist him to right a mistake. Help him plan the replacement or repair of broken, lost, or destroyed property—for example, by giving up part of an allowance or postponing purchase of a new bike. Repairing the damage gives him an opportunity to restore his relationship with you and the person injured and builds responsibility. Then the pressure of guilt for having committed a wrong is not prolonged. Habits of constructive action are begun.

FOUR

Keys to Better Discipline

Instant solutions are more imaginary than real. Acquisition of skills, arts, and the many habits comprising good character is arduous and gradual, and requires much practice. Emotional development, too, takes time. Some things learned may have to be unlearned, and this particularly is likely to require considerable time. Improvement occurs as the overall relationship with parents improves. Children are complicated creatures. We cannot expect one particular discipline to work all the time. Even a good idea may not work under all conditions.

SENSIBLE DISCIPLINE

A LITTLE REWARD GOES A LONG WAY

Reinforcing desirable behavior reduces undesirable behavior. In all conditioning, rewarded behavior tends to become fixed while unrewarded behavior tends to disappear. Using verbal reward as a stimulus, Hall, Lund, and Jackson (1968) retrained disruptive children in two elementary schools to produce more productive and fewer disruptive responses. The typical procedure in such schools has been to ignore contentment and give attention only when behavior becomes intolerable, and this has been the practice in most homes. Hall, Lund and Jackson reversed this procedure. They gave friendly attention and praise to the child who was quietly engaged in study. Disruptive behavior diminished, and great changes were noted in academic performance.

It's difficult to ignore whining, disruption, and lack of cooperation; and it is also difficult to remember to reward good behavior when all is going well. Parents are only too glad for an opportunity to work or rest without interruption. Nevertheless, your child is continually learning. Good behavior must be rewarded if we want to reduce chances for undesirable behavior to become fixed.

A RECONDITIONING PLAN

When a particularly troublesome behavior has been learned, a plan for its unlearning might go as follows:

During the next few weeks, reduce away-from-home concerns and household duties. Schedule a daily program of reading, art, games, and other interesting activities.

While he is cooperative, stay continuously close. Get down to his level on the floor. Engage in friendly conversation, fun, and play. Tell him, "That's good," "Well done," "You're doing fine." Reward cooperative behavior with smiles, pats, hugs, kisses, letting him sit on your lap, and showing interest in his work and play.

When he becomes uncooperative, walk away and direct your attention to other things. Remain only close enough to keep him in view. Become absorbed in other matters while you wait for the return of his good behavior.

Let name-calling, nonserious crying, quarreling, grabbing, pushing, noise, and rebellion remain unnoticed, reducing their pay-off value. If interruption becomes necessary, try to keep your involvement to a minimum. Interfere only if physical injury to himself, others, or damage to property appears imminent. Even then, largely direct your attention to the person or object being attacked.

At the first sign of improvement, even if it's only silence, give again the comfort of your interest, attention, and affection, until the next disruption occurs. Eventually you will approach him only during his good moods.

The success of this plan depends upon parents' ability to wait out uncooperative moods without giving them attention as in the past, and upon the persistence with which approval is given when due. Approval and attention are a powerful reward for children. When they get accustomed to receiving it, occasional approval is all that's needed to maintain cooperation. The trick is to avoid ignoring the child when he plays quietly and constructively.

Brothers and sisters, too, can learn to withdraw from provocation and respond to cooperation. When a child's problem behavior changes, all the family is likely to feel the effects.

SAYING NO KINDLY

This is necessary in many relationships throughout life. It is especially important at home, where the gratification of needs must be frequently postponed or relinquished.

When we remove an object from a child's hands, when we forcibly restrain him, correct intolerable behavior, deny his wishes, we must try to do so kindly. To do it in an angry or hostile way confuses him as to what it is we are intending to teach. For him to learn to cope with complicated wishes and feelings is difficult enough without this additional problem. Only maturity can enlarge his perspectives so he can understand that it is not he, but his behavior, or the object in question that his parents are protesting.

The preschooler is not ready for our concepts of conservation and postponement. The future does not exist. He comprehends mainly what he can see, hear, touch, and taste. He thinks of time in terms of daily routine, instead of clocks and calendars. Reality to him is now. He has difficulty putting aside immediate pleasure for future gain. His needs are more urgent, his disappointments more intense, his interests more consuming than are ours. When we must delay the satisfaction of needs that seem to him uncontrollable, he requires our understanding rather than our annoyance.

It's time for six-year-old Jenny's friend to go home. Jenny wants to continue the fun of the afternoon by accompanying her. You explain that one cannot invite themselves. This does not reduce Jenny's distress. She must express a certain amount of her disappointment before she can learn to tolerate and accept it. We help when we resist the anger we feel over the discomfort she causes us, and when we let her know we understand. "You wish Sara's mother would invite you right away, today? I know how that feels. . . . Come help me set the table. Maybe you can think of something interesting we can use as a centerpiece."

The child in the department store screaming for what he wants is reacting to the intensity of his frustrated wishes, and possibly to his view of your denial of those wishes as a lack of love. Pick him up and depart. Don't top off his frustration with punishment—giving more cause to feel unloved and not understood.

Delaying your no may reduce frustration. When it is obvious that an immediate no will provoke an inconvenient scene, to suggest postponement is sometimes helpful. In the interval, his interest may change. Say:

We'll talk about it later.
Perhaps we can do that some other time.
Let's sleep on it.

I think I see what you mean.
You may be right. Let's think it over.

Giving a reason with your no may make its acceptance easier.
It's worth a try to suggest:

> I'm sorry you're unhappy. I'm talking with father, and I can't give you your bath this minute. Go brush your teeth first and I'll be with you soon.
>
> I know how disappointed you must feel not getting a bike the same as big brother. You are young yet. We have to wait. It all comes in time.
>
> I know you'd like another candy bar, but our limit is one. Have a piece of chewing gum.
>
> They are very beautiful, but your dolly doesn't need clothes as much as you do.
>
> I understand how you feel. There are so many pretty things that you'd like to buy them all. I feel that way too sometimes.
>
> Someday we'll come shopping just to look at toys. We'll see if they are as useful as the TV says. We'll see if they have sharp corners that might break off and injure you. Some toys are not as big as the TV shows them to be. Others do not do all they appear to do.

Praise can reduce your need to say no. Praise often encourages a child to reduce the disturbing "I want" habits that make shopping with young children most difficult. You can say:

> How grown up you are when you resist the urge to put money in the gum-ball machine.
>
> Thank you, dear, for walking with me so quietly. That's a big help.
>
> You are wise to put the doll back and wait until you have saved enough for the one you really want.
>
> You are more grown up when you can walk through the store

without needing things. We have only enough money for necessary items: food, clothing, and things that we use. Fun things we buy on special occasions.

The many things we parents want do not seem more important to children than those they want. When your child is intent upon the shiny new beach ball, look into your grocery cart and see what you could put back on the shelf and easily do without: the package of cookies, the cinnamon rolls, the pickles, the hair spray. It is easy to feel that his wish is unimportant, but it can be more important to him than you can imagine. The values other people place on their desires are difficult to appraise.

APPEAL TO REASON

Democratic parents are most likely to use reasoning. Authoritarian parents expect children to do as they are told without question. Their ultimatums may sound like punishment: "Stop running this instant!" "Get your bed made!" "Do your lessons now!"

Using "we" or "let's" is a friendlier way to persuade children to follow our suggestions, and also makes it clear that many rules are for all of us, not just for the little people. "We aren't supposed to run in the house." "Let's get the beds made!" "We need to get the lessons done first."

Giving reasons builds goodwill and has the added advantage of developing reflective thought. Insight helps control aggression. Aggression is reduced when property rights are explained, when suggestions for how to solve a problem are made, when the wishes and feelings of one child are explained to another (McCandless, 1967). When the reasons for a particular behavior are clearly seen, a better chance exists for the generalization of that behavior to other situations. One learns the principle, not merely the particular application.

This is daddy's. Here is a book for you.

Let's draw a line across the sandbox. This will be your side,
the other is Randy's.

Mary doesn't like being pushed. She'll feel better if you tell
her how you feel rather than show her.

You feel concerned that we won't get home in time to see your
favorite TV program.

It's for your own good. Mother doesn't benefit when you wear
a sweater to keep warm.

Let's do your lessons now. Tomorrow we may go to the park.
You'll not have to worry about getting them done the last
minute.

Please put your toys away. You aren't using them now, and it
is lots more comfortable to have the house looking neat and
pretty.

MIRROR HIS FEELINGS SOMETIMES

Every person needs to share thoughts and feelings with
someone who really understands, someone who will accept his
feelings without always trying to change them. Deep relief
comes from knowing that we can be freely and honestly ourselves, secure in the knowledge that a particular person is with
us, understanding and accepting how we feel (Baruch, 1949).

Reflection helps parents become better as this kind of friend.
When we try to feel what our troubled child is feeling, we let
him know of our concern and sympathy. Sometimes we even
succeed in understanding him.

You wish you were going too.

It made you feel angry when mother laughed. You thought I
was laughing at you. People laugh from delight and joy,
too.

You don't want sister near you just now. Maybe we can get
her interested in something else.

It is sad to lose a pretty ring that you liked so much, isn't it?

You don't want to go to Mary's birthday party, but yet you do.

You are afraid that mother might blame you the way the teacher did.

You feel unhappy because big brother has a new tennis racket. You'd like to have one, too.

You feel angry when mother doesn't buy you the toy you want.

You don't like my suggestion. You think I'm trying to tell you what to do.

You want me to stop what I am doing and stay close to you.

"This kind of reflection helps one feel that he has the power of choice. It lets the child know that we are not shocked by his behavior nor do we regard it as weird or different" (Brammer and Shostrom, 1968, pp. 202, 203).

A word of caution. Sometimes a technique can be overdone. If we continually mirror a child's feelings back to him, he may come to fear that we can read his mind, know everything he thinks, know his feelings even before he does. He also may feel we are nothing but mimics, and give nothing of ourselves.

JOIN THE FUSS

There are times when parent participation reduces problems. Give your child five minutes in which you will join him in making all the racket, fuss, or muss he wants. Then he must be off with his interests elsewhere. Suggest an alternative: off to the sandbox, help make lunch, play with his blocks, read, work in his alphabet book.

KID HIM OUT OF IT

Funny words, dramatics, self-directed humor—these take the anger out of his sails and create a more joyous atmosphere.

Bet you can't make as funny a face as me.

What happened to Danny's smile? Let's go find it.

Ouch, I'll never be able to walk again.

There goes a mouse! See it running across the yard. Oh, it's
   gone now.

I'll bet you can't pick up these blocks before I count to twenty.

A parent who can joke when a child is bombarding him with
distress is less vulnerable. It's difficult to remain angry if your
opponent is good-humored and not angry. For the child to
regain his composure is easier when we avoid a strict disciplinarian approach.

When you are on the receiving end of name-calling, the following rejoinders are sometimes helpful in cooling the situation.
Use them only when they will not be taken as belittlement or a
denial of his feelings.

You must have the wrong house. There aren't any stupid
   idiots living here.

Save your compliments for later!

Now that you have me classified, let's get on with the work.

It takes one to know one.

I never said I was perfect.

What did you say your name was?

Welcome to the family.

Sure, isn't everybody?

Go powder your nose.

SAY HOW YOU FEEL

At times a child may seem insensitive to your feelings partly
because he does not know how you feel when he misbehaves or
is disrespectful. For instance, if you customarily remain silent or
fail to tell him or show him your hurt feelings, he cannot learn
empathy. If you frequently blame, scold, and correct, instead of
reasoning with him, he learns hostility rather than sympathy.
He learns best how his behavior affects others when we politely
tell him our feelings.

I feel that I'm being taken advantage of when you don't keep your end of the bargain.

When you speak that way, it hurts my feelings. If you're not interested in how I feel, do you think I should be interested in how you feel?

I feel let down when you take so long to do your work. It's almost time for our guests to arrive, and I still have to worry about the sweeping.

I was scared when I couldn't find you. Please stay close to me when we are shopping.

I'm disappointed that you did this when I asked you not to.

It hurts my feelings when you yell at me that way.

That noise is getting on my nerves. Please stop before I lose my temper.

Those marks on my wallpaper make me very sad. Help me try to get them off.

Gordon suggests that we may need to send a second, stronger message when children walk away from our first expression of how we feel:

Hey, I'm telling you how I feel. This is important to me. And I don't like being ignored. I hate it when you just walk away from me and don't even listen to my feelings. This doesn't sit well with me. I don't feel it's very fair to me when I really have a problem. [1970, *b*, p. 135.]

A SIGNAL

A stern glance, a shake of the head, or a hand signal may be all that is needed to let a child know that he's headed for trouble if he doesn't stop.

WORDS SPEAK LOUDER THAN ACTIONS

Help him learn to settle problems with words. The feedback of information enables one to better see another's point of view. It often brings about fairer treatment.

Tell Bill that you don't like being socked for no reason. Maybe
  he thinks he has a reason.
Tell Donald that you don't like having your toys grabbed
  away.
You want to hurt Jane because she is teasing. She needs to
  know how it makes you feel. Tell her that it hurts your
  feelings.
Ask Jack for your ball. He may be ready to give it to you.
Tell Art that you'll give him the truck as soon as you're
  finished.
Tell me why you feel angry; then, if it's my fault, maybe I can
  change what I am doing.
What other way do you think you could get Scott to quit
  teasing?
Have you tried telling Tom how his behavior makes you feel?
First ask Jean in a kind way to move from in front of the TV,
  so that you can see too. She may not intend to refuse you.

DON'T CALL HIM BAD

It's surprising that parents may still be heard using "bad" to
label children. A child hearing "bad" often enough over his
growing years may encounter increasing difficulty in thinking
himself "good" in any respect. Point out that it's his behavior of
which you disapprove, not him.

Mother loves you even when you do things she does not like.
  It's not you but what you are doing that distresses me.
No, mother doesn't think you are bad. She thinks you have a
  lot to learn. Mothers are for helping children learn.
When you love someone, you accept the not-so-good things
  that they do as well as the good things.
We all have feelings of anger. Most of the time our feelings
  of love are the strongest.

ENCOURAGE HIM TO THINK ABOUT HIS FEELINGS

Ask him questions. In answering, feelings are put into words. Considering the consequences of his behavior for himself and others may hasten understanding and empathy. Be a good listener. Stay calm even when he is not. Occasionally tell him how a situation appears from your point of view.

How did he happen to do that?

Do you think Ruth tramped on your foot on purpose?

How do you feel when you make such a mess of my magazines? How do you think it makes me feel?

Why do you think you wanted to push George?

You were all having such a good time until the ball game started. What happened then?

Can you tell me more about how you feel? I would like to understand your point of view better.

What does Mary do that bothers you? Have you talked to her about it?

What's the matter, dear? You don't usually get angry about nothing.

How do you think Dave's mother will feel when she tries to wash all that sand out of his hair?

IGNORE SOME MISBEHAVIOR

Depending upon the circumstances, it may be best to ignore much of a child's seemingly uncooperative behavior. More important is our ability to distract him and avoid giving to a situation more serious concern than it deserves. There are times when intervention only results in a tantrum, ending in the disruption of an entire evening. Ignoring a child's challenge to battle seems more sensible. Behavior that bothers you can be discussed at a more advantageous time. Ask later, "What made you so angry before dinner this evening?"

When he demands rather than requests that you do certain

things for him, depending upon the circumstances, let some of his demands remain unnoticed. It's not easy. His distress may be hard to tolerate; but so may the overcontrol that he can impose if parents too eagerly strive for peace. Try to sort out the reasonable from the unreasonable. Is it convenient? Could he more easily do it himself? Is his need a bid for parental attention that he has not received recently?

Shocking vocabulary can be ignored. "Apathy and disinterest in another's activity are effective means of extinguishing his responses" (Lundin, 1969, p. 73). Unless used by the parent in his hearing, embarrassing words are not likely to become a permanent part of his vocabulary.

A PLAN OF ACTION

Another way to reduce anger or misbehavior is to give it an acceptable outlet. A child having difficulty keeping disruptive impulses in check may need suggestions of more constructive ways to expend his energy:

Tumbling in the yard.
Tossing a ball with a friend.
A run, skip, or hop around the outside of the house.
Hammering scraps of wood together.
Jumping rope.
Blowing up balloons and bouncing them in the air.
Having a foot race with a friend.
Manipulating clay in his hands as he watches TV.

BE FIRM

If it's obvious that you mean business, children react to your intent. Guiding and limiting behavior in a considerate and respectful tone and manner usually will get results.

A family is a team. We don't kick one member of the team around just because he can't do something as well as the rest of us.

You can tell us how you feel, but you can't use words to hurt.

You have a choice. You can kick and cry as long as you want in the den, or you can stay out here and enjoy the game with us. We'd like you to stay here.

I'll answer you when you ask me kindly.

I'm stopping the car. I'll not move another inch until everyone starts cooperating.

I'll not let you hit Bill, and I will not let him hit you.

Out you go. Come back when you feel like cooperating.

I can't permit you to do that. If you feel like breaking things, go look for some sticks in the yard.

Sorry you don't feel like obeying the rules. I'll return the pail and shovel when you think you can use them properly.

Since you can't play happily together, play separately. Mary can go into the kitchen, and you can go into the family room.

REDUCE BOREDOM

When children are involved in increasingly intense disagreements, often the result of boredom, they may be glad for assistance in stopping. An idea or two may solve this form of problem.

Put on some records and dance for me.

Maybe Janice can come over to play.

Would you like to go to the park?

Your dolly is waiting for you to take care of her.

Here are some paints. Make me a picture.

Take this soap and water and wash the patio furniture.

How many things can you do with this piece of rope?

Make yourself a hideaway with these chairs and old bedspreads.

See who can keep quiet the longest.

Who can draw the funniest face?

How many different things can you do with this Hula-Hoop?

How many different ways can you get from one side of this
  room to the other?

How far can you kick this ball?

How high can you bounce the ball?

Can you walk while bouncing a ball?

How many times can you keep this ball going between you
  before it falls?

Can you bounce the ball and turn around in a circle before
  catching it?

Can you kick the ball into the air and catch it before it falls
  to the ground?

Here are some puzzles you haven't put together in a long
  time.

BE BRIEF

Talking too long in an effort to reduce distress, you may find
yourself rebuffed. Children appear unable to reflect upon as
many aspects of a situation as can adults. Carried away with
our wisdom, we may offer an overwhelming abundance of ideas
or suggestions. A child's ability to grasp more than one concept
at a time grows as he grows.

Big brother and seven-year-old sister have agreed to cooperate on an
art project. As the supplies belong to sister, she attempts to manage
the situation. Sister gets socked and brother walks away. Mother's
first brief explanation of brother's anger eases sister's distress. Encouraged, mother continues the discussion. Her helpfulness is met
with rejection. Sister is unwilling to conceptualize a variety of views
about the problem.

Efforts to keep three-year-old Jerry taking his afternoon naps were
violently opposed and resented for many months. He felt discrimi-
nated against as older brother was not napping. Reasons and explanations were not understood. At twelve, during a family discussion of
early experiences, he understood when mother explained that without

his nap, he often fell asleep without dinner and awakened late at night, and mother herself could not manage the day without her nap.

RESPOND TO HIS FEELINGS, NOT YOURS

You can't really know how important his feelings are to him. While he may be overreacting, his concerns may indeed represent a problem that has been bothering him for some time. There is no feasible alternative but to give due consideration to his comments.

CHILD'S COMMENT	PARENT'S RESPONSE
I'm going to run away.	That would make me very sad.
You don't love me.	You are wrong. You are more important to me than anything else in the world.
You think I'm bad.	No, dear. I was distressed to see your closet in such a mess. I guess I lost my temper. Throwing your clothes on the floor is not such a good thing to do, but you are not bad.
You are more fair to sister.	I wouldn't want to be. You mean just as much to me. Sometimes it may seem that way because she is little and must be protected.
I'm going to tear up this picture I made.	I would be disappointed. Daddy would like to see it, too. I know you worked hard on it. It is very pretty.
You get sister more things than you do me.	I want to get things for you, too. Maybe it seems that way because little girls need so many more clothes than boys.

"When actions evoke no response, a child becomes flooded with impotent rage. . . . The experience that his actions make no difference is what stops him from becoming a human being, for it discourages him from interacting with others and hence from forming a personality through which to deal with the environment" (Bettelheim, 1967, pp. 19, 25).

MAKE YOUR EXPECTATIONS DEFINITE

We must feel confident of our authority and impart that confidence. A child needs the strength of positive expectation, although he may test it to the limit. If he senses that we doubt the possibility that he will carry through, he may react to our feelings rather than to our words. Only by making our expectations definite and clear are we likely to gain his cooperation.

CHILD'S COMMENT	PARENT'S RESPONSE
I won't do it.	Yes, you will pick up the wastebasket. You were the one who dumped it.
You can't make me.	I don't intend to make you.
Why should I?	Because you are responsible for this mess, and it makes us uncomfortable to use an untidy room.
Make me.	I don't intend to make you. I'm leaving it to your better judgment.

Don't accept his challenge to make him do it. Nothing positive is gained by overpowering him. You can't hold a child's hand and make him pick things up piece by piece. Tell him instead that he has no option but to do it. "One of the attributes of the effective child-care worker is the ability to say no, mean no, and yet be able to save face if the child does not comply" (Trieschman, Whittaker and Brendtro, 1969, p. 92).

Having clearly stated what he is to do, don't directly supervise. Afford him the opportunity to carry out the task on his own. If instructions are not complied with within a reasonable time, repeat them. Tell him, "You have ten minutes to get the mess cleaned up." If this does not encourage his cooperation, suggest that you will help him. Finally, pick it up yourself. Some disagreements are won by losing. If it's not beneath your dignity to "lose," he learns from your example. Permitting the rebelling child to escape from a situation that you are obviously not going to win short of violence is sensible. Your expectations get your message across even though they may not, on this particular occasion, produce the desired behavior.

YOUR FAITH IS HIS BEST TEACHER

Your confidence guides his behavior. Children observe the persistence of their parents' faith. They tend to become what they are thought to be. Guidance is less of a problem when they know what parents expect—when they know that parents do not doubt their basic goodness. Our confidence is expressed when we support them in their relationships with ourselves—

I know you didn't intentionally forget.
You didn't spill it on purpose.
I know you didn't want to start such a fuss. It's difficult not
  to be angry when someone is teasing.
I know you didn't break it on purpose, but Dad may not
  know it. Tell him.
I know you didn't take his book. Let's help him find it.

—and help them understand others—

Dave will do his share of the work in a few minutes.
Ralph will help you with that task if you ask him. He is good
  at that.
Louise will move her seat if you ask her in a kind way.
Anne doesn't want you to be angry with her.
John didn't mean that. He wanted to return the hurt from the
  anger in your tone of voice.

AFFECTION AND FRIENDLINESS

An appeal to his need for friendship helps many a child who seems on his way to disruption. Put him beside you for a time. An arm around his shoulder, a smile, some words of approval, or just sitting on the floor with him and displaying interest in what he's doing may help to reorient him to more cooperative behavior.

PLANNED REPETITION

Irritating behavior such as purposeful drumming on the table, repeated tapping of his foot, tearing up newspapers, or provocative comments may be good-naturedly extinguished by urging their continuance, oversatisfying his need for the activity. Each time that he tries to stop, good-naturedly urge him to continue: "Come on; don't stop now," "Keep going." When he begins to beg "I'm tired, I want to stop," maybe he'll have had enough. Continuing an activity beyond one's tolerance reduces interest in it. As we become fatigued, behavior ceases to be satisfying.

AN APPLE A DAY

Hostility comes to the surface more frequently when children are hungry. Perhaps you have noticed how much more contented children are immediately following a meal than before. Pleasant feelings have been associated with food since earliest infancy. A light before-dinner snack can do much to forestall behavior problems that regularly occur while mother is busy preparing dinner.

LAST RESORT DISCIPLINE

Holding

We are concerned here mainly with small children. It is assumed that children in the ordinary home who are "too big to hold" have learned a degree of self-restraint and can be calmed without much physical contact.

Holding is necessary when a small child attacks parents, siblings, or personal property. Young children need physical support occasionally in getting strong emotions under control. No child is born with an appreciation of just how far his impulses should be allowed expression. He learns such limits from parents. If parental control is lacking, he has little reason for learning. In extreme situations he may come to fear that he will destroy himself or others.

It's not easy to restrain without anger a screaming child ready to bite, scratch, or hit. Nevertheless, a child feels more secure when a friendly parent takes over. An angry parent doesn't teach much of anything. He may make the child feel guilty, but not less aggressive. When you control him without descending to his level of violence, you set an example of good behavior. Your interference lets him know that you care enough to help him control his overwhelming emotions.

HELP HIM STOP

Try to anticipate when tantrum-like behavior has run its course. Each such occurrence has a turning point after which you may approach your child. If not helped to stop, he will sometimes whimper and cry long after his hostility is spent. Nothing is gained by prolonging negative feelings just to demonstrate that we can be equally stubborn. Extended distress upsets all the family. An overexerted child falls asleep before dinner. He may sleep until midnight and then be up for the rest of the night.

TALK TO HIM

Talk softly in a reassuring way while holding your distraught child. Although he may hear little of what you say, your voice helps calm him. Say:

Take it easy, dear. Everything is OK. I'm holding you because something might get broken. I don't want you to be hurt or my furniture damaged. You must calm down. Try to relax. I'll release you as soon as you think you can manage your anger. I will have to hold you again if you can't control yourself without my help. Your arm won't hurt if you quit jerking. I'll change my position to give that arm a rest. You aren't controlling yourself very well yet. As soon as you can be quiet for a few minutes, I'll be glad to release you.

Move with him into different rooms of your home. Movement and new things to see distract him. Show him various objects and talk in detail about anything that catches his or your interest. Your aim is to diminish the importance of the activity that originally stimulated his violent behavior.

HOLD HIM GENTLY

Use particular caution in your holding technique. A small child is made frightened and panicky by immobility. You can see this fear when a tight shirt gets stuck halfway over his head or a crib blanket twists and binds him. Prolonged restraint or complete immobility is unwise. Some movement must be permitted even if he does get in an occasional sock.

Removal

"Removal" means to briefly set apart (in a calm manner) the child whose behavior continues to be:

Dangerous to himself or others.
Annoying, unfair, or physically abusive.
Lacking in respect for the privacy of others.
Destructive to his own possessions or those of others.
Inconsiderate of the needs and rights of others.

He is set apart only for as long as he remains uncooperative, and only after appeal to reason has failed to gain his cooperation.

Locked out of brother's room, five-year-old Roger repeatedly kicks the door. Mother tells him, "I can't let you damage the door. Brother does not want to be disturbed while he studies. He will open the door when his lessons are done." Roger keeps right on kicking, so mother picks him up and removes him to another room. As soon as mother returns to her work in the kitchen, Roger returns to the door-kicking. Mother removes him again. This time she gives him ten minutes of her time, which may have been what he needed in the first place. They work a puzzle together and the door is forgotten.

From the battle that a small child puts up, it's difficult to believe that he ultimately feels increased security and affection from your interference. How you assert your authority is what makes the difference. To a degree, it depends upon your ability to hide "iron hands in velvet gloves." When reasonable limits are enforced without parental resentment and hostility, he knows that he matters enough to be worth the trouble. There are a number of advantages to removal.

> The child is not emotionally upset as he would be from a spanking. And a spanking affords no guarantee that he will not return to his door-kicking, which can bring on more spanking.
>
> It requires perhaps not more than ten minutes to remove a child and reorient his behavior. A child who has been upset by one or more spankings can disturb himself and the family for much longer.
>
> Parental rapport has not been markedly disturbed. Other children feel confident that they will receive the same consideration if their hostilities get out of hand. The child knows that he is part of an accepting family, realizing, nevertheless, that he will not be permitted to disrupt others.

WHAT TO SAY

Usually mother goes with the small child, distracting him to more peaceful activities in another location. She talks to him during this time and explains why it's better for him to move or change activities.

> Come with me. You'll feel better over here by yourself. Bring your truck if you like.

> Suppose you and I put this puzzle together. Sometimes we don't feel in the mood for playing with our friends. Then it's better to be by ourselves for a while.

> Bob, you seem to need more space. Let's move your things here.

> It made you angry—my taking the long stick away. It's too dangerous in the living room. Our lamps might get broken, or someone hurt.

> Freddy, here is something I think you will enjoy doing better.

> You've been asked to quit making so much noise while we are having dinner. We can't hear a thing anyone says when you play with that. If you aren't going to join us, please take your toy outside. Come back and join us when you've finished.

If you cannot stay with your preschooler, be sure that he knows of your wish for him to return as soon as he's recovered. You don't want to hurt him. You simply want to change a particular behavior. Seek him out if he fails to return soon. Tell him:

> Come join us. There's a good program on TV.
> Wash your hands. It's time for dinner.
> Come along to the store with me.

Your efforts toward reconciliation make clear your differentiation between his behavior and himself. When we restore good feelings quickly, we avoid educating our child on the care and feeding of grudges.

A word of caution about removal. For the child who is new to a situation, or the child who is not ordinarily disruptive, changing the activity of the group may be preferable to pointing out to all that his behavior alone is inappropriate—in other words, that he is different. For example, three-year-old Tommy, who has just entered nursery school, is disrupting the music class. We might ordinarily think it best to remove him separately to the swings or the sandbox so that the group's enjoyment is not upset. However, this could be unwise, particularly since Tommy is new to the school. The observations the group may make about him and his developing feelings toward the group should be considered in making this decision. It may be better to change the group's activity from indoor to outdoor play, from quiet games to singing games, than to remove the child, if we are interested in his developing self-worth and his status with the others. This principle should be as useful at home as in nursery school.

UNWISE DISCIPLINE

Spanking

A good leader uses respect and consideration to persuade his subjects to follow his example. Physical punishment arouses the desire to counterattack to even the score. As a method of influencing behavior, it belongs to primitive times. Today there are more productive ways to help children learn desirable behavior. Unfortunately, however, we cannot expect the practice of spanking children to disappear quickly and completely. It has been followed for many, many generations; and its sometimes quick suppression of misbehavior continues to mislead those unfamiliar with its undesirable side effects or with the success of more reasonable guidance.

There are other forms of discipline that are even less desirable than spanking. A slap in the face is decidedly more disturbing to self-esteem than a brief spanking. A quick swat on the bottom seems far kinder than verbal abuse. Persistent belittlement builds more inferiority than a spanking delivered without malice. Nevertheless, considerable evidence of the ill effects of spanking puts it in our category of unwise discipline.

Children learn by observation. "The aggression of parents in the context of discipline is not merely observed by the child. It is also directed at and experienced by the child" (Aronfreed, 1968, p. 320).

The child who is frequently punished inside the home often shows increased aggression outside the home.

A child learns to believe that force is acceptable if an adversary is angry or big enough.

A younger brother, sister, or classmate may later receive the physical abuse that a child cannot return to the parent. The force that parents use, he uses on others to get his way.

The physical punishment of one child may cause other children to fear a similar loss of love.

The punished child may feel hostile toward the unspanked children, whose accepted status is envied.

The frequently punished child may become identified as the "troublemaker" and suffer loss of family status.

Punishment tells the child what is disapproved but gives him no help on how to improve his behavior. He lacks even an appropriate adult example. As Redl (1966) points out, even if punishment results in the child becoming properly angry with himself, can he use this self-anger correctly? Does the punishment increase self-insight, or does he end up feeling worthless?

While punishment may temporarily inhibit undesirable behavior, tension remains high. Anxiety occurs as feelings

of hostility toward the parent and fear of further punishment increase. Fear, hatred, and anxiety may be what is
really learned.

Aroused hostility may find an outlet in aches and pains,
bed-wetting, increased thumb-sucking.

Punishment thwarts a child's right to be independent from
his parents. It says that he is wrong for having behavior
that is in accord with his own needs as he sees them.

For children who feel ignored or rejected, punishment may
lead to a repetition of the behavior that called forth the
punishment. If a spanking is the only way he can get
attention, he may try for such treatment.

Parental love seems less genuine.

Belittlement

Belittlement is the most frequently used form of behavior
control. Parents listening carefully to themselves may be surprised to note how often they use it. A brief written record of
daily expressions in your own family is very likely to demonstrate such consistency. Few of us are aware of the attitudes,
gestures, phrases, and expressions that are habitual in our
everyday communication.

Family members who feel that they have the "right not to be
bothered" by a younger member's need for attention come to
depend upon belittlement. In such interchanges they fend off
the irritable, attention-seeking youngster: "Don't be a crybaby!"
"Get out of my way!" "Who do you think you are?" The state of
a family's mental health is greatly influenced by the frequency
with which its members relate in a friendly or negative way to
one another.

PERSONALITY IS AFFECTED

Belittlement is more harmful than physical punishment as it
directly attacks a child's image of himself as a worthy person.

Normally, parents take special precautions to protect a child from physical danger. The same parents may be unaware that the psychological punishment they administer can be equally harmful. A child is sensitive to evaluation. "He seeks 'position' in the eyes of others" (Laing, 1969, p. 117). Frequent derogation undermines his self-confidence and inhibits his exploring, testing, and learning out of fear of further belittlement.

"The adult is not free to have any personality he wants" (Stagner, 1961, p. 106). Personality is almost entirely shaped in infancy and early childhood by the individual's most intimate associates, upon whom he is totally dependent. Consider the effects on self-image of a child frequently subjected to the disparaging comments of those whose opinions mean so much to him. The child must trust his parents. He has no other way of knowing what is real or unreal. He cannot disconfirm their evaluations. Comments such as the following sow seeds of self-doubt:

You have only yourself to blame.
My, but you are impatient.
You're not to be trusted.
Don't raise your voice to me.
Can't you remember anything?
Act your age.
You really think you're something.
What do you know about such things?
You're too big for dolls.
Can't you watch what you're doing?
You're old enough to know better.
Nice people don't say such things.
Don't be so sensitive.
Such a big boy to act like a baby.
Shame on you. Keep your dress down.
What's wrong with you?
You're nutty as your uncle.

What a braggart you are.
Don't act so shy.
You think you're so smart.
You're always complaining.
You don't get room and board for nothing.
You'll never learn.
You're impossible to manage.
You'll never be able to hold a job.
You are a demanding child.
Nice children don't fight.
Quit being a mommy's boy.
We've had enough out of you.
You'll never amount to anything.
I can't do a thing with you.
What are you good for if you don't work?
You don't know what you want.
People will laugh at you.
You are an ungrateful child.
What kind of person are you, anyway?
Big girls don't act like that.
Why can't you act more grown up?
You're just a little hoodlum.
Stop acting like a two-year-old.
You certainly have bad manners.
How clumsy can you get.
You drive me crazy.
You won't have any friends if you talk like that.

Parents are most unlikely to make public similar appraisals of their adult friends, who could defend themselves. Yet we behave as though we believe such comments will serve little children as guides to the improvement of behavior.

BELITTLEMENT AROUSES RESISTANCE TO AUTHORITY

Learning socially acceptable behavior becomes more difficult when the child must first deal with feelings of rejection. One does not feel like cooperating with someone who has humiliated him. It's not easy for a child to understand that parents are dissatisfied with only a part of his behavior, even when that is pointed out in a reasoning manner. Belittlement is often effective in unwanted ways. It may or may not suppress undesirable behavior, but it unfailingly damages self-esteem.

Our regard should be unconditional, not based upon a child's ability or accomplishment. Every child is lovable. If we desire that our child discard various behaviors, we should talk to him with the same absence of blame that we would express to a friend.

BELITTLEMENT TEACHES HIM THAT OTHERS ARE HIS JUDGES

Most injurious are those belittlements that teach a child that others are judging him.

What will people think? The outside world does not give a child self-esteem. This he learns mostly in early childhood from approving and accepting parents and siblings. Teaching that behavior must conform to the expectancies of the outside world produces self-consciousness, guilt, inferiority, and dependency, all more undesirable than the lack of conformity about which the parents may be worried.

Too great a concern for the approval of others narrows personal development. To become one's self, one must recognize, but not live in fear of, the opinions of others. Our goal is to help children learn to examine the standards of others without blind acceptance. It is the neurotic who spends much time and energy comparing himself to others in his search for self-appreciation.

Establishing the fear of being different is far too big a price to pay for conformity for the moment. Let a child remain undisturbed by social standards and public opinion until his maturity allows him to be objective, to judge freely, and to enjoy the values of his world unhampered by fears about his acceptability in that world. Let him first learn to be independent.

What does the Church think? Oddly enough, even the Church

uses a form of disparagement to influence good behavior. Some aspects of religion add to a child's guilt problems. Feelings of worthlessness flourish in the message that we are evil by nature. God may be perceived in the image of the parents who are accepting or rejecting. The love, lack of love, or criticism received from parents may be that which is expected of God. Children have been known to fear the wrath of God, who is watching from above and knows everything you do and think (Hodge, 1967).

Children do not understand many of the abstractions that for generations the Church has required them to memorize. Studies by Piaget clearly demonstrate that for the first seven or more years children grasp mainly thoughts and ideas related to real or concrete things. They come to understand the world around them more from perceptions in everyday experiences with people and things than from sermons or Scripture.

Significant differences are found among the attitudes of those who regularly attend church and those who do not. Authoritarian parents are likely to be regular churchgoers. Jones (1958) discovered that Protestant and Catholic parents are likely to be more authoritarian than Jewish or unaffiliated ones. In a study by Anisfeld, Bogo, and Lambert (1962) Jewish college students were found to have decidedly more favorable self-images than Gentile ones.

Banishment

Banishment here is used to mean separation from the family, usually in a specific location. It differs from "removal" in that the child is not free to return to his family until sentence has been served—one hour, two hours, or the rest of the day. The child's bedroom is often chosen as the location for such punishment. Supposedly a place for relaxation, sleep, and enjoyable play, it cannot serve as a prison and be enjoyable too. Since feelings often become associated with the surroundings in which they occur, the use of another location would be wiser.

BANISHMENT TEACHES HOW TO CARRY A GRUDGE

In banishing a child from our presence, we actually teach him to prolong angry feelings, to meditate in isolation on his dislikes.

WHAT IS BETTER?

Good behavior is more effectively taught when we search for ways to solve the problem within the situation in which it occurs:

When brother has kicked sister under the table, change seating arrangements. Tell him firmly, "If you don't like what sister is doing, tell her so, but no kicking." Since we cannot do anything about his first kick, ignore it. Try to prevent further attack. A child's unexpected angry impulses are not crimes. He does not need to suffer equal punishment.

When younger brother is leading up to a fight with big brother, say, "You seem angry with Robert. Tell him what the trouble is now. Your behavior is making us all uncomfortable."

Sister hits brother in a disagreement over the TV. Instead of banishment, let her find something else to do while brother gets the privilege of selecting the program.

Threats of Abandonment

THREATS OF ABANDONMENT ARE SEVERELY DISRUPTING TO
EMOTIONAL SECURITY

The very foundation of a child's well-being is the love and trust he has in his parents. Whether in jest or in anger, threats of abandonment are poor disciplinary techniques. Early in life children fear desertion, loss of love and approval, even when these things are not threatened. Brought up in the fear of being cast away, they are sometimes severely hurt emotionally. Many adult fears of rejection arise out of frequent childhood threats of abandonment, designed by parents to gain cooperation. Learning to feel loved, safe, and secure has its roots in early childhood.

It's terrifying to feel abandoned. Notice the alarm on the face of the infant who suddenly cannot find the mother who has momentarily stepped out of the room. Mothers sometimes make use of this fear. Impatient to get home from shopping, they may say, "If you don't come, I'll leave you here by yourself." Seeking peace in the midst of a family dispute, they may say, "If you don't behave, I'll give you away" or "If you can't settle down, I'm going to pack up and leave." Can you visualize the impact of such statements upon a small child? How much better simply to tuck a rebelling child under your arm and depart, or take time out to give the needed attention.

Parents sometimes confront an older child whom they cannot physically handle with comments such as:

You don't belong to me.
You can either behave or pack up and get out.
We'll get the juvenile authorities after you.
If you don't start behaving, we'll send you off to the
    detention home.

Imagine how such a child must feel. No matter how unkind his parents, no matter how poor or deprived the home environment, seldom does one find a child who wants to leave his home, even for a better one.

Withdrawal of Love

IT'S NOT REAL LOVE

Real love is neither given nor taken away on the spur of the moment. It is not conditional; it is not effective only when a child is being "good." Threats of love withdrawal tend to be made by rejecting parents who may not realize the full impact of their comments. They may:

Tell a child that he cannot have any more of something he is especially fond of.

Refuse to speak to or ignore the child until he does what they want.

Tell him that he's no good for anything or that they wish he hadn't been born.

Threaten to go away or to send him away.

Shame him for being ungrateful or unappreciative.

Tell him he isn't as nice as he used to be.

Tell him they don't love him because of some misbehavior.

Fail to make up following a disagreement.

A THREAT OF LOVE WITHDRAWAL IS UNFAIR AND UNREASONABLE

It may be even more emotionally devastating than a spanking, which at least is over and done with quickly. Have you noticed that a child able to endure considerable parental physical abuse will react with obvious distress and clinging when he's told, "You aren't my little boy anymore"?

Identification with parental values and the development of a healthy conscience depend upon a child's perception of parents as trustworthy sources of love and security. He needs to know that his parents are on his side. When we take steps to prolong anger, we cannot be perceived as persons who trust and believe in him.

Withdrawal of Privileges

As with the disciplines just described, when a privilege is withheld, a child may feel that a part of his parent's love is withheld. He cannot easily separate what we do for him from how we love him. It is especially difficult when the privilege withheld is unrelated to the specific rule broken.

PROLONGS UNPLEASANTNESS

As discussed previously, it's far more sensible to settle problems immediately than to teach a child that he must suffer for an extended period. Problems settled as they occur deny a child time to plan revenge, to feel sorry for himself, to feel unloved.

LACKS IMMEDIACY TO THE PRESENT

Moreover, the privilege being withheld may have little relationship to the offense committed.

Go to your room for the rest of the day.
We'll have to take Teddy away for a while.
No more TV for this week.
You must stay home from the camp-out this weekend.
No dessert tonight.
You cannot have any friends over for the rest of the week.

What does the child feel while others are enjoying privileges he is being denied? How certain of your love does he feel when you take from him a pleasurable activity or a prized possession?

WHAT IS MORE DESIRABLE?

In situations of neglect of responsibility or mistreatment of others, a chance to make up for behavior is more desirable. It lessens guilt and helps restore the rapport that may have been lost between the child and the persons offended. When hostilities have resulted in the destruction of another's property, restoration of that property should be made insofar as possible.

IS WITHDRAWAL EVER PRACTICAL?

The withholding of a privilege is desirable only in situations where the privilege itself is being seriously abused, where possessions continue to be mistreated, where health and safety are neglected. When requests for reasonable performance have failed, withholding something desired may encourage cooperation.

> You may play as soon as you pick up your toys.
>
> As soon as you pass a safe-driving test, you may ride your bicycle.
>
> When the dishes are put away, we'll be ready to go.
>
> The clothes you throw on the floor won't be washed unless you put them in the hamper.
>
> You can't go out until your boots are on.
>
> I'm putting this toy away until you feel that you can use it more carefully.
>
> No more soft drinks until empty bottles and glasses are cleaned up after you use them.

FIVE

Problem Prevention

DEALING WITH PROBLEMS
BEFOREHAND

Redl (1966) points out that misbehavior can sometimes be avoided by planning a program, a routine, a change in family policy, or an excursion in such a way that problems that might otherwise have been expected do not arise.

Help Him Accept His Physical Limits

It's frustrating when little fingers can't accomplish what the mind has set out to do. A small child's limited strength, speed, and dexterity often interfere with his goals. Typically, problems arise when:

Left-handed or ambidextrous children try too soon to use a hammer, cut with scissors, work with bolt-and-screw set. The latter offers particular difficulty. They forget that they must reverse the twisting movement when changing hands. Considerable tension accumulates for the child refusing to give up. When it's evident that hand preferences are frustrating, postpone those particular activities until he's older.

An activity is physically too advanced for him. Knowing how to make a clay cow doesn't necessarily enable him to make it.

Big brother's block houses look better than his own. He can't quite make his the same no matter how hard he tries.

241

WITHOUT YOUR ASSISTANCE

Problems become exaggerated when eager-to-be-helpful parents give too much assistance. Of course, it's difficult to resist a child's pleas for help, but it is a far greater kindness if you do. When we do not give him adult examples to follow, he can enjoy creating at his level. Keeping up with an older brother's talent is frustration enough.

After the occasion on which you consent to build that first elaborate castle with your child's building blocks, you'll find yourself repeatedly badgered for assistance. With more perfect examples available, your youngster's own work seems insignificant to him. He has seen your model car, your drawing of a house, your clay bird. Now he tries to do the same, "just like daddy's," and he can't achieve it. Not understanding his limitations, he feels angry with himself and is likely to give up. Resist his appeals for help. Give him your support instead:

That's the idea. You're getting it fine.
See—you put it together all by yourself.
Let me see what you can do with these.
You are learning very well. That's great.
Make it the way you think it ought to look.
If you want to change it, just draw right over it.
Just make one piece of the wagon if you want. That's good.
How many wheels does it have?
Where does the handle go?
That's a fine wagon.
How pretty. I like your flower.
That's a very nice design.
May I put this on the table for decoration?
Just let me sit here and watch.
I want to see your house, not mine.
That's a hard puzzle, but you can do it.
Where do you think this piece goes?

Put that piece aside. Maybe you'll discover a place for it
  later.

When you observe tension building over work obviously too
advanced, provide substitutes at his level of ability.

DON'T EVALUATE

When a child brings things to you for evaluation, don't point
out his mistakes. It isn't important if he leaves the arms off his
people or the windows out of his houses. He doesn't need to
imitate reality. Let him tackle his problems with only the most
limited assistance.

GIVE FREQUENT PRAISE

"The more a child expects approval for reaching a goal
unaided, the less will he tend to seek help" (Heathers, 1955, p.
286). Children whose parents provide encouragement while
refraining from giving impressive examples enjoy their own
work. They frequently strive for hours at all manner of artistic
endeavor.

Make New Learning Experiences Easier with "Closure"

Closure denotes the reduction of uncertainty about an unfamiliar experience by acquiring information about it. Lack of closure is responsible for much of a small child's resistance to new
learning. He resists because he is unable to visualize the beginning, the ending, or significant parts of an experience in which
he is to participate. He often prefers to do the same thing in the
same way he's been accustomed to doing it rather than face the
unexpected. New tasks, changed routine, strange people, new
cultural activities, travel, or nursery school may be resisted if
unfamiliar or insufficiently stimulating or if mother is not with
him. His concerns may be more realistic than we know. Lack of

closure even in everyday play can cause fears that may last a long time.

Three-year-old Betsy accompanied mother to serve refreshments at a Cub Scout meeting. According to the boys (playing a game of make-believe) an old shed on the premises is "haunted." The boys shriek, scream, and run, as they half-believe their own imaginations. Betsy becomes hysterical. Calming her takes over an hour. It is years before she will enter another home, basement, or strange building without mother. Playmates come to play, but not until first grade is she occasionally willing to visit at friends' homes.

To some degree, everyone needs to be able to predict how an experience is going to feel, look, or affect himself. Adults can predict fairly accurately. Children are not yet so equipped. They need the very experience they lack in order to gain "closure." Note some of the signals children give when closure is lacking:

The child afraid to walk to school needs a pleasurable exploration of the route in the company of a parent before he is willing to try it alone.

The child who refuses to ride in the nursery-school car pool needs to be driven by mother until he becomes better acquainted.

The child who wants to know who the baby-sitter is, what she looks like, whether she will make him eat all his dinner, what time she will make him go to bed, needs a brief visit with the sitter before his parents depart.

The infant with his first potty chair needs time to gradually become acquainted with its feel and appearance before he is ready to try it.

The kindergartner or first-grader who may spend considerable summer hours worrying about his new teacher needs a visit with her *before* summer vacation begins.

The first-grader afraid to buy his first school lunch may be reassured if older brothers or sisters act out lunch-buying at home: walking through the lunch line, ordering the food, handling the tray and the money, getting ready for what happens when the bell rings. A six-year-old is often afraid that he may drop or spill the heavy tray. Let him get the feel of an equipped tray at home. Preplanning helps prevent mistakes that could persuade him to withdraw from future participation.

- The child going on his first class outing needs to know who will take care of him, where he will eat his lunch, what he should do if he needs to go to the bathroom.
- The first-grader who doesn't want to ride to the zoo in a strange school bus needs to explore the bus first.
- The child afraid of the barber should accompany father on one or two of his routine visits. When his turn comes for a hair cut, let him sit on dad's lap and inspect the equipment.
- The child worried about attending the strange new school in the new community needs to visit the school. The sidewalks around the school, convenient for riding bikes, help him become acquainted with the new surroundings. Summer recreation programs held at the school are also a help.
- The child fearful of meeting a new and strange adult may be helped by knowing something about that person, what he looks like, what he does, how many children he has, what his hobbies are.

WHY ENCOURAGE NEW LEARNING?

Regularly allowing a child to stay home may deprive him of opportunities for physical, intellectual, and personality development. Children need opportunities for self-fulfillment in early childhood, while personalities are being shaped. They gain in self-confidence from being able to do and enjoy a variety of things, even though a state of expertness is not achieved. New skills offer new challenges for improvement and a sense of reward for accomplishment. As his horizons broaden, so must his self-image, as he comes to view himself differently, with new competencies for his age: as a good ball player, a fine musician, an excellent swimmer, a recognized member of the school honor roll, or an artist. "An individual grows whenever he moves out of the restrictions of his current life experiences into places, activities, and events in which he previously had no part, either because they lack appeal for himself or because they are frightening; he comes further into being a person" (Black, 1968, p. 178).

Your persistence in the face of his reluctance may someday be appreciated. In a recent interview study, young adults indicated that they were glad their parents had not given in to their pleas to give up musical activities. Some even regretted not having been exposed to a wider variety of experiences (Maynard, 1969).

HOW TO ENCOURAGE NEW LEARNING

Waiting until your child is older does not insure that new experiences necessarily will be approached with less resistance. When rebellion permits him to withdraw from such situations, it may appear with regularity.

Make some plans without his approval. "No, I don't want to go" should receive respect, acknowledgment, and sympathy, but not necessarily ultimate acceptance. Don't let concern for his immediate happiness dissuade you if you feel that he can benefit. The possibilities are greater than might be expected that once a child has begun to practice a new skill, the development of real interest will follow. Behavior that can be changed through some form of conditioning, even without early acceptance, is often followed by a positive change in attitude about the very concern supporting his reluctance to participate.

Provide security. First of all, don't expect him to undertake new experiences without mother's support. Make the transition an easy one. As Bowlby advises, no harm comes from a child's receiving as much of mother's presence and attention as he wants. "In regard to mothering—as to food—a child seems to be so made, if from the first permitted to decide, he can satisfactorily regulate his own 'intake'" (1969, p. 357). If mother cannot participate, perhaps a teen-age friend can provide the security necessary to help him take the first step. Unhampered by anxiety, he is more free to assert himself and enjoy the new experience. As it becomes less strange and unfamiliar, his need for support decreases.

Use a familiarization plan. Getting the rebelling child acquainted with a new experience, such as a summer recreation program, might go as follows:

Announce your plans shortly before departure. Pay no heed to his sulking, anger, tears, or rebellion. Reflect his feelings. Be reassuring:

> You are concerned about what is going to happen to you at play school. I will explain it to you.
> You are afraid that you might not like it. We are only visiting today to find out if we like it or not.

Let him know that he won't be forced to continue. If, after a few days' trial, he doesn't like it, he can stay home or try something else. Knowing of a way out, he doesn't feel so trapped and is more willing to give it a try. After all, we adults would also be unhappy if we could not escape from an uncomfortable situation.

Reassure him that you will be there as long as he needs you.

Provide "closure." Describe the events that will take place:

> After breakfast we will drive by and pick up Mary. She is going with us. Play school is being held in the school auditorium. Lots of children will be there. You will know some of them. Mrs. Adams is a very nice teacher. She will teach you tumbling and dancing. There will also be singing and

some arts and crafts. I will sit by the side and watch. When it's time for lunch, we will go home.

If necessary, combine the new experience with something he enjoys, such as a trip to the ice cream store or a picnic in the park.

If he refuses to participate, let him observe. Forcing will not increase his interest. If he doesn't take part within a few visits, you may need to search for another activity having more appeal to him.

When he has been participating and it is obvious that he is enjoying himself, you are usually free to leave. If he continues to be reluctant, try the gradual separation procedures described in the section on nursery schools.

Plan for In-Between Times

"In-between time," a particularly useful phrase contributed by Bettelheim (1955), refers to the interval between ordinary daily activities and also to the interval between the point at which the child first learns a particular event is to happen and the point at which it occurs. Some such "times" can be anxiety-building, as in the case of time spent waiting:

In physicians' and dentists' offices.

For parents to return home from a vacation.

Between knowing of a tonsillectomy and its actual occurrence.

In anticipation of moving from one community and getting settled in another.

The first few weeks before school begins in the autumn.

Just before a train, plane, or car trip gets underway.

For many children, such "in-between times" necessitate thoughtful preparation of interesting things to do while waiting. These times can be interesting while at the same time reducing tension and limiting the buildup of anxiety.

WHEN MEDICAL OR DENTAL ATTENTION IS NEEDED

Considerable time is spent waiting in doctors' and dentists' reception rooms. Upon admittance to examination rooms, more waiting often occurs. Your child, fearful and anxious upon arrival, may be ready to crawl out the window by the time the doctor arrives. If waiting times for you have proven to be lengthy, call in advance to make sure your appointment has not been moved back on a busy schedule. Stay with your child if he wants that during examination and treatment. Medical doctors are usually agreeable to this arrangement. For some reason dentists are less so. Nevertheless, it is not wise to separate a child from his source of security when he needs it most. Basic trust in mother is affected when she denies this need and submits to the decision of a professional "authority." The security of mother's presence reduces the child's anxiety while waiting. She can read and talk to him. Her presence gives him the courage to face the strange experience.

WHEN RIDING IN THE CAR OR SHOPPING

These "in-between times" are useful opportunities for learning. Many parents take them for granted, overlooking that they can be occasions for discovering that learning is fun. A child may spend many minutes a day in the car with mother. These are opportunities for teaching him to read street signs and traffic signals, the numbers and words on store signs and billboards. He enjoys jokes, riddles, and singing nursery rhymes. You can talk about the weather, how the wind blows the leaves from the trees and moves the clouds in the sky. The fog, rain, snow, or sunshine all make interesting conversation to a preschooler. How do you know when it is spring or fall? What happens to the water that disappears from the street?

Contrast this approach to what one ordinarily observes. In any place of business, note the various ways parents interact with the youngsters who accompany them.

There is the mother waiting in line at the bank with her three-year-old. The child is exploring the interesting movement of the red velvet rope controlling the lines of customers. He is obviously delighted by the way in which the rope swings. The mother, presumably striving to be a good parent, sternly informs her child that he is "bad, bad, bad, very bad."

There is the mother in the dress shop who points to a little boy sitting quietly in a chair and says to her son, "Why can't you be nice like he is?" You wonder what her boy is feeling as he stands in front of the seated child to stare at him.

How much more usefully could parents deal with youngsters if, instead of disciplining them to sit or stand quietly, they would use such occasions as opportunities for stimulating curiosity in the fascinating world of things around them. Let the small child be your companion—talk with him instead of down to him. He not only learns to think reflectively, but he feels more like a human being than a fixture that mother must cart along because she has no alternative.

WHEN AT HOME

In-between times at home are also opportunities for learning. Do you talk to your child as he toddles after you and as you care for his needs? He can learn a great deal before he can even speak. Let him hear you use the names of the objects he comes into contact with daily:

Here is your shirt. Let's hang the towel here. Open the door. See the soap floating on the water. Oops, the spoon fell on the floor. The milk is spilled. Oh, you lost a button.

Various concepts about movement, position, temperature, and texture can be incorporated into your conversation—what things are fast or slow, hot or cold, soft or hard, wet or dry, right or left, big or little, over or under.

Delayed Notification

FOR MEDICAL ATTENTION

The child who builds up anxiety over anticipated visits to a physician should not be told of them earlier than necessary. Going to the doctor can be casually accomplished in conjunction with a trip to the grocery, variety store, or ice cream parlor. Worry for weeks over a booster shot, a visit to the dentist, or a tonsillectomy, especially during formative years when attitudes are being shaped, is not really wise.

FOR PLEASURABLE EVENTS

Delayed notification can be helpful even for pleasurable events: a birthday party, a vacation trip, an excursion to the zoo. It saves the family much in the way of anticipation anxiety and hurt feelings should plans be canceled. Children not uncommonly become anxious even over the approach of Christmas.

Where family outings are concerned, delayed notification can be combined with advance planning to help reduce tension. Perhaps you've noticed the increased irritability, crying, quarreling, or thumb-sucking shortly before an excursion gets underway. Getting last-minute preparations completed early gets the family off while the children and parents are still in good spirits.

Plan Ahead

FOR AWAY-FROM-HOME BEHAVIOR

Knowing in advance what kind of behavior parents expect is helpful for the child in a variety of situations. Even if the message must be repeated later, it then gets across more effectively.

Let's have a practice session on table manners before we leave for Aunt Mary's.

Let me give you a few words of advice before we go to grandmother's. There will be no running in the house. Try not to interrupt when adults are talking. No loud talking. Take a toy that you enjoy playing with to entertain yourself in case you need it.

Decide now about the movie. If you want to go with the group, you'll be expected to sit through to the end. The theater is too far away for dad to bring you home if you get tired halfway through.

We are having company for dinner tonight, so be ready to leave Susie's house by five o'clock.

FOR AWAY-FROM-HOME SPENDING

Knowing in advance what his allowance will be helps the child act in accordance with decisions made. Too often parents find themselves saying no as their first reaction to a child's request for candy or an attractive object. Upon reflection and with the influence of a few tears, they decide that his request really isn't so unreasonable. As a usual procedure, this may prove even more frustrating for parents than children. The prepared parent can be more definite.

Before we go to the movie, let's decide now if we want to buy refreshments at intermission or save that money for a stop at the ice cream store on the way home. We can't have both.

We have just enough money for the dinner check. No candy or extras tonight.

Before we go to the grocery, remember that what you put in the coin machine comes out of your allowance for this week.

FOR AWAY-FROM-HOME HEALTH NEEDS

As mothers well know, preschoolers often need to visit every available bathroom as soon as they leave home.

A small potty that packs away in the back of the car can be both cleaner and more convenient than public bathrooms on a long trip.

A foldaway, under-the-dashboard tissue holder is a helpful convenience.

Premoistened towelettes or wet washcloths in a plastic bag are especially useful for sticky fingers.

Give Advance Notice to Stop

It is difficult to put one's interests aside immediately. You may observe that you yourself frequently say "Just a minute" before stopping whatever you are actively engaged in to answer a child's request for assistance. So, remember, a creative activity in which the child is absorbed may be more important than our instruction that he finish immediately. Advance notice makes termination easier.

You have five minutes to wash and be ready for dinner.

Your friends will be here shortly. You have ten minutes to get your room in order.

You have ten minutes to finish up before we go to your piano lesson.

Advance notice eases transition from active to quiet behavior. The child whose excitement over recent outdoor play has not subsided may have difficulty sitting quietly at dinner.

Know When to Go Home

When children are promised a day at the park, a picnic, or other outing away from home, the day should remain theirs, without the addition of a side trip to Aunt Martha's, to the nursery to pick up plants, or to the grocery. Returning home should be accomplished before everyone is tired and irritable and while the day's activities are still viewed as pleasant memories. Parents frequently get carried away with all they want to see and do. What started out to be a day for the children sometimes ends up being a day for the parents.

Reduce Hunger

Try food when children are becoming irritable. A small glass of juice or a cup of soup can forestall a multitude of problems and doesn't really interfere with mealtime. Mothers may have noticed that temper tantrums occur most frequently before dinner. Hunger and fatigue serve to sharpen other conflicts and frustrations.

Help Him Make Up His Mind

Vacillation may go on for days when a child is undecided about an event or an object. Considerable anxiety often builds up over his inability to make a choice among a number of alternatives. Tension may remain unrelieved until a decision is made. There are only a limited number of ways in which parents can be helpful. You may say which alternative you think would suit your child best. Occasionally, a listing of his alternatives may make one seem more attractive than any other. Sometimes the conflict may be resolved by setting a limit. A simple psychological explanation of the problem can be both interesting and tension-reducing. An older child benefits from being able to see how indecision may affect his tension level. Being less complicated than adults, his conflicts are often more obvious.

APPROACH-APPROACH CONFLICTS

Two goals are equally attractive. The child is pulled toward both simultaneously. Occasionally, more than two goals are involved. The difficulty arises in not being able to make a choice, as gratification of one goal means that the others must be abandoned. Tension is reduced when one alternative is sacrificed. For example, he must decide whether to:

Go to the movie or attend the track meet.
Enroll in German or French in high school.
Share his tent at the camp-out with John or Bill.
Buy one bicycle or another of equal value and appeal.
Put his nickel in the gum, the candy, or the toy machine.
Walk to school with Doris or with Hilda.

APPROACH-AVOIDANCE CONFLICTS

A single goal exhibits both attractive and unattractive features, or a number of goals may at the same time be desirable and undesirable. The child may:

Like desserts but be afraid of getting fat.
Love his parents and hate them, too.
Wish to make a date with a friend but be afraid the friend
    will refuse his invitation.
Wish to win the game but hesitate to have his friend and
    competitor feel sad from defeat.
Wish to masturbate but fear being immoral.
Wish to attend class but be afraid of the bully behind him.
Have difficulty choosing between two friends, both of whom
    have negative and positive values.

AVOIDANCE-AVOIDANCE CONFLICTS

Here the child finds himself forced to choose between two equally undesirable goals. As the saying goes, he is "caught between the devil and the deep blue sea." The situation is so structured that he cannot avoid both of them. He:

Doesn't wish to endure a toothache but is afraid of the dentist.
Doesn't wish to attend either summer camp or school, but his
    parents say he must make a choice.

Doesn't wish to study or fail.

Is afraid of the tough boy next door and afraid to say so for fear of ridicule.

Wants to quit music lessons but is afraid of the wrath of his parents.

Doesn't want to take either boxing or judo lessons, but his parents say he must make a choice.

Is afraid of the dark and afraid to admit it.

Know When to Stop

Each child differs in the amount of stress he can tolerate. What may be upsetting for one may not even trouble another. In any case, parental intervention is helpful when a child is continuing an activity to the limit of his endurance. Small children frequently continue play activities beyond the point of pleasure. The combined state of excitement and fatigue disrupts mealtime, sleep, and the family. Stopping an activity that has gone beyond its maximum usefulness keeps family harmony and later helps the child to learn to define and recognize his own limits. We can say:

Stop now. You are getting tired. Tomorrow is another day.

You have ten minutes to finish what you are doing.

I need some assistance in the kitchen.

Stop now and have a snack. I'll read to you while you eat and relax.

Reduce Home Responsibilities

When negativism and distress become uncomfortable and consistently evident, parents need to reduce the number of their demands. Children feel overwhelmed at times by the expectations of parents who have set goals based upon their own interests and capabilities. Activities should be planned so that children have periodic vacations from routine and some say about when it is needed. Schedules for piano lessons, household duties, or school homework that are seldom interrupted are discouraging.

Plan Reasonable Limits

Adults would expect the responsibilities of a new job to be outlined for them. So, too, do developing children feel more secure when they know what is expected. Reasonable and justifiable limits on their activities give children a sense of security, respect for the rights and opinions of others, and standards for judging their own performance.

LIMITS SHOULD BE FLEXIBLE

They should be used as guides for behavior rather than lines beyond which one dare not trespass. The result of careful planning rather than merely a series of spur-of-the-moment decisions, they contribute to making home a more comfortable place to be. Activities move more smoothly when there are a few basic rules for the daily routine and difficulties are not left to be solved as they arise.

A usual time for breakfast, lunch, and dinner.
A reasonable time for arriving home.
A sensible bedtime hour.
Selected TV programs.
Concern for property rights:
  Respect for home furnishings.
  Off limits for certain parents' possessions.
  Off limits for certain children's possessions.
Adequate effort applied toward schoolwork.
Responsibility for the development of certain cultural skills.
Respect for the needs, rights, and opinions of others.
Restraint from belittlement and physical abuse.
The right time and place for high-activity play.
Allowances spent with consideration.

Sharing of home responsibilities.

The observation of practical safety rules at home, on the street, at the beach, when riding bicycles, and riding in cars.

Limits set as a result of disapproval, without previous warning, are rightfully resented by children. An example is a parent's refusal to allow a child to return to the table for dessert when he left without previous knowledge that such a limit was in effect. To be fair, limits should not infringe upon the child's freedom to change his mind or to have some choice in matters touching his own welfare. Recognizing his rights and opinions when making decisions that concern him encourages his cooperation.

LIMITS GIVE SUPPORT

Have you noticed the relief of a small child when a friendly parent helps him discontinue an activity in which he has previously disregarded requests to stop? Limits are more believable when a parent is willing to interrupt his own activity, go see what the problem is, and help him end it. Directions called out from your seat at the kitchen table seldom accomplish the desired results.

LIMITS PROTECT

Limits protect the health, safety, and welfare of children. Tommy cannot go out to play with a fever of 101. Sally cannot ride her tricycle in the street.

Limits protect the self-images of younger family members from damage by older brothers and sisters. They do not have the right to belittle the needs of younger family members. Respect for the strengths and weaknesses of others starts at home. Carl should learn that he cannot frequently tell little sister that she is "too fat," "dumb," or a "crybaby."

Limits protect parents' own inner comfort when we become aware that we are resenting or avoiding a child rather than doing something about his disruptive behavior. The child learns that there are others outside of himself whose feelings and rights he must consider. Timmy must not habitually yell at his parents, complain about what they do for him, or disrupt their activities if he wants them to cooperate with him.

Limits protect property. But, as Holt suggests, "respect for property does not mean never touching what is not yours, but means treating objects carefully, using them as they were meant to be used, and putting them back where they belong. . . . It is only by handling and using objects that children learn the right way to handle them. Never being permitted to use or inspect the property of another may make a child too fiercely possessive of what is his own" (1968, p. 9).

Remove Temptation

CHILDHOOD IS A TIME FOR EXPLORING

What happens to a child's natural curiosity when he encounters too many don'ts, when adults act as though he may destroy everything he touches? How does he feel when adults at home and in the community are allowed to explore and inspect but he is not? "It doesn't make much sense, in a family that will later spend tens of thousands of dollars on a child's education, to get upset and to upset him because he may ruin objects worth twenty-five cents" (Holt, 1968, p. 9).

Why not keep highly prized, valuable, or breakable objects where he cannot be tempted by them? Children will in time learn to leave the possessions of others alone.

Don't Separate Mother and Infant

TRUST MAY BE IMPAIRED

Beginning around the age of six months, an infant's separation from mother of more than a few days is a very serious matter. A child's sense of trust depends upon his ability to locate mother when she is needed. It may be seriously impaired at a time when he is emotionally more vulnerable than at any other time in life. Mother is not only his source of love, protection, and security, she is an extension of himself. Through her he is able to communicate with the world. He feels helpless, abandoned, and incomplete without her.

Heinicke and Westheimer describe the behavior of a group of two- and three-year-old children separated from their parents for the first time in a community nursery. The children were away from their parents for periods varying from two to twenty weeks:

Crying dominated much of their behavior for the first three days. Most behavior was oriented toward desperately attempting to recapture the absent parent. Throughout the separation, behavior problems such as hostility, distress, self-injury, possessiveness, apathy, as well as biological disturbances in sleep, eating, and bowel control occurred.

The depth of hurt and despair experienced was expressed in varied ways upon first reunion with the parents. The children were described as turning away from the mother, refusing to recognize her, followed by desperate clinging, alternated with hostility. Upon returning home from the nursery, the children were at first unresponsive. Intense hostile feelings, temper tantrums, and negativism emerged at about the same time that the children began to again approach the mother for affection. Strong mixed love and hate behavior extended from zero to seventeen weeks, with the median at nine weeks, a considerable time for a child to be under stress when ordinarily he is busy formulating persistent attitudes toward life. Impairment of trust showed up in the desperate clinging and the intensity of the ambivalence toward the mother. Recovery varied with the severity of the child's anxiety and the length of separation. Extended separation was likely to be the most traumatic and disorganizing. (Summarized from 1965, pp. 162–179, 230–248.)

When trust in mother as a source of love and protection is impaired, dependency increases. The child dares not separate himself from mother for fear that she may disappear again.

With so much time thus devoted to protecting his source of love and security, psychological development is impaired. Interest in his surroundings is reduced and new learning is resisted. We cannot seem to undo easily disillusionment that has been done in the early years. "In the first three or four years of life, certain impressions become fixed and ways of reacting to the outside world are established which can never be robbed of their importance by later experiences" (Freud, 1964, pp. 41–42).

Bowlby (1961) points out that even species of birds and mammals show signs of anxiety when removed from their parents. Their survival in the wilderness depends upon mother's protection. The lower primate tries to prevent mother's absence in the same manner as the human infant. Upon separation he makes the same desperate attempts to find the lost parent, followed by mourning, despair, and detachment. Upon the return of the mother, self-protecting rage and anger are expressed, possibly to discourage future abandonment.

Hinde and Spencer-Booth studied the long-term effects of separation in naturally mothered monkey infants separated from their mothers when between twenty-one and thirty-two weeks of age:

The various brief separation experiences were concerned with the removal of the mother, with infants remaining in a familiar environment. The effects of the separations were similar to those of human infants. The infant monkeys who experienced shortest separations suffered the least depression of activity and recovered more quickly, were more active when active, and gave fewer distress calls than did the infants with the longer separations. As long as two years later, the separated infants continued to be less active and differ from the controls in various ways. (Summarized from 1971, pp. 111–118.)

Suomi, Harlow, and Domek studied the effects of separation anxiety on infants reared with each other rather than with the mother. The young monkeys were separated not once but many times—four days for each of twenty experimental weeks spread over a six-month period.

During each separation period, the infants exhibited severe protest-despair. Each time they were reunited, mutual clinging was their primary activity. Their behaviors following the separations were as infantile at age nine months as they were prior to the first separation. Severe maturational arrest occurred. Complex infant play activities which normally mature from ninety to 180 days had not appeared at nine months. The experiments appeared to have stopped the monkeys' biological calendars. (Summarized from 1970, pp. 161–172.)

Other forms of separation may also damage a child's sense of trust. The sudden loss of an accustomed symbol of mother love, such as the bottle, may lead to infantile depression (Erikson, 1963). "We may fly too swiftly through the process of mourning over the little separations that occur in childhood—the unexplained absences of mother, every crisis that feels like a desertion, such as weaning, toilet training, and the birth of a brother or sister" (Freeman, 1969, p. 106). Unable to express the emotions that accompany such separations, a person may mourn for a lifetime without knowing why.

WHAT TO DO

With the exception of possibly the first six months of life, it may be wise for parents of preschool youngsters to postpone separations of more than a few days. Even then, mother should not just disappear. A child's faith in her concern for him requires that he be informed. Mother's care, like her promises, should be reliable. Separation should not be abrupt. He needs to become accustomed gradually to mother's absence. He can better tolerate absences of increasing length. With time and experience, "he gradually becomes able to interpret her absence and reassure himself of her return" (Kagan, 1971, p. 10). For children who have been infrequently cared for by others, nursery school offers the best opportunity for gradual separation to take place.

Attachments developed for persons other than mother who

may have played and communicated with him since early infancy will reduce anxiety in some children, but should not be counted on in the case of extended separation.

Protect your child's faith and trust. Consider all of his feelings as important. Our inability to distinguish serious anxieties from his everyday problems will not then be significant.

Increase Contact-Comfort

Adults and children alike are warmed by the comfort of being close to someone they genuinely care about. It may be as important a need as nourishment. Harlow's (1958) landmark research with monkeys raised in cages with dummy mothers, some constructed of wire and some of cloth, demonstrates that, when frightened or in need of nearness-comfort, young monkeys will cling to the cloth-covered mother even though only the wire mother, containing a nursing bottle, provides any real nourishment.

Although most important during infancy, comfort derived from nearness to another significant person is calming and tension-reducing at any age. Embarrassment about closeness is learned. Even the adolescent feels contact-comfort need. An occasional hug, an arm around his shoulder, an arm linked in his—these help to let him know that he's valued. The nine- or ten-year-old is not too mature to occasionally enjoy being held close and comforted. The young child thrives on physical comfort and tenderness and will seek it through most of childhood.

The small child seeks substitutes when the real thing is not available. Increased demands for his bottle, his blanket, his food, frequently arise from his need for contact-comfort that mother is too busy to supply. At other times, as he watches TV, plays with his blocks, goes to bed, he may prefer his blanket or his thumb because it is more convenient and maneuverable than mother.

When his need is strong, an increase in aggressive behavior may be his way of saying that he would rather have your angry attention than none at all. A little extra cuddling each day makes a big difference in the most persistent of negative moods. Look for his positive moments. Be careful that affection does not immediately follow uncooperative behavior, thus reinforcing it.

Sympathize with Failure

Although our bodies generally grow to physical maturity with relative ease, emotional maturity is more difficult to achieve. Parental insight and understanding are continuously needed to keep a child's emotional health developing smoothly. When conditions outside the home threaten to undermine self-confidence, we can suggest ideas to older children that help them look beyond themselves and view the situation more objectively:

Sometimes we think about the whole job at once, and it makes us tired before we even start.

Sometimes we may not receive what is rightfully ours; at other times we get more than we deserve. Things usually balance out in the long run.

Not succeeding this time does not mean that you're not good enough. It may be that you are just not good enough *yet*. Each new day gives us another chance.

Much of our distress is caused by the view we take of things rather than by the things themselves. Few objects or events may be as important as we might imagine them to be.

Talent helps, but it's not the only prerequisite. Sometimes there are unknown circumstances over which we have no control.

Because we must go to school, eat, sleep, and care for our
personal needs, there isn't time for all we might like to do.

Doing a job as well as we can is a good way to find satisfaction in life.

The world doesn't guarantee us anything, not even life itself.

Whether we win or not—a game is fun, an exam is a challenge, a good chess partner makes for a good game, a good athlete improves physical condition.

SIX

Social Concerns

THE IMPORTANCE OF FRIENDS

Preschool Friends

Two-year-old Sally has no friends in her neighborhood. At three she attends nursery school but stands and observes most of the time. The teacher reassures mother that she will join when she is ready, but Sally remains distant. With younger children at home, mother makes no effort to find outside friends. Sally follows a more or less distant pattern throughout childhood.

Even before the age of two, children begin to want friends. They don't play much with them at this age, but they enjoy watching and playing alongside them. This is the time to begin encouraging sociability. Children entering kindergarten without such experience adjust poorly, and may remain socially distant. Perceptions of one's self as popular or unpopular already may be firmly fixed.

Becoming acquainted with other children is important. A child's social self-image is shaped early. Parental companionship and siblings may ease the problem, but it cannot be counted upon totally to prevent social retardation if play with other children comes too late.

Research supports this theory. Even monkeys need playmates early. Deprived of experience with other monkeys in early life, they have difficulty in mating and make poor mothers. Those raised by mothers but denied playmates adjust in differing ways—some make essentially normal adjustments, others show extreme reactions in their relationships. For example, they may stay for long periods in corners by themselves and when they do contact other monkeys, fight excessively (Harlow and Harlow, 1969).

FIRST PLAYMATES

These are more or less chosen by mother. They usually come from the immediate neighborhood, but a youngster's closest friends, including school and kindergarten acquaintances, may live a considerable distance away. Mother becomes the chauffeur.

Insofar as possible, give children full opportunity to enjoy companions. Their formative years are spent with them. Avoid expressions such as "Mary acts like a spoiled brat," "Jane is a little know-it-all," "George is a crybaby." The preschooler guided by his own personal yardstick will most likely accept his friends as they are and reject others he cannot accept.

VARIETY IS IMPORTANT

In the same way that children learn from their parents, they learn from each other. Their differences are valuable. A variety of playmates with differing backgrounds, cultures, and personalities have much to offer one another. Baldwin describes a child's companions as the raw material from which he adds to the structure of his present personality. "Give the children room. They need all they can get and their personalities will grow to fill it. Give them plenty of companions. Fill their lives with variety—variety is the soul of originality and its only source of supply" (1968, p. 342).

Even at the age of three there is wide variation in playmate personality and capability. Associating almost exclusively with one child may leave some personality needs unfulfilled. Aggressive Bert may never give shy Ronald a chance to lead or make a decision. It may be impossible for dainty Sara to keep up with the athletic maneuvers of Janice. Friction increases when two children cannot share each other's strengths or cope with each other's weaknesses. Variety eases the stress of learning to deal with different personalities. Two children play more peacefully than three, but there is also less friction when children do not see too much of each other. Most mothers can locate a fair number of suitable playmates of their child's age in the average community. But to do this requires the interest and attention of mother. She must cultivate friendships with neighbors, often inviting children to play without any expectation of a return invitation.

Elementary School Friends

By the time a child begins elementary school, he will be making friends on his own. If he's had numerous playmates in the pre-school years, his need for mother's assistance will be lessened.

PLAYING TOO LONG

Children do not always sense when they are tired, a fact often overlooked by parents. They may play for hours, become irritable with each other and still be unwilling to part. It helps if mother has a reason: "It's bathtime," "We need to get our lessons done," or "Tomorrow is another day." Occasionally, a child may wish to be alone but doesn't know how to tell a friend that it is time to go home.

Also, too much play with friends interferes with creative and intellectual skills which can better be accomplished when one is alone.

ENCOURAGE VARIETY

A close relationship that exists for years may create problems of guilt and rejection when one of the children chooses to make new friends. You may have to help ten-year-old Jerry comprehend that he has not caused all of the unhappiness of the friend who frequently seeks him out to ask, "Why don't you play with me anymore?" or "Why don't you like me as well as Mike?" It may be difficult for Jerry to understand that he is not responsible for his friend's inability to reach out and enjoy others. A child not standing on the edge of self-doubt cannot be pushed over the edge by his friends, but Jerry probably does not know this. Jerry may need to be helped to devise ways to reassure his friend that he does like him still, although he is playing with other children, too.

SOCIAL NEGLECTS

Usually preschoolers are not concerned unduly about being overlooked socially. The party invitation not received, the friend who speaks unkindly, the invitation to play that is not returned—these often are accepted casually if parents show no special concern. Of course when a child is hurt, it is difficult for a parent not to identify with his hurt feelings. Nevertheless, depending upon the circumstances, mother may need to be reassuring or to imply that the incident is of only minor significance.

PARENTS' COMMENTS

Children sometimes are distressed when we speak disparagingly of a friend, relative, or acquaintance—probably more often than they let on and more than adults realize. A comment as uncomplicated as "Roger didn't use very good sense" or "Bill isn't very bright" may be met with considerable opposition. Lacking fully developed self-images, perhaps children fear that their traits are similar to those that parents criticize in others. They may wonder too when the parent is going to turn on him and say harsh things about him behind his back. If Uncle Roger (who is so wonderful) is being criticized harshly, who is safe?

Correspondingly, children may resent attempts to justify the character of persons they disparage. We may make them angry by saying, "George isn't so bad," "Andy has some good points, too," "Dick wasn't trying to make you angry," or "I don't believe he has a funny laugh." Our observations are sometimes difficult for them to comprehend. Possibly they feel we are doubting their ability to perceive accurately a situation. Perhaps they believe we are not fully on their side or doubt their truthfulness, or simply that we are entirely wrong. At first just listening and being sympathetic may be most helpful when a child is expressing displeasure with regard to a friend. We might say, "That's interesting," "I know how you must feel," or "Why do you think he does that?" After we have listened and made clear that we understand and know something went wrong, we can try to point out what else might be true, if we can be reassuring.

Some friends and classmates are indeed difficult to tolerate. Ronnie is nice one minute and unkind the next. George's bragging just seems too much at times. It seems impossible for Harold to play fairly. For your child to be able to talk about the problem may be all that is needed to help him tolerate the frustration. Occasionally, a few words of helpful advice are accepted. It is when we add too much to the situation that our child is likely to withdraw or rebel, or when we make judgments only, rather than offering suggestions, understanding, and comfort.

Loners

While popularity may add to a child's personal esteem, it does not determine his value as an individual. Without parental expressions of alarmed concern, being alone may well not bother him. Our regard for him should be independent of his status with others. Social ambition is usually ours and not the child's. Some children do not seek out close companions until the later years of high school, especially if they were not accustomed to numerous playmates during the infancy and preschool years.

BASIC PERSONALITY IS ESTABLISHED BY ELEMENTARY SCHOOL AGE

By then, lack of acceptance by age-mates or the child's acceptance of them probably will have become matters over which you have little control. Also, the supply of compatible friends may be limited in your particular environment. The children available simply may not share similar interests. Your child may be a perfectly well-adjusted youngster; but if others do not stimulate him, being alone may be his preference. His inner security may be such that he enjoys independence of action and thrives on it.

IT COSTS LESS PSYCHOLOGICALLY TO BE ALONE

He may find that he can pursue interests alone more efficiently than when he has to consider the wishes of a friend. Friends mean doing what they want to do occasionally, whether one wishes to or not; it means playing games of their first choice, letting them use one's bike part of the time, inviting them home and repaying social obligations when one would rather read a good book. Some children are sufficiently happy and interested in reading or other solitary hobbies that friends are secondary. This is fortunate for all of us, since much in the world worth doing must be done alone.

PARENTAL CONCERN MAY CREATE PROBLEMS

Parents may not recognize his wish to remain independent, a desire of which he himself is unaware. "Why don't you go out and make some friends?" they may frequently ask. If Albert is dispositionally a more solitary person or if he has tried without success, their repeated and worried concern may influence him to believe that he really is personally inadequate.

YOU ARE HIS FRIEND

Limited social communication with others does not seriously affect the child who grows up in a companionable family, where interests and activities are shared. He doesn't need outsiders too much. Ironically, not needing them so desperately, he is quite likely to acquire them. Having parents who afforded him ample opportunity to express himself at home, he will in time develop the social skills necessary for acceptance by others. Approving of himself, he will not need the constant approval of others as a substitute for self-respect and self-worth. A favorable self-image liberates him from an excessive need to meet the often conflicting expectancies of society. The ordinary contacts at school, in club work, and in recreational activities may satisfy his outside social needs.

WHAT YOU CAN DO

It takes only a little extra family effort to encourage most children to grow into interesting persons, socially competent in any group. This is an area where small investments pay large dividends.

Enjoy family conversation, storytelling, and occasional word games at the dinner table or on trips. This does much to promote reasoning, intellectual curiosity, and confident self-expression.

Give him a home environment where books are plentiful and are read, where he is free to follow creatively interests and hobbies. Support his interests. A creative child is self-actualizing and moving toward a healthy self-image.

Offer opportunities for responsibility inside and outside the home. Express your appreciation and praise work that he does well.

On occasion, participate in various sports and club activities with him. Successful performance enhances social status.

WHAT THE SCHOOL CAN DO

If opportunities within the home are inadequate, consult with school counselors and teachers.

He can be placed in classes with children whose interests and intellect are similar to his own.

Being assigned classroom responsibilities increases his opportunities for getting acquainted.

Teachers can identify children whose interests seem more similar to his own. They can be placed on special projects together.

Teachers can refuse to let him totally isolate himself. He can be placed in areas other than the last seat in the room, which he might seek out. He can be seated beside children who will respond to him.

He can be called on to recite whether he volunteers or not. Teachers can reinforce a shy student for class recitation. A smile, verbal approval, and increased attention usually have high reward value.

In research with children of nursery school age, Harris, Wolf, and Baer (1964) trained isolate children to become more social. This was achieved by rewarding movement toward social behavior and withholding adult attention from solitary play. Whenever the isolate child was approaching or had joined a group, the teacher rewarded him with interest and conversation, provided in such a way that attention was not drawn from the children to the teacher. The findings showed that isolate play declined markedly while social play increased two- and three-fold.

Neighborhood Ruffians

Ten-year-old Frank lives in a neighborhood surrounded by hostile children. He can't walk to the corner for the school bus without being insulted, shoved, or bullied.

SHOULD HE FIGHT?

While encouraging a child to "stand up for his rights" may help in some situations, telling him to go and literally fight for himself may increase his problems rather than solve them. He does not always need to hit back. When the other guy is twice his size and more capable physically, it is sensible to ignore some kinds of injustice. Hitting back today is not so important for public respect as in primitive times when brawn rather than intellect or skill was the usual means for solving a personality issue. The rational use of language is a more civilized way to circumvent conflict.

In any case, in the presence of your child, restrain the anger you feel toward neighborhood bullies. A child's vivid imagination may stimulate him to believe that he is in more danger than he really is. He is less vulnerable when less afraid.

VARIOUS SOLUTIONS

When another child is frequently provoking your child to fight, it may be wise to:

Let him know that he can stay home if he prefers, and that is possible. Let him make the decision as to whether he wants to fight or not. Being subjected frequently to a neighborhood nuisance can be traumatic, whether he is capable of defending himself or not. If he is capable of defending himself, quite often one all-out successful fight will terminate forever the bully's behavior.

Discuss the problem with the other child's parents. In extreme instances, talk to community juvenile authorities. They are there for your assistance when other parents persistently demonstrate inability or disinterest in controlling the violent behavior of their children.

Boxing lessons may be practical. The experience of hitting and being hit in a controlled situation may relieve some fear of aggression. Father and son can act out the bully and the intimidated. Ways for defending himself can be discussed and practiced. A punching bag may help.

Ignore some disturbances of mild aggression or disagreement.

When children are equally matched, as in the case of pre-schoolers, and mother is nearby to interfere if needed, children can work out many of their own problems of dominance, sharing, and competition.

Change environments. As a final solution, moving to a new community makes sense when a family lives uncomfortably in an area totally dominated by hostile parents and children. There are times when a move, drastic as it may seem, is certain to be an improvement.

Both at home and in the community, provide your child with an environment where he is free to develop a reasonably positive outlook on life. The hostilities of a particular neighborhood may not be characteristic of the world in general, but your child does not know this. He will react to society in line with the social experiences acquired in childhood. Attitudes once learned are more or less permanent. It's wise to refuse to let others add unnecessary fears and negative attitudes to your child's developing images, social or otherwise.

School Ruffians

Seventh-grade Leo is being intimidated by certain eighth-grade boys. His books are grabbed away and hidden. He is poked from behind in class. In various ways they make his life uncomfortable. Mother is aware that something is wrong, but Leo will not disclose the troublemakers.

Where intimidation by others is making the child uncomfortable and interfering with schoolwork, counselors and teachers should be consulted. They may be able to discover the source of your child's frustration. New seating arrangements can be adopted. A change of classes sometimes makes a difference.

The old-fashioned idea that one should learn to tolerate adversity is fine for adults whose personalities are shaped. It is far less appropriate for the growing child. Our ancestors did not well understand how daily experiences shape the expectancies of a young child, influencing his image of the world and himself and later his reactions to himself and society. We know with certainty that harsh treatment does not strengthen personality, but instead undermines it. Our mental institutions are well-populated with people who have been treated harshly. An early environment with a preponderance of happy, agreeable experiences is the best insurance of a child's later ability to tolerate unpleasantness.

The Problems of Friendship

The following principles can be the basis for advising the child of middle years, who often needs to view his friends in a more objective way:

Acquiring friends:

- Assume that others like you. Don't wait for them to be friendly first.
- Take the chance of making a fool of yourself. It won't bother others if it doesn't bother you.
- Don't be afraid to ask for assistance. Lincoln is reported to have remarked that if he wanted a person to like him, he asked that person to do him a favor.
- Unless they are engaged in something private, don't ask permission to join your friends. When you say, "May I join you?" or "Let me play," it is tempting for others to say no. Risk joining in without getting permission.
- Realize and remember that others will accept your mistakes if you do.
- Arrange for "chance" meetings with no other purpose than to be friendly.
- Be aware that how others see you and how you think others see you may not be the same.
- Finding a congenial friend may not be something over which

one has a great deal of control. Time, work, and our environment limit the number of people we have opportunity to meet regularly. And yet with a modicum of luck, congenial friends do turn up.

Make social invitations without concern for whether they are equally returned. Sometimes you are more capable of taking the initiative than a friend.

Assume indifference to be the other person's loss. Their judgment, past experiences with other friends, and emotional problems are factors over which you have no control. They are looking into the mirror of their own experience.

Most people are not concerned with judging you. They are either "friendly or indifferent" (Streitfeld and Lewis, 1970, p. 44).

Be willing to be different. It shows strength of character to stand alone. It also may turn out to be where others also wished to be but were reluctant to go along at first.

Troubles with friends:

Don't prolong angry feelings. When you have fallen out with a friend, make up when an excuse for doing so arises. If no opportunity arises soon, make an opportunity.

Realize that responding to an insult with anger is your own decision.

When we politely and honestly tell others how we feel and they are angered or offended, that may be their problem, not ours. Or it may be that we too often express negative feelings while seldom expressing favorable or appreciative feelings.

Name-calling may be compared to fishing. When a fisherman doesn't get a nibble from the fish he is after, he usually is smart enough to go elsewhere.

If you are distressed over a disturbing situation with a friend, call him on the phone and politely tell him of your concern. When we inform ourselves, we often find relief from our anxieties.

Good guys don't call people names. They don't need to humiliate others in order to feel more important themselves.

Sometimes you are just unlucky enough to be on hand to receive the anger a friend has generated toward someone else. When people's feelings are hurt, they sometimes say things they don't mean and which aren't true.

We are not required to answer the remarks of those who are being rude.

Realize that others have spent many years becoming the way they are. Acceptance of them as they are is more likely to alleviate drawbacks and disabilities than is rejection.

Evaluating friends:

We often ascribe to others influence, power, and abilities they do not have.

It is easier to accept the faults of others when we realize that they have the right to be wrong, except when intentionally seeking to disturb us.

People are what they do more than what they say.

It is not important that you like a friend all the time. It's what you feel most of the time that's important.

It is not important that you like everything about a friend. It's the preponderance that matters.

Usually it's a particular behavior or trait that you do not like, not the whole person.

A friend is not all one thing. He is not all good, bad, indifferent, arrogant, selfish, generous, mean, or lovable. At different times, he may be a little bit of any of these things. We are hodgepodges.

How we perceive the motives of another and what his motives really may be are not always the same.

SEVEN

Developing Responsibility

WORKING TOGETHER IN A
FLEXIBLE WAY

Steven (nine) ignores the note mother left telling him to sweep the patio. Linda (ten) needs to be reminded every day to set the table. Jerome (twelve) half-finishes assigned tasks, then disappears.

Although a child will resist responsibility, he needs experience as a contributing member of the family. Being able to consider oneself a responsible and capable person is of major significance to a healthy self-image and a satisfying adult life. "Human beings are naturally productive—and, it hurts us to do nothing. It damages our feelings of being worthy, of being needed and useful—upon which our adult self-esteem and inner confidence depend" (Missildine, 1963, p. 123).

Analyzing Yourself

We first should look at ourselves in determining what we expect of children. Perhaps we demand too much or too little. Knowing exactly how we feel and what goals we have in mind will simplify the problem.

WE MAY JUDGE CHILDREN BY UNREALISTIC STANDARDS

In our unconscious envy of the freedom children enjoy, we forget their inequality. We forget too that in every generation responsible parents have emerged from the rebellious years of childhood. Kids the world over rebel against work. What is important to us may not seem important to them. We do not wish to dig holes in the sand. They may not wish to clean house or work in the yard.

WE MAY EXPECT TOO MUCH

A task that seems simple to us may be a complex learning experience for a child. Merely sweeping the floor requires the handling of an awkward tool, which necessitates the fine coordination of a variety of movements.

WE MAY HAVE DIFFICULTY ACCEPTING INDIVIDUAL DIFFERENCES

The child with a high level of activity may be easy to persuade and quite helpful around the home. The more passive child may need to be nudged into task completion. Although he seldom gives trouble in other ways, his physical slowness may try your patience to the limit. Attempts to speed him up, slow him down. Anger makes him drag even more. It is difficult to refrain from labels such as "slowpoke," which only discourage him further. The child whose room is never clean was not born resenting orderliness. He may be merely acting out family labels such as "Bill always has a messy room" or "Mary is the neat one." Adopting our labels and appraisals of his work performance, he may fail to excel physically or intellectually. Believing himself incapable, he becomes incapable; he avoids work and other exertion. Expected failure is embarrassing. Thus he retreats from situations in which his performance is likely to receive critical evaluation.

A VARIETY OF PROBLEMS

It's not easy in our push-button society to help children learn to enjoy routine work. Not really needing a young child's assistance, we may:

Find ourselves critical and impatient.
Fail to persist in following through on assignments.
Insist on a child's cooperation only to discover that we can't keep him busy. He stands around waiting to be told what

to do next. Or he is delegated the task of handing dad
the tools while dad does most of the real work. It's easier
that way.

Never consider it "enough" no matter how much the child
accomplishes.

Insist on perfection, directing his every movement, allowing
little freedom to make even simple decisions. Self-expression is restricted and the work provides little pleasure as
an accomplishment or completed task.

Not know how much and what to expect of a child at various age levels, how to control his distractibility, what to
do when he resists work.

Teaching responsibility does pose a problem, but it's not as
serious a problem as we may imagine it to be. Besides, we do
need the older child's assistance, as all parents discover.

Likely Solutions

EXPECT TO GIVE REMINDERS MOST OF CHILDHOOD

If reminding is all you find necessary, you are fortunate. Lack
of interest in the routine work of household duties is normal.
You have become adapted to boring tasks such as sweeping,
cleaning, cooking, washing, picking up, and dusting. Don't be
disappointed when he shows lack of interest in your work. If
he's busy, let him enjoy spending his energy discovering that
the world is an interesting and pleasant place to be. A curious,
creative child is not lazy. He is working hard.

Realize that lack of enthusiasm for home duties is not usually
related to feelings for us. A child is naturally self-centered but
not unloving. Gratitude develops as he matures and observes its
expression by parents and others.

WORK WITH YOUR CHILD

Ignore his complaints. Kids can always find an excuse for not
wanting to do dull routine work. Whether your child is six or

sixteen, you may have to involve yourself personally. For a youngster there is more satisfaction in doing a job with others. Cheerfully help him clean his room. Overlook resistance. Recognize instead his accomplishments. Even if all he gets done is one drawer cleaned while you do everything else, tell him how nice his drawer looks. When accomplishments are noticed, the habits supporting them are strengthened. As your compliments increase and your resentments decrease, his interests will grow.

Working with your child helps keep first experiences from becoming disasters, which are discouraging to future effort. With learning-how-to-cook tasks, especially, mother should be at hand to give necessary assistance. If busy with other work, she won't distract with too much supervision.

Don't be angry with the child who fails to carry out a task to your satisfaction. Remarks such as the following discourage future effort:

How many times do I have to tell you?
I can't see a thing you've done.
Can't you ever do anything right?
Do you call that "clean"?
Anyone can do better than that.

Tell him instead, "Looks as though you had trouble. Let's see what we can do about it."

Within the familiar home environment, we sometimes forget the effectiveness of the word "please." "Please answer the phone," "Please pick up the papers," "Please shut the door" can gain cooperation and at the same time teach courtesy. And, simple thank-yous have high reward value.

PLAN TOGETHER

Teamwork makes the activity more interesting. Tasks are divided up more evenly. Children feel a greater sense of participation when allowed an opportunity to express their preferences about certain chores and the way in which they wish to accomplish them. Obedience to direction alone does not develop the kind of responsibility that can come from being part of the decision-making.

BE FLEXIBLE

Children feel trapped with daily duties that must be accomplished without fail. Let them change jobs occasionally. Fit the responsibility to the situation that exists. If other plans interfere, a job can remain undone or be completed at another time. Home tasks should not be considered as important as schoolwork, outside job responsibilities, or social engagements.

PUT THEIR DECISIONS IN WRITING

Children pay closer attention when there is an assignment sheet on the bulletin board:

MARK	JOHN
Keep coffee table, couch, and floor clean.	Keep the TV room in order.
Empty kitchen wastebasket after dinner every day.	Empty all wastebaskets, and put out the trash on Wednesday.
Set the table. Help put dinner on.	Clear the table. Load the dishwasher.
Run the sweeper in the living room and halls once a week.	Run the sweeper in the bedrooms and TV room once a week.
Water the plants on Saturday.	Mow the yard on Saturday.

BOTH

Help bring groceries in from the car.
Return in-between-meal dishes to the sink, rinse, and stack them.
Keep your own room and bath in order.
Each day:
> Brush your teeth.
> Put your clothes away.
> Keep the sink and bathtub clean.
Neatly hang up your towel and washcloth.

For regular tasks, a checklist is often a help, so the young person can check off each day when he has finished each task. This gives him a satisfying sense of accomplishment and also gets him into the habit of looking at the list.

Motivating the Child

MAKE HIM FEEL NEEDED

You encourage cooperation by the way in which you ask for assistance. Warmth, courtesy, and appreciation are key ingredients here, as in so much of life.

> I have worked hard all day getting your clothes ready. Please clean up the living room for us.
>
> I like your idea about the doll corner. Let's fix it that way.
>
> Be my helper and carry these books to the car.
>
> Dave, you're good at this. Would you help me, please?
>
> Could I get a big strong boy to carry this to the garage? Thanks heaps, Son.
>
> I'd enjoy having your company. Come help me plant these flowers.
>
> Look at Bill! He needs help. You are big and strong. Help him.
>
> You are just in time. I need some help getting the table set.
>
> Oh, there you are. How nice of you to come help me put the dinner on.

Clue him in on why his help is needed. Why do you want his help? What difference does it make whether he does any household tasks or accepts any responsibility? Answer these questions for yourself and your youngster as you deem best. These are not simple questions, and it is little wonder a four-year-old or even a fourteen-year-old cannot figure out the answers all by himself.

DEVISE A PLAN OF ACTION

Ten-year-old Craig barely moves the broom as he sweeps the patio. Every movement seems to come with great effort. He stops occasionally to rest, or to disappear if mother is not looking. With patience, persistence, and a plan, you may be able to get his cooperation.

- Assign work that doesn't interfere seriously with what he wants to do. Respect for us does not obligate him to do our bidding without a similar expression of our respect for his situation.
- Work with him. Children who are inclined to abandon projects before they are finished are more likely to persevere in the company of others (Jersild, 1942).
- Stay calm, if you can, even when he is angry and rebellious. Supply casual small talk, although it may not be returned.
- Put instructions in writing if necessary. They cannot be ignored so easily, nor are they so easily forgotten.

    > Craig, clean the garage. Stack the newspapers in a neat pile behind the door. Put all the tools on the workbench in their proper place. Sweep the floor. Break up the paper boxes, flatten them, and put them in the trash.

- Don't expect a perfect job. Be encouraged by the fact that he has started and is bound to improve after a year or more of experience at the same job.
- Compliment those parts of a job well done; and if you appreciate it, say so!

Accept slowness, lack of interest, and even his rebellion as beyond your complete control. He doesn't have to like the work, and you can't really force him to do it. If he hasn't received an abundance of ridicule from distressed parents, he'll develop more skill and assume more responsibility for home duties as he matures.

When repeated requests to pick up clothing or other possessions remain ignored, you may want to try the following more emphatic measures.

Put all "discarded" items in a lost and found box. Charge five cents to get them back.

Collect discarded possessions and neatly pile them in the middle of his room. Warn him of your plans.

Postpone the purchase of the new party dress until present clothing is attended to.

Put uncared for toys and games away for a few weeks.

For one day, make a list of all the things you do for him that he should have done for himself. Ask him to write down what he does for you.

Withhold permissions (often most effective).

> Come back. You can't go outside until you've picked up your blocks. No painting until the dolls are put away. When your bed is made, we'll be ready to go.

Some of the above are somewhat unconventional methods for gaining a child's cooperation. Depending upon the child, they may increase resistance. You must be willing to give them up if they don't work. Giving up is sometimes wise. Occasionally, a respite is all that is needed to enable matters to go more smoothly later.

Monetary Reward for Home Responsibilities

When a child is accustomed to being paid for immediate efforts, satisfaction for job completion alone may not be learned. Money becomes the goal. The result can be lack of incentive and refusal to work when external reward is not forthcoming.

Financial reward for work essential to the welfare of the

family is not a necessity. An allowance can be a regular occurrence that is not related specifically to work completed. As a member of the family team, each person has responsibility to do his share of the work necessary for keeping the home and family functioning smoothly.

An orderly home has a restful effect upon its members. It is also prettier and saves much futile searching, added bumps and falls, and other needless frustrations. There are added blessings: when children are helpful, parents have more opportunity to share in the leisure so plentiful to children. There is more time for the family to do things together. Parents feel more free to allow children full use of the home when they help with the cleanup.

Ideally, a child learns to derive pleasure in an activity. The activity becomes satisfying to him for its own sake alone, whether its achievement is in the form of an object, a state of affairs, or a school lesson prepared; and whether or not there is some additional extrinsic reward. Accepting responsibility for the requirements of everyday life is a necessity for which one's own satisfaction must ultimately be one's only reward. The interest and approval of companionable parents help a child discover this sense of satisfaction and pride in achievement.

EIGHT

The School Situation

PRESCHOOL

You Are His First Teacher

Two-month-old Johnny's crib rattles periodically on into the night. Johnny has too much fun to sleep. With hands and feet he bats at the toys hanging over his crib. He rests for a while, then starts in again. Not until his parents remove the toys does he settle down to more peaceful sleep.

INTEREST IN LEARNING BEGINS IN THE CRIB

If supplied with interesting objects to explore, your infant will amuse himself for hours. On the other hand, if sensory and motor needs are ignored, he may cry in restlessness and boredom for hours. If encouraged, his natural curiosity grows. The infant is interested in the sounds he can make with a rattle attached to a string, the movements that occur as he bats at the toy attached to his high-chair tray, the way the ball bounces when it drops to the floor, the way his Teddy bear doesn't bounce when it drops to the floor. He explores with mouth, hands, and eyes the physical properties of any object within his reach.

As early as 1901, Groos described the paper-crumbling, spoon-throwing, puddle-wading child as demanding a knowledge of effects, while seeking to be the producer of those effects. This kind of behavior is noted also by Piaget as he describes his infant son breaking off one piece of bread at a time and watching it fall to the floor. "The child gives evidence of sensing, perceiving, attending, learning, recognizing, probably recalling, and perhaps thinking in a rudimentary way" (White, 1959, p̄. 320).

Early mental stimulation is noted regularly in the preschool homelife of children with high ability and achievement scores. In general, the greater the variety of pleasurable social and intellectual stimulation in infancy, the greater his capacity for development later.

> Give him windows from which to look out at the world. The child who is able to crawl spends much time at the windows.
>
> Let the tiny infant stay with you during the day. A port-a-crib easily rolls from room to room.
>
> Hang toys from his crib. Replace these with new ones occasionally. A baby of two to three months will make swiping movements toward an object attached to the side of his crib. White and Held (1966) suggest that moderate stimulation is better than elaborate gadgets. Objects should be hung from the side of his crib rather than directly over it, dominating the view.
>
> In any event, don't let toys take the place of your own play with your child. From the first days of birth, give him adequate handling. As noted earlier, gentle handling can increase your child's later ability to tolerate emotional stress.
>
> Talk to him frequently, but not in baby language and not in a loud and high-pitched voice.
>
> Play with him. Crawl with him. Go for walks with him. Roll balls to him.
>
> Cut pictures from magazines of animals and children. Attach them to the wall near his crib. Give him new ones occasionally.
>
> Let him investigate, build, and explore. He wants to touch and see for himself. Curiosity about the world is not encouraged if he is regularly confined to a playpen.

Let him hear the names of objects and things that he can see,
hear, touch, and hold. He is learning, even though he cannot yet repeat what he hears.
Smile, cuddle him, sing to him.

EVIDENCE SUPPORTS THE THEORY OF EARLY LEARNING

Preschoolers who have a strong desire to master intellectual
skills retain this motivation during adolescence and into early
adulthood (Moss and Kagan, 1961). Animals given an enriched
free environment after weaning are advanced in adulthood,
having greater facility in perception, problem-solving, cognition,
and neural activity (Denenberg, 1969). The most crucial phases
of physical and mental development may occur very early in
life, the brain by the age of six having grown three sizes larger
than it was at birth (Dubos, 1968). Livingston (1968) sets
forth the view that the brain is molded by the age of twelve.

In a 1969 study sponsored by the United States Office of
Education, Schaeffer trained eight college-educated women to
tutor infants of low-income families on a one-tutor, one-child
basis. Beginning at fifteen months of age, twenty infants received five one-hour-a-day lessons each week in their own
homes until they were three years old. The tutors concentrated
on intellectual and verbal stimulation. They talked, played
games, read books, taught new words, assisted in puzzle con-
struction and picture-drawing, and used anything else available
to keep the child's interest. Significant results were obtained in
verbal and perceptual development, with an IQ gain at three
years of seventeen points over the children who did not receive
the instruction and personal attention.

The authors of this book recorded the early learning of their
own firstborn. From five weeks of age on, the names of foods
being consumed were vocalized to him. At six months of age,
picture books were examined daily with mother pointing to and
giving the names of objects viewed. Things the infant came into

contact with daily around the home were verbalized to him: bed, chair, ball, shirt, spoon, cup, and so forth.

Given below are excerpts from the behavioral history of this early training, some of which may be the result of these early experiences:

At six months: Clamps his mouth closed upon hearing the names of foods he does not prefer.

At nine months: Books turned upside down are righted immediately. He has learned to turn the pages by himself.

At sixteen months: Likes to identify the names of objects heard and pictures seen. He does this by pointing to objects in the room that are the same as he hears or sees in his books as mother reads. Jumps down from his seat to find and point to items not in view, such as telephone, broom, clock, bed, toy truck, cup, flowers, car. He goes to the bathroom on the word bath. Comes to the kitchen for water to drink.

Points to animals and objects on TV that he has learned to identify in books and around the home.

Can pick out many of the correct alphabet blocks floating on his bath water as we call out the letters.

Does not destroy or tear up books or magazines. Leafs through books alone, although he prefers company and having the pictures explained to him.

At sixteen months and the arrival of a baby brother, intensive lessons were discontinued. Crawling, walking, and speech developed normally; intellectual skills were advanced.

DON'T MISS YOUR OPPORTUNITY

If you wait for the school to teach your child, he loses. His most impressionable years are bypassed. Intellectual curiosity not exploited in infancy may resist stimulation later. By five or six years of age a child begins to resist instruction from parents. Whether he knows a fact or not, he now frustrates you with comments such as "I know that already. Mother, I know how to do that." He prefers to repeat what he already knows, as though our asking him to learn something new suggests he is ignorant. Such independence mixed with parental impatience may fuel itself. For more detailed suggestions toward raising your infant's ability to achieve, read Genevieve Painter's book *Teach Your Baby* (Simon and Schuster, 1971).

What Should He Learn?

A child of nursery school age, if given the opportunity, can learn many things. He may be reading first-grade work by the time he is in kindergarten if parents or others have the time and patience to teach him. If this is not possible, knowing at least how to do the following gives him a good start in school.

Read and write his own name.
Read and write numbers up to ten.
Read and write the alphabet.
Recognize and read words describing colors and use colors
    correctly.
Answer questions about number, size, and position.
Differentiate between variously shaped objects: round,
    square, oval, rectangle, triangle.
Use the proper reading movement from left to right in the use
    of simple picture storybooks.
Express himself verbally. Dictate letters to grandparents and
    friends while mother writes or types them.

The self-confidence gained from such knowledge helps a child perceive first experiences in elementary school as easy and fun. Consequently, he expects future learning to be the same. Such expectation can be as important for successful learning as IQ. If your child is interested, why not give it a try? It costs hardly more than a little parental time and patience.

How Should You Teach Him?

USE HIS "IN-BETWEEN TIMES"

Use the time he impatiently waits for a friend to arrive, when he's ready for nursery school thirty minutes too early, when he's eating a leisurely lunch, when he's sitting in his bath or traveling in the car. The more variety, the more interested he'll be. Why not be as dedicated to his intellectual development as you are about his health needs. A few minutes of number writing can be a time for togetherness. When he's not in the mood for learning, skip a day or two. For the preschooler, the completion of a specific task is not as important as his sense of satisfaction over what is being learned, his discovery that learning is pleasant, invigorating, and fun.

KEEP HIM NEAR YOU

As mentioned earlier, aloneness does not encourage creativity in small children. A desk or table of his very own, located where you spend much of your time, is a helpful incentive. Supply it well with crayons, papers, and simple workbooks.

BUY PRESCHOOL WORKBOOKS AND TABLETS

Even the grocer sells tablets showing the correct writing for letters of the alphabet. School supply stores have a wide selection of materials for early learning.

He can learn to write his ABC's by tracing over perfect outlines, or connecting the spaces between dots made in the shape of letters of the alphabet. In this way visual and motor faculties work together to help him learn. Although he will not learn to write all letters quickly, seeing them in sequence each time he elects to practice provides closure and speeds learning. A few minutes daily provide the repetition necessary for learning to take place.

The average five-year-old easily learns to recognize the alphabet. Sing the alphabet song with him. Point to the letters as you sing.

WHAT CAN YOU DO ABOUT REBELLION?

Your preschooler may resist lessons in the same way that he resists face-washing, teeth-brushing, naptime. If he senses your anxiety and determination, he rebels. Keeping his frustration to a minimum is imperative.

If routine meets opposition, look for the "teachable moments," times when he is in-between other interests.

Recognize that the preschooler doesn't work consecutively through a workbook. He's as likely to begin in the middle as anywhere. Make extra copies of those pages you believe he will especially enjoy.

Don't wait until his work is complete to give praise and affection. Give him approval for the smallest accomplishment. That is what motivates him to learn.

Ignore mistakes. Let him view correct examples in future lessons. Just as his mistakes did not stop him from learning to speak, they will not stop him from learning to read and write.

Make lessons short. The shorter the lesson, the better it's learned.

Before he begins to show loss of interest by scribbling or saying that he's tired, discontinue the lesson for the day. Thus he leaves the project with a pleasant attitude toward it and happy anticipation of returning to it.

Don't stand over him when he is working on a lesson that may be difficult. He may not want to admit that he doesn't know. Be aware that he tolerates only a minimum of correction, direction, and interruption. He resents lack of opportunity to figure it out himself. Although it is not easy to remain silent when a child hesitates as he reads or writes, interest remains high as our assistance remains low. Too much help is experienced as pressure and lack of faith. It's mainly our approval and confidence in him that he wants.

Give your help in as few words as possible. The instant he achieves insight, he may resist every extra word of explanation you give, and rightly so. Our assistance is distracting and interferes with his continuing.

Occasionally assist the child likely to rebel by saying, "Do you mean this way?" Thus it becomes more his doing than ours.

Don't let momentary rebellion upset you. Move out of the picture when you are uncomfortable. His distress doesn't bother him as much as yours will. Even though he may be causing much of your annoyance, he cannot work well unless he feels accepted.

If rebellion is chronic, terminate the lessons and wait for the child to become older and readier for these activities. There is no need to learn everything at once.

Never push the preschool child to do lessons to the point that they seem like punishment to him. He learns best if the activities are interesting and fun. This takes planning, interest, and patience on the parents' part.

NURSERY SCHOOL

As discussed earlier, in the critical periods of early childhood there is a time for socialization. If a child passes through this period without opportunity for play with other children, he may remain socially distant throughout life. Nursery school supplements other ways of meeting social needs and offers a range of broadening experiences not possible at home. Although it comes after definable personality traits have been established, the available social and other learning will be helpful.

A degree of social adjustment, emotional security, verbal capacity, athletic skill, and physical dexterity must have been acquired if a youngster of five is to satisfactorily adjust to elementary school. Retardation in any one of these areas can interfere with school progress. If he has had a constructive nursery-school experience, it will ease the task facing him.

Selecting the Nursery School

Choose school and teacher carefully. These years, too, are critical to personality development. Negative attitudes learned here are difficult to change. Give serious consideration to the following:

> The teacher's experience should include training in child psychology.
>
> The teacher's personality should be pleasing to both mother and child. For one thing, he needs a pleasing personality upon which to model his own.
>
> School buildings, play equipment, and other facilities must be adequate, safe, and convenient.
>
> Choose a school where mothers are allowed to participate. Your child benefits from knowing other friendly and helpful mothers. So do you.
>
> Choose a school where you are permitted to stay with your child if he needs you. Unpleasant first separations may seriously affect a child's sense of trust in you as well as interfere with his confidence in the school. "The adult's presence nearby encourages rather than discourages independence" (Swift, 1968, p. 153).

Study the school organization. All children should not be in one large group with the same activities. Their interest, physical skill, and social development are not the same. Even the members of an apparently homogeneous group of three-year-olds are in various stages of development. Older children fail to be stimulated by the activities of younger members. Play equipment may be outgrown. With separate programs, a child can view his own maturation and that of the other children from one age level to the next.

Getting to Know the School

MOTHER SHOULD GO WITH HIM

Nursery school is often a child's first extended time away from mother in a strange environment. As his primary source of security, she should share the experience with him. His empathy with her helps him make many of his decisions. If she enjoys the school and seems pleased with it, he will more likely feel the same.

Plan to go with him for a week or even more if your child has been distraught over past separations. If necessary, reassure him daily that you will be there as long as he needs you, though you expect that he will prefer to have you go home so that he can be on his own like the other children. Without fear of your leaving him, he feels free to enjoy his new surroundings. Movement to or away from you is then his decision and not something forced upon him.

As he becomes acquainted, he begins to appraise the school. Notice how he watches the teacher as she communicates with the other children. She is carefully scrutinized in every activity. When more secure, he tests out his observations, approaching her as he has seen others do with their questions and attention-seeking behavior.

The cooperative nursery is usually most congenial about helping with separation anxiety. In a program where mothers share the work, the parents become more interested and involved. Becoming acquainted along with your child, you can talk with him about school activities. He feels happier belonging to a school in which parents participate.

EXPLORE THE SCHOOL WITH HIM

On your first day, take a look at the facilities: bathroom, playyard equipment, games, coat closets, storage shelves, the kitchen. Show him how the doors, windows, and lights work. Talk to some of the children and learn their names. What is interesting and fun for mother will more likely be fun for him. Your leaving when he feels secure and familiar in surroundings he has shared with you does not generate the anxiety he would feel in a strange environment.

GIVE REASSURANCE

Reassure the hesitant child that he is going to school because it's fun to learn and play and be with other children. If he is not worried that you are banishing him to get more time for younger family members, he is likely to be more receptive to nursery school or any other experience.

Emphasize to him that teachers are people who like children and enjoy taking care of them. Point out the ways in which the children are protected, how there is time to rest and time for a midmorning snack, how teachers stop children who might start to hit or be rude.

PARTICIPATE

You should be permitted to participate in some way while accompanying your child, especially if sitting and watching is boring and uncomfortable. Observing such feelings, your child may share them with you. If mother works, the child becomes accustomed to having her occasionally disappear from view. Mother learns more about the school and what is expected there on her work day.

However, if sitting and watching are interesting to you and your preference, one can learn much about the school this way too.

TAKE A SPECIAL TOY

Special toys or objects from home provide extra comfort and add to a child's feeling of security. Notice the rapport with others that a new toy stimulates. All children gather around in a friendly way to inspect the new possession.

TALK ABOUT HIS SCHOOL

Talk at home about the interesting things observed at school. Encourage your child to tell about his day. Talking about his experiences helps him to remember them more pleasantly, and helps you stay in touch with each other.

DON'T WORRY ABOUT HIS FEAR OF LEAVING YOU

Archer and Hosley point out that mothers sometimes feel that they have failed when a child has trouble leaving them for nursery school. These researchers offer the reassurance that "the better the mothering has been, the more a child is bound to miss her if plunged too quickly into a place with unfamiliar adults and children for several hours a day" (1969, p. 45). "Too quickly" varies from child to child. Long enough may be a few minutes or it may be several days, depending in part upon how many prior pleasant separations there have been.

When Mother Leaves

When mother finds school a familiar and pleasant place, her child usually feels the same. When he is obviously enjoying many of the school activities, when he is playing with selected friends and can let mother out of sight occasionally, he is ready to try going it alone. Make separation a gradual experience. How gradual it needs to be depends upon the child. In many cases, a schedule similar to the following is useful.

Five minutes the first day
Ten minutes the second day
Twenty minutes the third day
Forty minutes the fourth day
Sixty minutes the fifth day

For many children, a plan as gradual as this would not be necessary. Individual differences are huge here. For some children one could jump from five minutes to sixty minutes to all morning with confidence and nonchalance in both child and mother.

Some ways that will facilitate beginning such gradual separation are given below. You will think of others, too.

Decide with the teacher what part of the school routine is most suitable. For some, separation is less stressful if it begins when the child is involved in an activity he enjoys. Outdoor playtime is convenient if other children are apt to be disturbed by his distress.

Let him know that you will notify him when it is time to leave for a short errand. This way he is free to enjoy himself rather than worry that you may disappear at any moment.

Upon departure, alert the teacher to his possible need for comfort. Of vital importance is your promise to reappear and its fulfillment at the designated time.

Don't increase your absences beyond twenty minutes if he cries for the whole time you are gone. Lengthen your absences as he ceases his crying within that time period.

Tell him exactly where you will be while he is in school. Be sure these are places he knows well. If you will be at home, describe what you will be doing at home so that he can visualize you in the familiar home situation. Let him know that those things you enjoyed together will be saved for when he is home.

Don't introduce the car pool until he is willingly attending on his own. An unpleasant car pool experience can set him against the school as well.

If a child can at least fairly cheerfully participate in a week or more of short separations, he often discovers that increased independence from mother is a satisfying experience. This is one of the advantages of gradual separation. Some other advantages are these:

Gradual separation does not interfere with his perception of school as an enjoyable place to be.

Nursery school is introduced with a minimum of anxiety at a time when important attitudes about the world, particularly the world outside the home, are being learned.

It is not difficult for him to manage by himself short separations from mother.

He is able to test his own ability to be without mother's security under conditions of not too great tension and stress.

When mother returns as she promises, he is reassured of her reliability.

Mother is not away long enough for him to be seriously upset. With crying limited to twenty minutes, it's not so difficult for him to regain his composure and enjoy the remainder of the day.

Other children are not disrupted by a child who otherwise might scream or sob for most of his time at school.

When independence is finally achieved, it seems like something he has accomplished on his own, rather than something that happened to him or was forced upon him.

SHOULD PROBLEMS DEVELOP

If your child continues to be troubled, repeat the week of short separations. Try a week of thirty-minute absences before lengthening the time to one hour. Each child's needs are different. In any case, if school is enjoyable and no other problems arise, even the most hesitant child will finally accept gradual separation from mother.

Should he persist in efforts to get your promise not to leave, tell him:

> You think you need me a lot more than you do. You haven't had a chance to discover yet how well you can get along without me. Your teacher will be here to help you and take care of you, and I'll be back soon.
>
> I'm sorry, dear, but I have errands to run. I'll let you know before I leave. I'll be gone such a short time you'll not need me. Your teacher will be here to help you with anything you need.
>
> Nursery school will help you get used to being away from me for short periods, such as when you go to kindergarten.

Largely ignore his threats that he is not going to school anymore. Tell him, "We'll talk about it in a week." Spend additional time getting him dressed in the mornings, chatting with him and not rushing. Overcoming his refusal to participate may require increased warmth, companionship, diversion, and considerable patience. Keep in mind that he will resist an angry parent even more.

As a final alternative, let him stay home a day or two. Then be busy with housework. Let finding something to do be up to him. If such mornings at home are less than interesting and playmates are not readily available, school may become more attractive. Such a day may give him different perspectives about school and serve to remind him of what you are doing while he is away.

With some children, shortening the school day is helpful. A full morning almost certainly will be too long for a child wholly unaccustomed to being away from mother.

When your child finally makes it alone, give extra attention. Greet him cordially upon his return home. Have a special lunch ready. Let him know you are pleased to see him and proud of him.

Perhaps it sounds like a lot of effort. On the other hand, these few extra weeks helping your child face his first major separation from you can be important for years to come.

ELEMENTARY SCHOOL

Getting to Know the Teacher

IF THE TEACHER KNOWS YOU, SHE BETTER UNDERSTANDS YOUR CHILD

You and your child's teacher are the most important people in his life. He benefits when you know each other. The teacher who sees and talks with you gets to know your child better. She's interested in his problems, his study habits, what he likes to do at home, how he gets along with others, what he likes or dislikes about school. Knowing more about your child improves her ability to communicate with him. Parents in turn discover ways to be more helpful to the school's program at home.

YOU BETTER UNDERSTAND THE TEACHER

Personality is important. Academic skill is not all that a teacher imparts. Your child may spend more hours each day in the same room with his teacher than he does at home in the same room with you. All teachers have some influence upon personality whether they wish it or not. Like parents, they repeatedly respond to particular children in a characteristic way. Knowing your child's teacher can make it easier for you to point out ways in which your child may be misunderstood, or ways in which your child may be misunderstanding the teacher.

Personality conflicts should not be ignored. Don't invariably accept the rationale that your child should tolerate particular teachers in order that he may learn to cope with different personalities. Davidson and Long (1968) have experimentally demonstrated that the more favorably a child judges his teacher's opinion of him, the more favorable is his perception of himself, the better his academic work, and the more cooperative his behavior in class.

YOUR CHILD'S PROBLEMS GET CONSIDERATION

When parents communicate with their child's teacher, inaccurate perceptions are not so apt to remain untested. Problems not talked out may interfere with personality development as well as school performance. When a problem develops that you and your child cannot solve, accompany the child who will not go alone to talk with his teacher, or go yourself. When teachers understand they often can correct unpleasant situations or restructure the environment so that a problem is more tolerable.

The child who runs home from school with his hand puppet, because he is afraid the teacher will make him perform in front of the class, discovers that the teacher is sympathetic to his feelings.

Inflated fears about the teacher's being angry with him over a problem incident at school are dispelled as they are talked about.

The disappointing grade may be changed when the teacher discovers that all of Jimmy's papers do indeed indicate that he did better.

The child who feels left out because of the classroom buddy system, which has placed him in a group with markedly different interests, finds that the teacher can plan a more comfortable arrangement.

Why Help with Lessons?

SCHOOLS ARE NOT IDEALLY STAFFED AND EQUIPPED

Teachers in the ordinary classroom do not have the time to insure that children learn each lesson well before going to the next. A child falling behind may remain there indefinitely. Having come to expect mediocre achievement by himself, he may never really extend himself fully.

As a parent you want the best for your child. At the same time, you must understand that other people—most notably those in schools—cannot be expected to accomplish your goals for you totally. Schools are not financially able to exploit fully the individual capacities of each child.

INTELLECTUAL PERFORMANCE IS RAISED

As mentioned earlier, children who come from homes that afford them intellectual stimulation have higher IQ's and do better in school than those from other homes. Parents who take an active role in training, who establish high but realistic standards of performance, who encourage children to believe that goals can be reached, and who give warm approval for good performance are likely to have children with high levels of motivation to achieve (Berkowitz, 1964).

NUMEROUS ADVANTAGES CAN ACCRUE

When all is going well for your child academically, he will need no special help at home beyond furnishing him an appropriate place and time to do his school assignments. If he is falling behind or in other ways having trouble academically, added help at home can be advantageous.

Brief study periods at home help your child go from one lesson to the next fully prepared. Work not completed in a first lesson interferes with his ability to accomplish in the second lesson, etc.

Poor study habits are a major problem for underachievers. You may be able to help him improve his technique.

Assistance at home helps him avoid the unpleasantness of failure in front of classmates, discouraging to future effort.

The discouraged child, lacking faith in his ability to learn, may discover his self-estimate is inaccurate. A student's opinion of his own academic ability plays a crucial role in academic performance. Equally as important as IQ may be one's ability to recognize his capacity to learn, find satisfaction in his own efforts, self-initiate and maintain effort for extended periods (Bailey, 1971).

Parents have additional time for praise and approval. A positive relationship exists between intellectual competence and parental interest, praise, and lack of criticism, especially where mother is concerned and interested.

Through parental example, he can learn to do more than the minimum requirements of a task. This can be rewarding both at home and at school, as well as satisfying for its own sake alone.

Children dislike recopying. Parents can teach tolerance for repetition with examples of their own persistence. In the world of business, science, or education, data are often copied and recopied many times before final results are ready for evaluation. The school seldom provides time for proofreading.

Our expectancies are significant in helping a child set goals for himself. If we believe that he has a responsibility to strive, within his ability, toward successful scholastic achievement, he more probably will assume the same. We should ignore protests about lessons in the same way that we ignore protests about cleaning his room. Firmness is not coercion. If your child is capable, expect and enforce reasonable scholastic performance. He will discover ultimately that it is not his parents but he himself who benefits most from these efforts.

WHY DO PARENTS RESIST?

Interestingly enough, some parents quite capable of helping a child learn avoid giving assistance out of fear of the authority the school represents. The child is the one who loses when parents worry that the teacher may find out and disapprove.

Seriously needed attention is not given also out of concern that the child will become unduly dependent. Such a concern lacks reality. It will be obvious to both parent and child when a tutor is no longer needed. Your child will be quick to say, "Mother, I can do it myself." Once he discovers that it is fun to accomplish, he will strive on his own to excel.

How to Help with Lessons

READING

Make flash cards from the word lists accompanying daily reading lessons. The text used in class may be borrowed from the teacher, purchased locally, or ordered from the publishing company. The child who learns well the words accompanying each day's reading won't be overwhelmed by the new words of succeeding lessons. Work will not pile up on him. As classroom reading improves, his opinion of his scholastic abilities will rise. Thereby he develops a new willingness to try.

A supplementary text, different from the book currently used in class, does not challenge interest effectively. Supplementary material lacks apparent relevance to the present. Future proficiency is too vague an incentive, except for the gifted child who without assistance is doing well.

Feeling overwhelmed has a great deal to do with a child's resistance to learning. We caution you not to let him see the whole box of flash cards, the complete vocabulary list for the year, or all the books he will read. To a first- or second-grader, it may look like an impossible mountain to climb. That learning is to be spread over a long period of time is difficult for him to comprehend. Teaching materials and long-term goals are best not called to his attention. He need only know his assignments one day at a time.

SPELLING

It should be noted that the child who can recite his spelling lesson doesn't necessarily write it correctly. Mistakes made when a lesson has been ostensibly well-learned are particularly disappointing. Writing each spelling word at least once at the close of a home-study period helps catch unsuspected errors.

ARITHMETIC

Many children resist proofreading or checking their work. Time for review is limited at school. Your willingness to go over his work sets a good example. If you don't mind it, he is less likely to object. Rather than pointing out all errors, note the number of mistakes each line contains, but let him find the errors.

CREATIVE WRITING

In this category, parents may help with ideas. Trips to local points of historical interest make useful subject matter. Literature saved from summer vacation trips contains pictures and other useful information for school reports. Libraries are a source of almost unlimited data.

Learning to express oneself in writing comes with practice. Children are particularly reluctant to accept parental advice about how something should be written. They want to do it their way.

OUTSIDE READING

At about the fourth grade, children often begin to read more on their own. They sometimes can be encouraged to do so earlier if pressure is not too obvious. Joke and cartoon books, or any other books containing more pictures than words, are a good start. Get them for trips in the car, for reading in the doctor's office, or just to put on his bookshelf. As long as he is reading, don't be too concerned about the subject matter. If you are dissatisfied on that point, increase the supply along other lines.

Unfortunately, rows and rows of library books that seem too much to choose from can discourage interest in reading. Having selected several uninteresting books in succession, he may be disinclined to try again soon. Teachers and librarians can help insure that first selections are stimulating enough to tempt him further.

GRADES

Refrain from expressing strong disappointment over low or failing grades. They are not an indication of your child's worth. Overconcern causes him to feel that he fails not only himself but you as well. More useful is your continued assistance, coupled with your optimism that he will do better in time. "So you got a D plus. That's a nice improvement. You'll make a C next time." If there's only one good mark on the grade card, praise it highly and be encouraging. If this can't be done, say nothing, or point out that "Sometimes we win, sometimes we lose, but we keep on trying."

How he believes he will perform has a great deal to do with how hard he will try. Encourage him to improve his own record, not to compete with the grades of others. This is an excellent idea for any child.

Motivating Home Lessons

Our interest is the key to his motivation. We must not look upon his work as a chore, a nuisance, or an interference in our lives. Sensing such feelings, a child will resist learning. Our feelings combined with the frustration of the work itself can cause a mental block in him against learning. If it is difficult to work with him, seek assistance. Sometimes a high school or college student is a helpful tutor when parents are overly tense and anxious.

Plan home lessons so that they are pleasant, and as easy and free of frustration as possible:

Arrange a pleasant, quiet place for him to work undisturbed and happily.

Arrange sufficient time so that study is not rushed. Just as a child will not eat for the hurried, tense, or impatient mother, he also will not learn.

Depending on the lesson and the child, it may be necessary to work at the same table with him or nearby. Have your sewing or other work at hand so you are not scrutinizing his every movement.

Plan a time for study that does not conflict with other interests, his or the family's.

Unless he asks for assistance, wait until a lesson is complete before reviewing it.

Knowledge of results facilitates learning. Point out what he has done well. Praise his improvements.

Organize each lesson so that it gives practice on errors made in previous lessons. This is better than pointing out his mistakes. Workbook pages can be duplicated when you feel that more practice on certain lessons will be needed.

Change the time and the location of his study periods occasionally, unless he very much likes the current arrangement.

Have other members of the family help with some parts of his lesson, if their help would be welcomed and they are willing.

If he resists offered assistance, ask him to give a signal when he wants help.

Periodically reward the slow child with candy, special foods or events, or an inexpensive gift. Rewards will become less important as he begins to find satisfaction in excelling.

Serve a special dessert or favorite dish upon the completion of a particularly difficult project. Let him select the dinner menu occasionally.

Praise is a powerful stimulant. In general, the more he receives of it in the beginning, the less he will need of it later. Tell him:

Good going! You figured that out all by yourself.

Very good. You are doing fine.

How well you are reading after only a few lessons.

Your circles are nicely rounded.

Those are well-written capital A's.

That's fine! You followed the directions just right.

A few weeks ago, you didn't know these words. Now they seem easy.

That was a very good lesson. You are writing so much faster
now.

I enjoyed helping you. It's my time just to be with you.

Research with animals shows how first-learning that can be
easily accomplished may lead to strong motivation and much
improved chances of later success.

Young puppies were tested to see if they could learn to get a dish of
food from under a cover, either by pulling a string or by reaching
with their paws or teeth. The test purposely was made easy. If a
puppy failed, he made only half-hearted efforts on the second try. If
he failed on the third try, he would take one look then simply go to
the door, sit down, and wait for release. A puppy that succeeded on
the first trial would usually go on to succeed on subsequent trials. If
a difficult problem developed, he would keep right on working. If a
puppy failed repeatedly, he was extremely difficult to motivate.
(Summarized from Scott, 1969, p. 67.)

We humans are much more complicated creatures; nevertheless, we too are motivated by success. When we help our children over the rough spots of learning so that they are more
likely to succeed, we increase their motivation.

Monetary Reward for Schoolwork

Learning should be largely its own reward. Material gifts are of
secondary importance. A dollar for every A is not what we want
to teach our children. Financial reward as a continuing motive
for scholastic success may put satisfaction of a job well done,
the challenge of a good grade alone, the fun of excelling farther
into the background. Then, too, many of our child's efforts will
receive reward only in the distant future; for example, a college
diploma, a satisfying job, success in work. Immediate pleasure
must often be postponed in the interest of later gratification.
The unwillingness of the capable teen-ager to strive scholastically may in some measure rest upon his view that the monetary

reward accompanying a college diploma seems too far in the future. He may prefer a lesser goal in order to have his financial reward sooner.

On the other hand, Rich (1969) suggests that discouraged children who don't see themselves as "succeeders," or disadvantaged children who don't believe in the payoffs of the outside world, may very well be stimulated to greater achievement by a system of immediate tangible rewards. She refers to the work of Harold Cohen, of the Institute of Behavioral Research, who stimulated student interest in learning by awarding points for completed tasks. As the child accumulated points, he was able to choose from a variety of immediate rewards, such as books, shirts, times-out, and money.

D. Leon Smith uses rewards of food to train bears to play basketball. The bears are rewarded for every correct move they make. They are never punished or starved. Food, the original stimulus for their learning, subsequently becomes secondary to their love for the game. As Smith describes, "They've become so fond of playing basketball that I'm afraid if we took the balls away from them, they would rip their cages apart" (see Hillinger, 1971, p. 1).

NINE

New Views on Some Old Child-Care Problems

BEDTIME PROBLEMS

Nighttime Separation

Fear of the dark and of being left alone are two of the most common fears of childhood. The natural bond that causes the human infant to cling to mother does not cease at bedtime and begin again in the morning. It is perfectly normal for children not to want to be separated from parents, especially at night. Human babies are perhaps the only young ones who must tolerate such separation from the mother at any time before weaning. As Bowlby writes:

The first thing we discover about young monkeys and apes is that they spend the whole of infancy very close to their mothers, and for much of the time actually clinging to her. . . . The two stick together, and any attempt at forcible separation is met with violent resistance from both parties.

The clinging of young monkeys and apes has its parallel in human young. It has been known for a long time that human infants at birth are able to support their own weight by clinging. . . . At one time it was imagined that this clinging of newborn babies is a relic of a time when we inhabited the trees, but a more probable explanation is that it represents the human version of the clinging to mother that is seen in every one of the other six hundred primate species. [1970, p. 23.]

Before the age of electricity, parents and children usually went to bed at the same time and often slept in the same room or even the same bed. Separation was not as noticeable as today, when electricity gives parents longer evening hours and

homes are designed with adult sleeping quarters as far removed
as possible from the children's.

GETTING HIM TO BED

It is not easy to deal with our children's natural resistance to
separation from us, nighttime or otherwise. We need ways to
simplify the task. Here are some suggestions:

Plan in advance:

> Have a usual time for going to bed. Avoid excitement and
> other stimulation. Devise a quiet, soothing routine for
> twenty minutes or so before bedtime and follow it con-
> scientiously.
>
> Strive for pleasant experiences where bedtime is concerned.
> Dressing, bath, and getting ready to retire can be a time
> for companionship and warm communication.
>
> A roommate, human or animal, can ease a going-to-bed prob-
> lem. So can a Teddy bear or favorite doll.
>
> A bottle of warm milk helps the infant drop off to sleep.
>
> If he is afraid of the dark, a soft light may help. His psycho-
> logical well-being is well worth the extra cost.
>
> A reading light over his bed is convenient for looking at books
> for a few minutes and may make going to sleep easier. It
> is also reassuring to know that a light is within easy
> reach.

Try persuasion:

> When he climbs out of bed, return him in a friendly way. Tell
> him, "All little children are in bed now."
>
> Inform him that eight o'clock is bedtime and time for both
> parents and children to get rested up for the next day.
>
> Acquaint him with your own needs. Tell him how you need
> your sleep, that he is now big enough to stay in his own
> bed at night. If there is something he needs, put it beside
> his bed.

Involve yourself:

When infants and small children become overly tired, they have trouble falling asleep. Gentle rocking, soft singing, reading softly to them, or walking are often helpful.

If your child persistently refuses to leave you at night, go to bed with him until he feels more secure. If his bed isn't large enough for both of you, set up a foldaway cot and lie down with him. Your companionship may solve the problem sooner than persuasion. Stay with him until he falls asleep.

Some parents use this time for communication. The sound of the parent's voice is security-building and relaxing, providing you are not teaching or correcting. Talk about pleasant things. Make up stories. Sing songs.

If nothing else works, rather than have nightly battles over bedtime, you may have no alternative but to let him stay up. Provide a quiet environment near you so that he becomes sleepy. Carry him to bed after he falls asleep. Children of school age do not resist our limits as strongly as does the very young child.

If it is the parents' bedtime and you do not wish to go to his room, let him sleep in your bed. The contact-comfort of being close to his parents is sleep-inducing. Return him to his own bed when he sleeps. Again, this is a last-resort measure.

If he is a late-night riser, talk soothingly to him, and tenderly return him to his own bed. He may be merely checking to make sure you are still there.

The vividness of his dreams may cause him to seek out his parents. Comfort him and cuddle him and return him gently to his bed. If it has been a very bad dream, stay with him for a while talking softly of not much about anything to help soothe away the terror of his nightmare.

In spite of his resistance to separation from you at night, your child will ultimately be going to bed by himself. Few such problems last beyond kindergarten. In any event, don't give him labels such as "Louie is a light sleeper" that he can act out indefinitely.

Afternoon Separation

Four-year-old Donald has given up napping. When three-year-old brother observes this, he battles furiously at the discrimination he isn't mature enough to understand. If your daily efforts to keep younger brother napping are without success, it's wise to give up. Sleep is not one of his needs that you can control. A daily battle of wills between you and your child when attitudes toward life are being shaped can have long-lasting effects. Usually, it is mother who most needs the rest.

A quiet time may be substituted for the abandoned naps. During this time, the child rests quietly in his own room, listens to soft music, plays quiet solitary games, colors, looks at his picture books, and the like. Often he will drop off to sleep during these periods.

CLOTHING PROBLEMS

He Wears Only One Outfit

When you take off five-year-old Tommy's trousers, they look as though he were still in them. You can almost stand them up in the corner.

If your child refuses to wear anything except one or two familiar pieces of clothing, let him. Save your battles for more important things. Time broadens his clothing preferences.

When most of his old favorites are outgrown, he'll go on a shopping trip.

Choose a variety of items that meet the qualifications you feel are important for wear and comfort. Let him make the final selections. If you want him to wear them, be sure that he is happy with the feel, color, fit, and texture. A child in the habit of wearing the same things feels uncomfortable in anything new. It seems at first as strange as a new home. He may complain that his trousers are too stiff, the seams too scratchy, the waist too big, or the legs too long. Keep your good humor. In spite of his early resistance, he probably will be wearing an appropriate selection of clothing later.

A daughter may be more agreeable about clothing. Getting her to save certain clothing for a special occasion may be as difficult as getting brother into his. Clothing appropriate for any occasion seems the best answer. Party outfits and dress-up clothes are often outgrown before they are outworn.

Dressing for a Special Occasion

Forcing a rebelling child into dress-up clothes may not be worth the trouble. Even should you succeed in getting him into the new clothes, watch how fast he can get out of them!

"What will people think?" was the plea past generations often used to get children dressed appropriately. They were unaware of the self-consciousness it could produce. Influencing a child to perceive others as his most important judges, just to get him dressed, is hardly desirable. In the formative years, building inner self-esteem is more important than outer appearance. For that special occasion try the following techniques for getting him dressed:

Select his outfit a day in advance.

Hang it in the kitchen or family room where he can see it as he plays. This gives him time to get used to the idea. Don't discuss it unless he asks. Point out its attractive

features. Ignore threats that he is not going to wear it. If
he demands a reply, say only, "I heard you."

When it's time, announce the various getting-ready preparations: bathing, teeth-brushing, putting on clothes, hair-
combing, and departure time.

If resistance occurs, say, "I know how you feel, but you can't
wear your around-the-house clothes to this party. Wait
until you see how handsome you look."

Periodically let him know how much time remains. Allow for
last-minute bargaining if nothing short of an all-out
battle will get him into his clothes.

Have on hand acceptable substitutes in case your first selection is completely rejected.

Compromise. He may wear the shirt but not the pants.

He can wear his old shoes but he must take the new ones
along. He can put them on in the car before getting out.

If success is finally achieved, guard against comments such as
"Well, you finally made it. It took you long enough." Tell him
instead how nice he looks. You'll find future occasions not so
difficult to manage.

BATHING PROBLEMS

Bathtime

Have you ever tried to force a screaming, fighting, kicking child
to take a bath? It can't be done without damaging consequences. The strong-willed child will redouble his resistance.
The ensuing battle reinforces unpleasant feelings that can become a continuing source of repeated conflict.

At other times, bathing can be such fun that Junior wants to bathe two or three times a day. You are wise not to overreact to either extreme, as such fluctuations usually do not last.

A youngster's concern about cleanliness doesn't usually begin until early adolescence. Until then, you may need to content yourself with giving reminders and playing bathtime games with little ones. When your best efforts fail, forget it until another day. If he tells you, "I'm not going to take baths anymore," you have time to plan ahead, to make his next bath a more interesting occasion.

Resistance to bathing may also arise as a result of fear. A child's vivid imagination can trigger fears difficult to comprehend.

Evelyn (four), unable to see the bottom of the tub because of baking soda mother has added to ease the discomfort of a rash, imagines alligators in the water. Her visualization is so vivid and frightening that nothing entices her back to tub bathing. For many weeks, other facilities are used: the shower, the kitchen sink, the laundry sink. When the bath is again approachable, only a small amount of water is accepted. She wants to see the bottom clearly. A collection of household gadgets to play the game "What's under the washcloth?" helps reduce her anxiety. The incident is forgotten by the time she is in kindergarten.

Hand-Washing

Make small talk as you carry your resisting child to the bathroom. Talk in a soothing, friendly tone of voice, but don't mention hand-washing as such. With a resisting child, the mere mention of the word may increase his opposition. As he dips his hands into the water, make a game with the slippery soap. Call attention to its color and scent and to the rainbow bubbles that float on the water. For the older child, use hand-washing as a signal that lunch is ready. "Wash your hands. It's time for lunch."

Face-Washing

Face-washing is particularly disliked by children, perhaps because we mention it so much. We can't seem to resist remarking about a child's dirty face. Our child comes happily in from play eager to see us and we forget even to greet him, saying instead, "Oh, look at your dirty face." It must head the list of our most frequently used comments.

Then, too, we go at the job with much vigor and little hesitation. Children's discomfort is more understandable when we visualize ourselves being led regularly to the bathroom for a thorough scrubbing, especially when we are fatigued, sleepy, or particularly interested in an unfinished activity.

If you have a thoroughly disgruntled child, teaching him to wash his own face may reduce his resistance:

> Let him experiment first on sister's doll. Applying soap, rinsing the washcloth, wringing out the water, and removing the soap are easier to do for dolly than for himself.
>
> If he's afraid of the soap, let him use water only for a while.
>
> Give him a small washcloth. It's easier for small hands to grasp and twist.
>
> Use face-washing as a prerequisite for something more pleasant. "If you hurry and wash your face, you can come to the market with me."

MEALTIME PROBLEMS

Firstborn children may be the fussiest eaters, perhaps because we worry more about their behavior. As we discover that children survive in spite of food resistances, we become more relaxed with each succeeding infant. Food problems arise out of our excessive concern, impatience, and pressure. If we force, worry, bribe, coax, punish, or ridicule at the table, we must expect unpleasant feelings to become associated with food. Anything unpleasant occurring at the same time food is served tends to take the fun out of eating. Just being regularly ignored at the table is enough to keep some children from wanting to show up for dinner.

Refusing to Eat

Understand his reasons. All children have days when they don't feel like eating. Appetites return to normal if we don't coax and worry too much. As with all of us, a number of conditions may affect our desire to eat. For example:

He may be too sleepy or tired.

Worry, upset, and friction over naptime, toilet training, or even nursery school may be interfering with his appetite. Eating is one task parents can't make him do.

Curiosity about a new toy, excitement about a trip, or any intense stimulation reduces appetite.

One good meal a day, or two very small ones, may be all that some children need.

He may not be hungry at the same time every day. He may be hungry at three o'clock rather than twelve noon. How hard he plays or how much he ate at his last meal has much to do with how soon he is hungry again.

Whether the parent is relaxed or tense and rushed affects him. A five-year-old may push his food aside if mother is in a hurry to get him off to kindergarten on time.

Young children stop eating, sometimes for extended periods, during and after illness. Our pressure at such times is often the beginning of food problems.

If older children eat and leave the table quickly, younger children want to do the same.

The preschooler may copy the likes and dislikes he hears older brothers and sisters expressing about food.

Parental pressure can make food seem more like punishment than pleasure. Note how often you say, "Eat your food," "Sit up straight," "Say please," "Wipe your mouth," "Don't be so slow," "Keep your mouth closed when you chew," "Use your napkin." He feels under constant scrutiny.

KEEP MEALTIME PLEASANT

Be relaxed and have fun. Mealtime is the principal occasion for all family members to be together. It can be a very special time. Emotionally healthy children are likely to come from families that communicate collectively around the dinner table (Westley and Epstein, 1969). Mealtime is a great opportunity for the development of self-expression through word games and conversation. Although it may be difficult at first to avoid dominating the conversation with your own interests, children are happier when included. Let each child have his chance to shine and tell the family what he found most interesting and enjoyable about his day. We can reserve for coffeetime later our adult talk about subjects of minimum interest to children.

Keep your cool. Don't let food spills put mealtime out of commission. It is unfair to humiliate a child for poor coordination, for being naturally awkward. He is not clumsy on purpose. We have all experienced the unease and chill that anger can put on mealtime. If we are too easily upset, our child is deprived of participation in the pleasant, free-and-easy exchanges of a happy environment.

Don't make an issue of what he eats. Take no obvious notice of what your preschooler eats. If his diet appears unbalanced, offer him appropriate food later. The middle of the morning, the middle of the afternoon, or just before bedtime are opportune for reordering his diet. Thus your family's dining remains free of the unpleasant associations that result from excessive coaxing. Anyway, four or five small meals may be a better arrangement for some children until they are older.

Polish up manners some other time. Instruction in table manners should be given considerably before or after dinner, when food is not being served. Bring up your special concerns then, one or two at a time. Trust that what is not learned immediately will come with practice and your example. Within limits, what the neighbors or relatives think is not so important as the positive attitudes you want your child to have toward food.

Give him more. When youngsters ask for "more" of the foods they especially like, such as desserts, prevent a contest of wills by giving them more, in small portions. A teaspoonful at each request keeps mealtime an occasion to be looked forward to. When three-year-old Carol screams for dessert before dinner, tell her, "I understand how good the cake seems to you right now, but dessert comes after dinner. Have a taste. We'll put your piece here until dessert time."

Add variety. You can do much toward helping your child become interested in food by the approach you take. Children cooperate with parents who give them considerable freedom and make things interesting.

Let little ones make their own lunchtime sandwiches. Prepare the ingredients ahead of time and attractively arrange them on small plates.

Get a step stool for the kitchen. Let children help themselves to certain foods when they are hungry. The mother who guards too closely her refrigerator and grocery shelves makes food appear unpleasant.

Let children help and taste while food is being prepared. A spoonful in a small bowl does not destroy their appetites.

Try serving meals family style. You'll be surprised at how much children like to serve themselves.

Occasionally let your child choose items to be on the dinner menu.

Don't serve his meal on the same plate every day. Look for variety in pattern and design in plates, cups, place mats, and napkins.

Serve at least one food that you know he likes at each meal. Post a list of each child's food preferences for your easy reference.

At breakfast, let him pour the milk on his cereal from his own individual pitcher.

Let children eat in front of the TV occasionally. Old mattress pads make good tablecloths for the floor and can be washed easily. Low wooden foot stools make the right size tables.

Have lunch in the yard or the park. Sometimes a party on play dishes makes an interesting change.

Enjoy conversation at the table longer if it encourages the slow eater to finish.

Eating out builds new food tastes. Served in a new setting, food takes on more interest appeal.

Arrive at the restaurant ahead of the dinner-hour rush. When possible, phone your order in early so that it's ready when you arrive.

Have all food and liquids served at the same time. Otherwise, young children fill themselves on ice water, rolls, and crackers before the dinner is on the table.

A bag of washable toys helps keep the high-chair-age youngster contented. When one drops on the floor, replace it with another.

Take turns walking the child who can't stay seated until others are finished with their meal.

The infant who resists food may eat if intellectual stimulation is provided. Collect a box of noninjurious washable toys: rattles, rubber beads, squeeze toys, plastic play animals, balls, blocks. From the kitchen find plastic bottles, brushes, jar lids, food strainer, funnel, spools, plastic cups. Sitting in his high chair, he likes to explore the shape, taste, and feel of these fascinating items. Or sit beside him and talk about the pictures in a book while you feed him. He will listen, look, and learn while he eats.

Should these efforts fail, put the food before him and let him eat what he will, as best he can with his fingers. You will find that almost invariably he will give himself a fairly adequate diet within a short time.

Refusing to Eat with the Family

Eight-year-old Roger's indifference to eating at the table with the family is quite an aggravation. He either refuses to eat at all, takes his food elsewhere, or waits until later in the evening to eat.

You feel that he may never join the family for meals, but he will. He may go for some time without joining you, but he eventually will return if mealtimes are happy occasions and it is not more enjoyable elsewhere.

Let him go his way. Continue to set a place for him regularly. Cheerfully invite him to join you. But don't interrupt your own dinner to serve him elsewhere. Regardless of the ruckus he raises, kindly inform him: "We are having our dinner now. We'd like you to join us. If you don't want to, that's all right. I'll be glad to take care of you when I am finished."

If he serves himself and takes his plate elsewhere, let him. Be thankful that he eats. You will have more luck getting him to the table for dessert. Friendly persuasion, without pressure, will ultimately convince him that he should join you. Tell him occasionally, "We miss you," "We'd enjoy having your company." He will want to join in if he observes that others are enjoying themselves and his rebellion has not succeeded in upsetting anyone.

Don't be overconfident when he does return to the table. He may only briefly or periodically join you, testing the situation to see how he feels about it before getting back to the routine of eating most of his meals with you. Don't force him to stay or call undue attention to his return or absence. Welcome him with a smile when he returns and continue the meal as usual.

It's difficult to judge the depth of his rebellion, or even whether it is rebellion, or a feeling of being unneeded or unwanted. Occasionally, it can be tested without serious consequences. Being very firm may gain cooperation. It is worth a try sometimes to tell him, "You are having dinner at the table with us. We want you with the family. Here is your place." If a power struggle is obviously in the making, be willing to accept defeat. You can't tie him to his chair. Conformity is not particularly desirable if it means more unpleasant feelings about food.

Keeping Your Child Well-Nourished

There are various ways for you to make sure that your child is getting adequate nourishment. Some of these may be useful:

> Meat not eaten at mealtime makes a convenient between-meal snack. Children enjoy cold beef or chicken sliced in strips that can be picked up in the fingers and dabbed into a spoonful of mayonnaise.
>
> Season cooked and drained vegetables or noodles with chicken bouillon.
>
> Lightly sweeten and butter peas to make them more appealing.
>
> Omit the table salt and season hamburger with beef bouillon.
>
> Use bread sliced extra thin. Reduce the size of hamburger buns by removing a thin slice from the center. A child eats more of his sandwich when it is not so large.
>
> Serve drinks in five-ounce glasses. Children then do not fill up on fluids rather than food. Give them plenty to drink between meals.

Serve vegetables raw as between-meal snacks. Potatoes, carrots, celery, cauliflower, and turnips are just as good uncooked.

Occasionally serve meat and vegetables only. Skip starches, which quickly fill a child.

Use skimmed milk. It contains more protein than the same amount of whole milk. Give him the butterfat he would ordinarily get in his milk on his vegetables.

Limit sweets by serving ice cream, puddings, and other desserts in small custard bowls.

Let children eat green salads before dinner. This tides them over until dinner is on the table. The salad gets eaten when it may ordinarily remain untouched on the table.

Let the preschooler who is a problem eater keep his bottle. We do not agree that you can starve a child into eating. A bottle at bedtime or in the middle of the afternoon doesn't interfere with meals, and it may be your only means of getting nourishment into some children.

BOTTLES

All mammals except man nurse their young until they can find food for themselves. A child not forced to give up his bottle will try out for himself various stages of independence from it. There is no evidence to support its discontinuance at any particular time. In fact, its limited use has a number of advantages about which you might like to know:

The bottle soothes the distressed child. Along with his blanket, it is one of his first substitutes for mother and provides much comfort and solace.

An ill child will take liquids from a bottle when he will reject liquid from a cup or food from a plate.

The bottle is convenient for traveling. Today's family spends a great deal of time in the automobile. It's a lot easier to drink from a bottle in a moving car than from a cup.

An irritable, hungry, or tired child often refuses to eat and falls asleep hungry. Although sleepy and tired, he'll drink from his bottle. The milk is often satisfying enough to let him sleep undisturbed, preventing a nighttime feeding problem and interruption of the parents' sleep.

A bedtime bottle is comforting and sleep-inducing.

It gets extra food into the problem eater, and it doesn't interfere with meals if solid foods are ready when a child is hungry.

SECURITY BLANKETS

Blankets and bottles, possessions children often cling to most determinedly, seem to be the very things parents most want to be rid of. If children need them so desperately, they must serve a purpose. Adults find security in the favorite old jacket or dress they hate to give away, in the particular chair they wish always available, in the cup of coffee they cannot do without. We would be much distressed to learn that we must give up these pleasures.

His blanket (or a favorite cuddle toy) is probably a child's first substitute for mother, representing both the comfort and the security that mother may not always conveniently supply. The average mother ordinarily cannot supply the great amount of comfort needed. Civilization has made her less convenient. His blanket becomes her substitute. It appears to ease the transition from strong infant attachment to mother to independence.

You may have noticed that your child is more content to go to bed alone when his blanket is available. It comforts him when he is lonesome, unhappy, tired, ill, hungry, or bored. When he is unhappy, the blanket is frequently sought out in preference to mother. It gives quiet solace whereas mother might try to talk him out of his unhappiness. When he is drawn simultaneously to mother's comfort and a wish for independent play, he often settles his problem by using the blanket, which is more maneuverable than mother. While he plays with his blocks with one hand, he conveniently comforts himself with his blanket with the other.

The fragmented remains of the blanket may be lost and retrieved many times. When it is lost, the child may be unconsolable. Perhaps a few rules for its use may make it more acceptable to parents who are bothered by his great need for it:

It should not be dragged on the floor.

It should be washed once a week.

It should not be permitted outside the house except when the family is making an overnight stay away from home.

THUMBS

Like blankets and bottles, thumbs also provide comfort. A bored, unhappy, tired, lonesome, or sleepy child may put his thumb in his mouth. There is a great deal of concern that this will affect the shape of his teeth or jaw. Heredity is believed to have a greater effect. The way in which the thumb is sucked may also make a difference. Some children apply pressure upward. Others who suck fingers instead of thumbs may apply pressure to the lower teeth and tongue.

If you want to reduce sucking, insist that he wash his hands before putting his fingers in his mouth. It helps him learn to postpone sucking until washing is convenient. Appealing to his maturity is sometimes helpful: "Now that you are older, you will want to practice getting along without your thumb more of the time." Requesting that he do his thumb-sucking in his room may limit the activity even further.

By elementary school age most children begin to cooperate with parents in trying to reduce sucking. In any case, it is best if parents don't overreact. If it really troubles you, your dentist may be able to help.

TOILET TRAINING

Children enjoy acquiring bowel and bladder control if they are not rushed or pressured and are given sufficient praise. Unfortunately, just knowing this is not enough. Parents need more precise information than has been generally available. The following suggestions may make this task easier.

First of all, don't use potty chairs with arms. Such chairs resemble those seen in living rooms. Children are fearful of restraint. Chairs with arms and straps give them a hemmed-in feeling. A child's potty chair should resemble the one he has seen his parents use. It should permit his feet to rest firmly on the floor so that he may get on and off as he pleases.

Place the chair in the bathroom months before you expect him to use it. Don't mention its purpose. Let him discover that. Later, when he displays sufficient interest, you may point out that it is his, just like mommy's and daddy's. He will first use it as a seat. When it is evidently a familiar part of his life, you will be more successful in your efforts to explain what he is to do with it. Training usually begins sometime in the child's second year, when he is dry upon waking in the morning or after his nap. Make your training program an hour a day planned activity for perhaps two or three weeks.

Don't race to the bathroom. Take him in an unhurried, quiet way.

Unpin his diapers and sit with him. Reading or looking at pictures keeps him seated a few minutes longer. Don't force him to remain. Stay only as long as he will sit.

If nothing happens, pin him back together and set the alarm for another try in ten minutes. Don't plan to accomplish much else during this hour except taking him back and forth to the bathroom, until you either catch it or you don't.

His first success usually will be accidental. It will be your enthusiastic approval that helps him discover what it is that he is supposed to be doing. Later, he will start waiting for your approval, letting you know when he needs to go to the bathroom.

Sometimes your child has a natural rhythm that you can observe. Time your trials to coincide with these rhythms.

Temporarily move the potty chair into the kitchen or family room if it makes these timed trials easier.

Don't pass over his accomplishment quickly. Your child has

done something you wanted. Let him know you appreciate it.

Don't be disappointed if you don't succeed. Tomorrow is another day. Give it a few weeks' trial. If there are no results, try again at a later date.

It takes time for him to learn a completely new way of behaving. When you start having fairly consistent success during your trial periods, you may want to give him an opportunity to try at other times during the day. He will begin to enjoy the comfort of being dry if he hasn't built up anxiety over the disappointments that his failures have caused you. Parental impatience to be done with this distasteful task is a major cause of toilet-training problems.

TEN

Some Health and First-Aid Concerns

HEALTH FEARS

Parental attempts to worry a child into conformity often are successful in unwanted ways. Regular and frequent warnings about failing to wear hats, getting chilled, being wet, staying up late, falling, and getting dirty may make him oversensitive.

If you don't eat, you'll be ill.
Don't eat the dirty candy; it will make you sick.
You will fall and hurt yourself.
You will get an earache if you don't wear your hat.
You always get sick when you play in water.
You need your sleep to stay healthy.
You will get sunstroke.

How else can we handle the situation? We can remove him from unsafe situations and put necessary clothing on him without such comments. We can give instructions rather than explanations.

Eat your lunch.
Don't eat candy that falls on the floor. I will give you another piece.
Our rule is no walking on fences.
Put your hat on. It is cold outside.
On with your coat if you are going out to play.
Time to come out of the water now.
Ten more minutes until bedtime.
You've been in the sun long enough.

If you are troubled about your child's health, take precautions that will reduce your worries. Children readily adopt health habits that are a required part of their daily routine. It's a good idea for every family to take a few safety precautions. A few family health rules such as the following will have beneficial results:

Wash hands before eating.
Wash hands after going to the bathroom.
Wash hands before handling or preparing food.
Wash hands upon arriving home from school, grocery, parks, theater, visiting friends, or any public place.
Check little friends who arrive. Colds and flu can be reduced significantly if runny noses are not allowed to stay and play.
Take soapy washcloths along on outings away from home.

From the varied bits of health information given to them, children sometimes arrive at worrisome conclusions. Complaints and symptoms are practically sure to increase when they begin to study health in the fourth and fifth grades. Concern often is aroused in them when they hear parts of family conversations about deaths, illnesses, or tragedies.

When a child is worried about his physical condition, investigate his complaints. Be reassuring about his health and strength and about his body's ability to repair itself.

Gardner sees health fears as probably being arrived at in the following way: "He acquires a conception of the possibilities of harm, but his experience is too limited to give him an idea of the probabilities" (1970, p. 50). Moreover, the news media are not particularly helpful. Only the unfortunate makes interesting reading or viewing. Thus they do not offer a similarly vivid picture of those unafflicted.

When his concern for his body is great, parents may point out:

Sometimes we exercise muscles that are not frequently used. These may be sore for a day or two.

The pains in our limbs when we are young are often called growing pains. We go to the doctor when they do not go away.

The body is a remarkable machine. It repairs, without much assistance, the many cuts and bruises we get.

The doctor's report of your examination indicates that you are in excellent health and a very strong little boy (or girl).

People live a long, long time before growing old. It is so far away we just don't worry about getting there.

HOSPITALIZATION

Hospitalization can be a severely traumatic experience. Knowing something about it can reduce his anxiety and yours, too. It is natural for unknown surroundings and strange people to cause children concern. They often fear even experiences likely to be pleasurable simply because they are strange. The anticipation of pain produces much greater anxiety and fear. Hospitalization usually involves pain. And it confronts the child with unpleasant medical treatments, unfamiliar diagnostic procedures, and separation from the family, any one of which can arouse anxiety and fear.

Emotional health is important. Properly preparing your child for a hospital stay reduces the possibility of long-lasting fears. "If a normal person is given accurate prior warning of impending pain and discomfort, together with sufficient reassurances so that fear does not mount to a very high level, he will be less likely to develop acute emotional disturbance than a person who is not warned" (Janis, 1969, p. 313).

Delayed notification reduces anxiety for some children. Does a child really need to know of his planned hospitalization three weeks in advance? Depending upon the child, three or four days may be sufficient. Most important is providing "closure." Help him become familiar with what is going to happen.

Make a visit to the hospital. Let him see:
The nightgown that ties in the back.
The beds that crank up and down.
The food that comes on trays.
The button that brings the nurse, should he need her.

Talk to him about:
Why the hospitalization is necessary.
How long he will be there.
How long the parents will be with him.
When the parents plan to leave and return.
Other children who might be in the room with him.
The medication that will relieve his discomfort and help him get well fast.
The favorite toy or blanket that will accompany him.

Give him something to anticipate upon his return home. That new toy he has always wanted may make it all seem worthwhile.
Have sleep induced in the hospital room before he leaves his parents for surgery. This is less frightening than being wheeled away on a stretcher and put to sleep by strangers in a strange operating room. Being strapped to an operating table while awake is especially traumatic.
Be there when he awakens and is returned to his room.
The father or mother who can remain calm and not overly

solicitous should remain with their preschooler during his hospital stay, even with an older child if he desires it. Adults too are comforted by the presence of a friend in a difficult situation. Staying overnight should be your prerogative. It is especially important for the child who is unaccustomed to being away from his parents. This may be a time when he needs you most. When you know that you can be of comfort to your child, you should not accept any other alternative. If a bed or chair is not available for you, take your own fold-up chair or cot. It can help insure that a hospital experience is not overly traumatic for your child. Of course, there are exceptions. There may be children who are better off when a parent is not there.

When he gets home, encourage him to talk about his experience. This helps prevent the repression of anything particularly frightening. No matter how well-prepared he was, there is generally a certain amount of reaction he needs to work out.

CUTS, ABRASIONS, SPLINTERS

We tend to be provoked by the apparent stupidity resulting in his fall off a swing, the shutting of a door on his fingers. Some children seem to manage to hurt themselves while sitting absolutely still. We usually can't resist commenting:

Why can't you watch where you are going?
That's certainly nothing to cry about.

I told you not to do that.
That didn't hurt bad enough for you to make all this fuss.
A big girl like you shouldn't be so scared.

The child with the bleeding toe cries for mother because he knows that her presence relieves his fear and comforts him. We should not humiliate him because of his need for sympathy. When we belittle feelings that may appear exaggerated to us, we put distance between our children and ourselves. Without an "I told you so," let him cry out his hurt. An injury is quite a strong lesson in itself. What seems like a small hurt to us may seem enormous to him. Being able to reach out for our love and sympathy with his smaller problems, he will feel confident to bring his larger ones to us. Tell him:

I'm right here to help you.
I know how it must hurt. I've done that too.
Cry it out if it helps you to feel better.
You'll be all right soon.
I realize how annoying it must be, but it's not dangerous.

Sometimes it's not the bleeding toe they cry about. They may cry because they are disappointed in themselves, or disappointed with a world that goes suddenly awry when everything had been so lovely, or embarrassed by their recurrent clumsiness, or humiliated that they can't even run without falling down. Swift and cheerful reassurance and a certain nonchalance can ease their heartache and often prevent heartbroken crying. Setbacks then become just one of those things that crop up off and on and do not signal the end of the world.

Psychological First-Aid

Caring for the physical injuries of our child can't be accomplished without his cooperation, and often he is unwilling to give it. The following suggestions, not ordinarily found in a first-aid manual, may help ease your problem:

Six-year-old Christopher, who refuses to have the dirt washed from his scraped knee, may be willing to soak some of it off in a warm bath.

Eight-year-old Jimmy can learn to take out many of his own splinters. Use of needle, tweezers, and antiseptic are easily demonstrated. A warm bath calms him and may aid in the removal.

"Take it off" screams five-year-old Louis, who believes that the medication you applied is making his injury hurt more. The function of antiseptics is often difficult to get across to the small child. It's best to try to warn him in advance that, although the medication aids healing, it does not stop the hurt or make it worse.

Cut away much of the adhesive on Band-Aids before application. It makes removal from hairy arms and legs less painful. Soaking in warm water also aids in removal.

Let the fearful youngster apply his own local medication. If he fears the strange appearance, texture, and odor, transfer it to a cup or other familiar container. Describe its characteristics as being similar in sight or feel to something he is familiar with: Vaseline, paste, or milk. Of course, caution him not to drink or taste it.

Medication warmed to skin temperature is not so noticeable when applied. It can go on even during sleep.

In recent years, medical science supports the applying of cold to burns. The pain of a burned finger is relieved immediately when immersed in a cup of ice water.

ORAL MEDICATION

Colds and infections occur so frequently that mothers and young children often become oversensitive to the every three hour bottle-and-spoon routine. It is a chore—for both mother and child. There is not much one can do except find a way to make unpleasant medicine easier to tolerate or combine it with a more pleasant experience. Have you tried the following?

> Follow up each dosage with the reward of a cookie, ice cream, or maybe even a piece of his favorite candy.
> A pill in a spoonful of jelly, followed by a drink of juice may make the medicine go down.
> If he still uses the bottle, he may drink the medicine in a small amount of juice.
> Disguise the medicine in cola or root beer. It is not as noticeable in these drinks as in his familiar juice.

Whatever you do, don't force it down. He will resist harder on succeeding occasions. Usually, you get more all over the child than into him. Ask the doctor for a medication the child is less likely to fight. Be aware that he may not know you have a problem.

Sometimes children are upset by taking medicine because they have the feeling this is going to go on forever, unless they do something about it. If you suspect this has happened, tell your youngster how many times this pill or medication will be necessary and check the times off together. This can be profoundly reassuring to both of you. Tell him too, of course, that this will help him get all well and strong again, real soon. You know this, but he doesn't. He may even fancy that the medicine is a punishment for being sick. Children do not know much about the world. They are new here.

DENTISTS

In the sensitive and formative preschool years, dental experiences should not be taken lightly. A preschooler has enough to handle in merely coping with the everyday frustrations of his environment and his ineptitude. For some youngsters, the trauma of a dental appointment can create fears far more serious than any ordinary problem with the enamel on his baby teeth. Adults have forgotten how strange the scene and the odors of a dentist's office seem, including the chair, equipment, and tools being used. A feeling of being trapped is quite likely for a child when he is restrained in a dentist's chair. Anxiety is a common reaction to an unpleasant situation from which one cannot escape. The situation here is made even more fearful for the child if the dentist refuses to permit mother's presence.

Few dentists permit mother past the reception room. How must a child feel when mother is not present at a time when he needs her most? What is the psychological cost to our child when we submit to the authority of a strange dentist? Parents may not realize that the same security they receive when their spouse is there to help them through a trying experience is similarly helpful to a child.

The authors of this book examined what appeared to be the most fear-arousing aspects of the dental treatments received by their children.

Anxiety increased as waiting-time in the reception room increased.

The insertion of the cardboard-covered X-ray film aroused anxiety, and sometimes resistance.

Anxiety increased according to the amount of time the children were left unattended in the dentist's chair between the various dental tasks.

Anxiety bordering on panic occurred for John (three) while waiting for the four-minute fluoride application to set.

Mark (four), who had agreed to receive his fluoride treatment without mother's presence, could be heard screaming as far as the reception room.

Another dentist's angry rebuke, "Hush up, stop that," to four-year-old John's crying, resulted in his absolute refusal to return.

Anne (nine) refused further fluoride treatments after an experience in which she felt that the fluoride was escaping from the containers in her mouth and gagging her.

Parents should consider how really important the various dental treatments are before the age of five or six. With the new fluoride toothpastes, do children need as much early care as in the past? In any case, a parent has a right to remain with the child while he is in the dentist's chair. The parent should insist upon it.

Select a dentist who will permit you to stay with your child on his first visits. Your presence should be agreed upon with the dentist prior to the appointment, and (of course) not in the child's presence.

Question the dentist about his techniques for reducing tension. A limited number of dentists offer the patient a buzzer that can be pressed when he wants the dentist to stop working.

Let your child accompany you on your routine checkups

before being scheduled for his own appointment.

Combine a necessary trip to the dentist with another more pleasant experience, such as a stop at the dime store or the soda fountain.

Encourage children to talk about their experiences with the dentist so that unpleasant feelings (if any) can be worked out.

SAFETY

Crossing Streets

Mothers whose little ones accompany them around the community on various errands have excellent opportunity for teaching street safety. Let your child be your eyes and ears for you. Although you are checking also, let him tell you when it is safe to cross the street. Children enjoy pretending to be grown up. Even toddlers learn to recognize and understand street signs, street lights, and how to cross at unmarked corners. The words "wait" and "walk" become meaningful even before they know the letters that make up the words. By the time your child is ready for school, he can be a good pedestrian. The problem is in remembering to let our child remind us.

Bicycles

Children should not ride bicycles on city streets without first having taken a safe-driving test. Even more than adults, they need to demonstrate their ability to drive safely. Many of the habits and skills they learn as bicyclists will be useful later, when they receive a driver's license. They should know the rules they will have to observe when they get behind the wheel of the family car. A child's knowledge of safe-driving rules is still the responsibility of parents.

In Case of Fire

Why not have a fire drill in the home? More accidents with fire occur in the home than in the school. Parents can demonstrate the proper use of appliances; the use of short sleeves near stove and fireplace; what kind of electrical equipment to keep away from water; how to turn pot handles so that they do not stick out from the stove. On a tour of the home, point out rugs to wrap in or roll on should clothing catch fire. Point out windows and doors that make an easy escape route from a burning home. Discuss ways to escape if trapped in upstairs bedrooms. Teach older children to keep a pail of water or a fire extinguisher nearby when building a fire in the outdoor barbecue. Do they know where the fire extinguisher is kept and how to use it?

Around the age of nine or ten children want to build fires. This need can be satisfied by supervised experience at the barbecue, or on camping trips, or by building fires in the fireplace. At the same time that we teach them how to build and care for a fire, we can teach them how to properly extinguish a fire.

For the child distressingly curious about fires, an hour or two lighting and burning wooden matches over the kitchen sink in his parent's presence may extinguish his obsession. When he begs to stop, he probably has had enough for some time.

IN CONCLUSION

And so, we reach the end of our endeavor to identify guides useful for parents, some perhaps just beginning this most significant effort of their lives. If there is a single, central message in this volume, it is that of trust. We believe that much of the problem of and for children flows from the difficulties that parents have in freeing themselves from their own early learning, which may have been less than desirable. These difficulties are displayed most dramatically in the way parents talk to and about their youngsters.

If the duties and obligations of real friendship come to characterize parent-child relationships—courtesy, respect, responsibility—then the exciting, illuminating, and challenging features of parenthood will more fully benefit the child as he learns about the world for which he is being prepared.

We wish all parents a happy and rewarding child-rearing experience, hopeful that we have helped you understand children a little better.

Bibliography

Adorno, T. W.; Frenkel-Brunswik, Else; Levinson, D. J.; and Sanford, R. N. *The Authoritarian Personality*. New York: Harper & Row, 1950.

Allport, Gordon. *The Person in Psychology*. Boston: Beacon Press, 1968.

Ambrose, Anthony, ed. *Stimulation in Early Infancy*. New York: Academic Press, 1969 (participating psychologists: Hamburg, D. A.; Ainsworth, M. D. S.; Schaffer, H. E.; Kagan, J.; Ginsburg, B. E.; Papousek, H.), pp. 196–201.

Anisfeld, Moshe; Bogo, Norman; and Lambert, Wallace. "Evaluational reactions to accented English speech." *Journal of Abnormal and Social Psychology*, 65, 1962, p. 230.

Anthony, E. James. "On Observing Children." *Foundations of Child Psychiatry*. 1st ed. Edited by Emanuel Miller. Oxford, New York: Pergamon Press, Ltd., 1968, p. 91.

Appel, M. H. "Aggressive behavior of nursery school children and adult procedures in dealing with such behavior." *Journal of Experimental Education*, 11, 1942, pp. 185–199.

Arasteh, A. Reza, and Arasteh, Josephine. *Creativity in the Life Cycle*. Leiden, Netherlands: E. J. Brill, 1968.

Archer, Lois, and Hosley, Eleanor. "Educational Program." *The Therapeutic Nursery School*. Edited by Robert A. Furman and Anny Katan. New York: International Universities Press, Inc., 1969, p. 45.

Arkoff, Abe. *Adjustment and Mental Health*. New York: McGraw-Hill Book Co., 1968, p. 190.

361

Aronfreed, Justin. *Conduct and Conscience.* New York: Academic Press, 1968, pp. 21, 320.

Arsenian, Jean. "Young children in an insecure situation." *Journal of Abnormal and Social Psychology,* 38 (April, 1943), p. 225.

Bach, George, and Wyden, Peter. *The Intimate Enemy.* New York: William Morrow and Company, Inc., 1969.

Bacmeister, Rhoda W. *Growing Together.* New York: D. Appleton-Century Co., Inc. 1947.

Bailey, Roger C. "Self-concept differences in low and high achieving students." *Journal of Clinical Psychology,* 27 (April, 1971), pp. 188–191.

Baldwin, A. L. "Socialization and the parent-child relationship." *Child Development,* 19, 1948, pp. 127–136.

———. "The effect of home environment on nursery school behavior." *Child Development,* 20, 1949, pp. 49–61.

———. *Behavior and Development in Childhood.* New York: Dryden Press, 1955.

Baldwin, James M. *Mental Development in the Child and the Race.* New York: Augustus Kelly Publishers, 1968, p. 342.

Bandura, Albert, and Kupers, C. J. "The transmission of patterns of self-reinforcement through modeling." *Journal of Abnormal and Social Psychology,* 69, 1964, pp. 1–9.

Bandura, Albert, and Walters, Richard. *Adolescent Aggression.* New York: The Ronald Press Co., 1959.

Bandura, Albert; Ross, Dorothea; and Ross, Sheila. "Imitation of film-mediated aggressive models." *Journal of Abnormal and Social Psychology,* 66, 1963, pp. 3–11.

Baruch, Dorothy W. *New Ways in Discipline.* New York: McGraw-Hill Book Co., 1949, p. 14.

Baughman, Earl E., and Welsh, George W. *Personality, A Behavioral Science.* Englewood Cliffs, New Jersey: Prentice-Hall, Inc., 1962.

Baumrind, D. "Child care practice anteceding three patterns of pre-school behavior." *Genetic Psychology Monograph,* 75, 1967, pp. 43–88.

Baumrind, D., and Black, A. E. "Socialization practices associated with dimensions of competence in preschool boys and girls." *Child Development*, 38, 1967, pp. 291–327.

Bayley, N., and Schaefer, E. S. "Correlations of maternal and child behaviors with the development of mental abilities." *Monograph of the Society for Research in Child Development*, 29, No. 6, 1964.

Beadle, Muriel. *A Child's Mind*. New York: Doubleday and Co., Inc., 1970, pp. 59–60.

Beck, Joan. *How to Raise a Brighter Child*. New York: Trident Press, 1967.

Becker, Ernest. *Angel in Armor*. New York: George Braziller, Inc., 1969, p. 183.

Becker, Wesley C. "Consequences of different kinds of parental discipline." *Review of Child Development Research*. Vol. I. Edited by M. L. Hoffman and Lois Hoffman. New York: Russell Sage Foundation, 1964, p. 169.

Becker, Wesley C., et al. "Relations of factors derived from parent-interview ratings to behavior problems of five-year-olds." *Child Development*, 33, 1962, pp. 509–535.

Benedict, Agnes, and Franklin, Adele. *Your Best Friends Are Your Children*. New York: Appleton-Century-Crofts, Inc., 1951.

Bennet, E. A. *What Jung Really Said*. New York: Schocken Books, 1967.

Bergman, Rita E., ed. *Children's Behavior*. New York: Exposition Press, 1968.

Berkowitz, Leonard. *The Development of Motives and Values in the Child*. New York: Basic Books, Inc., 1964, pp. 40, 41.

Bernhardt, Karl S. *Discipline and Child Guidance*. New York: Mc-Graw-Hill Book Co., 1964.

———. *Being a Parent: Unchanging Values in a Changing World*. Edited by David K. Bernhardt. Toronto: University of Toronto Press, 1970, p. 5.

Bettelheim, Bruno. *Love Is Not Enough*. New York: Free Press, 1950, pp. 27, 105.

———. *Truants from Life*. New York: Free Press, 1955.

———. *Dialogues with Mothers.* New York: Free Press, 1962, p. 203.

———. *The Empty Fortress.* New York: Free Press, 1967, pp. 15, 19, 25.

———. *Children of the Dream.* Toronto: Collier-Macmillan Ltd., 1969.

Beverly, Bert I. *In Defense of Children.* New York: John Day Co., 1941, p. 108.

Beyer, Evelyn. *Teaching Young Children.* New York: Western Publishing Co., 1968.

Bijou, Sidney, and Baer, Donald. *Child Development.* New York: Appleton-Century-Crofts, Inc., 1961.

Bing, Elizabeth. "Effects of child-rearing practices on development of differential cognitive abilities." *Child Development,* 34, 1963, pp. 631–648.

Black, Sister Kathleen M. "An existential model of psychiatric nursing." *Perspectives in Psychiatric Care,* 6, No. 4 (July–August, 1968), p. 178.

Blatz, W. E. *Human Security.* Toronto: University of Toronto Press, 1966.

Bloom, B. S. *Stability and Change in Human Characteristics.* New York: John Wiley and Sons, Inc., 1964.

Bonham, Marilyn. *The Laughter and Tears of Children.* New York: Macmillan Co., 1968.

Bower, T. G. R. "The visual world of infants." *Scientific American,* 215, December, 1966, pp. 80–97.

Bowlby, John. "Childhood mourning and its implications for psychiatry." *The American Journal of Psychiatry,* 118, 1961, pp. 481–497.

———. *Attachment and Loss.* London: Hogarth Press, 1969, p. 357.

———. "Security and Anxiety." *The Formative Years.* Edited by David Edge. New York: Schocken Books, 1970, p. 23.

Bradburn, N. M. "N achievement and father dominance in Turkey." *Journal of Abnormal and Social Psychology,* 67, 1963, pp. 464–468.

Bradbury, Dorothy, and Amidon, Edna. *Learning to Care for Children.* New York: D. Appleton-Century Co., Inc., 1943.

Brammer, Lawrence M., and Shostrom, Everett L. *Therapeutic Psychology*. Englewood Cliffs, New Jersey: Prentice-Hall, Inc., 1968, pp. 202, 203.

Bricklin, Barry, and Bricklin, Pat. *Strong Family Strong Child*. New York: Delacorte Press, 1970.

Briggs, Dorothy. *Your Child's Self-Esteem*. New York: Doubleday and Co., Inc., 1970, pp. 237, 238.

Bronfenbrenner, Urie. *Two Worlds of Childhood*. New York: Russell Sage Foundation, 1970, p. 102.

Brown, P., and Elliott, Roger. "Control of aggression in a nursery school class." *Journal of Experimental Child Psychology*, 2, 1965, pp. 103–107.

Burnett, Dorothy K. *Your Preschool Child*. New York: Holt, Rinehart, and Winston, 1961.

Burton, Linda. *Vulnerable Children*. New York: Schocken Books, 1968.

Button, Alan DeWitt. *The Authentic Child*. New York: Random House, 1969.

Byrne, Donn. *An Introduction to Personality*. Englewood Cliffs, New Jersey: Prentice-Hall, Inc., 1966.

Chandler, Caroline A.; Lowrie, Reginald; and Peters, Anne. *Early Child Care*. New York: Atherton Press, 1968.

Chapman, A. H. *Management of Emotional Problems of Children and Adolescents*. Philadelphia: J. B. Lippincott Co., 1965.

————. *Put Offs and Come Ons*. New York: G. P. Putnam's Sons, 1968.

Chess, Stella; Thomas, Alexander; and Birch, Herbert. *Your Child Is a Person*. New York: Viking Press, 1965.

Clarke, Paul A. *Child-Adolescent Psychology*. Columbus, Ohio: Charles E. Merrill Publishing Company, 1968.

Cobb, Stanwood. *The Importance of Creativity*. Metuchen, New Jersey: The Scarecrow Press, Inc., 1967, p. 132.

Coffman, Judith Ann. "Anger." *Perspectives in Psychiatric Care*, 7, No. 3 (May–June, 1969), p. 104.

Combs, Arthur, and Snygg, Donald. *Individual Behavior*. New York: Harper & Bros., 1959.

Coopersmith, Stanley. *The Antecedents of Self-esteem.* San Francisco: W. H. Freeman and Company, 1967.

――――. Personal communication, January 12, 1973.

Cox, Frank. *Psychology.* Dubuque, Iowa: Wm. C. Brown Co. Publishers, 1970, p. 46.

Crandall, V. C.; Katkovsky, W.; and Crandall, V. J. "Children's beliefs in their own control of reinforcement in intellectual-academic achievement situations." *Child Development,* 36, 1965, pp. 92–109.

Crandall, V. J.; Preston, A.; and Rabson, Alice. "Maternal reactions and the development of independence and achievement behavior in young children." *Child Development,* 31, 1960, pp. 243–251.

Cranford, Peter G. *Disciplining Your Child.* Englewood Cliffs, New Jersey: Prentice-Hall, 1963.

Cratty, Bryant. *Movement Behavior and Motor Learning.* 2nd ed. Philadelphia: Lea and Febiger, 1967.

――――. *Social Dimensions of Physical Activity.* Englewood Cliffs, New Jersey: Prentice-Hall, Inc., 1967.

――――. *Psychology and Physical Activity.* Englewood Cliffs, New Jersey: Prentice-Hall, Inc., 1968, pp. 18, 19, 40, 41, 56, 63, 65.

Crile, George, Jr. *Naturalistic View of Man.* New York: The World Publishing Company, 1969, p. 13.

Dallett, Kent. *Problems of Psychology.* New York: John Wiley and Sons, Inc., 1969.

Daniels, Marvin. "Pathological vindictiveness and the vindictive character." *The Psychoanalytic Review,* 56, 1969, p. 182.

David, Myriam, and Appell, Genevieve. "Mother-child interaction and its impact on the child." *Stimulation in Early Infancy.* Edited by Anthony Ambrose. New York: Academic Press, 1969, p. 183.

Davidson, H., and Long, H. "Children's perceptions of their teacher's feelings toward them related to self-perception, school achievement, and behaviour." *Children Growing Up.* Reprinted from John Gabriel. London: University of London Press, Ltd., 1968, p. 46.

Davis, Carroll. *Room to Grow.* Toronto: University of Toronto Press, 1966.

Denenberg, Victor H. "Different effects of pre- and post-weaning stimulation in rats." *Stimulation in Early Infancy.* Edited by Anthony Ambrose. New York: Academic Press, 1969, pp. 65, 21.

Deutsch, H. *The Psychology of Women.* Vol. I. New York: Grune and Stratton, 1944.

Devereux, Edward C. "The role of the peer group experience in moral development." *Child Psychology.* Vol. IV. Edited by John Hill. Minneapolis: The University of Minnesota Press, 1970, pp. 94–138.

Dinkmeyer, Don C. *Child Development.* Englewood Cliffs, New Jersey: Prentice-Hall, 1965.

Donovan, Frank R. *Raising Your Children.* New York: Thomas Y. Crowell, 1968.

Dreikurs, Rudolf, and Grey, Loren. *Logical Consequences.* New York: Meredith Press, 1968.

Dubos, René. "Environmental determinants of human life." *Environmental Influences.* Edited by David Glass. New York: Rockefeller University Press, 1968, p. 153.

Erikson, Erik H. *Childhood and Society.* New York: W. W. Norton & Company, Inc., 1963, p. 418.

Eron, L.; Walder, L. O.; Torgo, R.; and Lefkowitz, M. M. "The relationship between social class and parental punishment for aggression and of both to an independent measure of child aggression." *Child Development,* 34, 1963, pp. 849–867.

Evans, Ellis, ed. *Children: Readings in Behavior and Development.* New York: Holt, Rinehart, and Winston, Inc., 1968.

Fass, Jerome S. *A Primer for Parents.* New York: Trident Press, 1968.

Ferguson, Lucy Rau. *Personality Development.* Belmont, California: Brooks/Cole, 1970.

Finch, Stuart M. *Fundamentals of Child Psychiatry.* New York: W. W. Norton and Co., Inc., 1960.

Fowler, Harry. *Curiosity and Exploratory Behavior.* New York: The Macmillan Company, 1965.

Fraiberg, Selma H. *The Magic Years.* New York: Charles Scribner's Sons, 1959.

Freeman, Lucy. *The Cry for Love.* New York: The Macmillan Company, 1969, p. 106.

Fremon, Suzanne. *Children and Their Parents*. New York: Harper & Row, 1968.

Freud, Anna. *Normality and Pathology in Childhood*. New York: International Universities Press, Inc., 1965, p. 117.

Freud, Sigmund. *Leonardo da Vinci and a Memory of His Childhood*. Translated by Alan Tyson. New York: W. W. Norton and Co., Inc., 1964, pp. 41–42, 67.

Frey, Sherman H., and Haugen, Earl S. *Readings in Classroom Learning*. New York: American Book Company, 1969.

Fromm, Erich. *The Art of Loving*. New York: Harper & Row, 1956, p. 26.

————. *The Crisis of Psychoanalysis*. New York: Holt, Rinehart and Winston, 1970.

Fromme, Allan. *Our Troubled Selves*. New York: Farrar, Straus, and Giroux, 1967.

Gabriel, John. *Children Growing Up*. London: Unibooks, University of London Press, Ltd., 1968.

Gale, Raymond. *Developmental Behavior*. London: The Macmillan Co., 1969.

Gardner, George E. *The Emerging Personality*. New York: Delacorte Press, 1970, p. 50.

Geber, Marcelle. "The psycho-motor development of African children in the first year and its influences on maternal behavior." *Journal of Social Psychology*, 47, 1958, pp. 185–195.

Giffin, Kim, and Heider, Mary. "The relationship between speech anxiety and the suppression of communication in childhood." *The Psychiatric Quarterly Supplement*, 41, Part 2, 1967, p. 317.

Gillham, Helen L. *Helping Children Accept Themselves and Others*. New York: Teachers College, Columbia University, 1959.

Ginott, Haim G. *Between Parent and Child*. New York: The Macmillan Company, 1965.

————. *Between Parent and Teenager*. New York: The Macmillan Company, 1969, p. 104.

Glass, David C., ed. *Environmental Influences*. New York: Rockefeller University Press, 1968.

Glasser, M. D. *Reality Therapy*. New York: Harper & Row, 1965.

Glidewell, John C. *Parental Attitudes and Child Behavior.* Springfield, Illinois: Charles C. Thomas, Publisher, 1961.

————. "The child at school." *Modern Perspectives in International Child Psychiatry.* Edited by John G. Howells. New York: Brunner/Mazell Publishers, 1971, pp. 736, 737.

Gnagey, William J. *The Psychology of Discipline in the Classroom.* New York: The Macmillan Company, 1968.

Goldfarb, William; Mintz, Irving; and Stroock, Katherine. *A Time to Heal.* New York: International Universities Press, Inc., 1969.

Goodman, David. *Emotional Needs of Children.* New York: Hawthorn Books, Inc., 1959.

Gordon, Ira J., ed. *Human Development.* Chicago: Scott, Foresman and Company, 1965.

Gordon, Thomas. "A theory of healthy relationships and a program of parent effectiveness training." *New Directions in Client-Centered Therapy.* Edited by J. T. Hart and T. M. Tomlinson. Boston: Houghton Mifflin Company, 1970, pp. 408, 420.

————. *Parent Effectiveness Training.* New York: Peter H. Wyden, Inc., 1970, pp. 117, 119, 135.

Grant, Eva H., ed. *Guiding Children as They Grow.* Chicago: National Congress of PTA, 1962.

Groos, K. *The Play of Man.* Translated by E. L. Baldwin. New York: D. Appleton, 1901, pp. 96, 105.

Guerney, Bernard G., Jr. *Psychotherapeutic Agents: New Roles for Nonprofessionals, Parents, and Teachers.* New York: Holt, Rinehart and Winston, Inc., 1969.

Hall, R. V.; Lund, D.; and Jackson, D. "Effects of teacher attention on study behavior." *Journal of Applied Behavioral Analysis,* 1, 1968, pp. 1–12.

Halpern, Howard M. *A Parent's Guide to Child Psychotherapy.* New York: A. S. Barnes and Company, Inc., 1963.

Harlow, Harry F. "Mice, Monkeys, Men, and Motives." *Psychological Review,* 60, 1953, pp. 23–32.

————. "The Nature of Love." *American Psychologist,* 13, 1958, pp. 673–685.

————. "Primary affectional patterns in primates." *American Journal of Orthopsychiatry,* 30, 1960, pp. 682–683.

Harlow, Harry F., and Harlow, M. K. "Social deprivation in monkeys." *Scientific American,* 207, No. 5, November, 1962, pp. 136–146.

——. "Learning to Love." *American Scientist,* 54, 1966, pp. 244–272.

——. "Effects of various mother-infant relationships on rhesus monkey behaviors." *Determinants of Infant Behavior.* Vol. IV. Edited by B. M. Foss. London: Methuen and Co., Ltd., 1969.

Harris, Florence R.; Wolf, Montrose M.; and Baer, Donald M. "Effects of adult social reinforcement on child behavior." *Young Children,* 20, 1964, pp. 8–17.

Harris, Sydney J. "Last to get waited on." *San Francisco Sunday Examiner and Chronicle,* Section B, May 24, 1970, p. 3.

Hartrich, Paulette. *You and Your Child's Health.* New York: Harper & Brothers, Publishers, 1955.

Hauch, Paul A. *The Rational Management of Children.* New York: Libra Publishers, Inc., 1967, p. 21.

Havighurst, R. J. *Human Development and Education.* New York: Longmans, Green and Co., 1953.

Heathers, Glen. "Acquiring dependence and independence: A theoretical orientation." *Journal of Genetic Psychology,* 87, No. 2, 1955, p. 286.

Heinicke, Christoph M., and Westheimer, Ilse J. *Brief Separations.* New York: International Universities Press, Inc., 1965, pp. 162–179, 230–248.

Helper, M. M. "Learning theory and self-concept." *Journal of Abnormal and Social Psychology,* 51, 1955, pp. 184–194.

Hershey, Gerald L., and Lugo, James O. *Living Psychology.* New York: The Macmillan Company, 1970.

Hess, E. H. "Imprinting." *Science,* 130, July, 1959, pp. 133–141.

Hillinger, Charles. "Man trains animals by remote control, hopes to revolutionize human education." *Los Angeles Times.* Part II, September 28, 1971, p. 1.

Hinde, R. A., and Spencer-Booth, Yvette. "Effects of brief separation from mother on rhesus monkeys." *Science,* 173, July 9, 1971, pp. 111–118.

Hodge, Marshall Bryant. *Your Fear of Love*. New York: Doubleday and Company, Inc., 1967, pp. 46–50, 122.

Holt, John. *How Children Learn*. New York: Pitman Publishing Corp. Ltd., 1967, p. 9.

Hymes, James L. *Understanding Your Child*. New York: Prentice-Hall, Inc., 1952, p. 29.

———. *Teaching the Child Under Six*. Columbus, Ohio: Charles E. Merrill Publishing Co., 1968.

Ilg, Frances L., and Ames, Louise Bates. *Parents Ask*. New York: Harper & Brothers, Publishers, 1962.

Jakubczak, Leonard F., and Walters, Richard H. "Suggestibility as dependency behavior." *The Journal of Abnormal and Social Psychology*, 59, 1959, pp. 102–107.

James, Howard. *Children in Trouble*. New York: David McKay Co., Inc., 1970.

Janis, Irving. "When fear is healthy." *Readings in Psychology Today*. Del Mar, California: CRM Books, 1969, p. 313.

Jenkins, Gladys. *Helping Children Reach Their Potential*. Chicago: Scott, Foresman and Company, 1961.

Jersild, Arthur T. *Child Psychology*. Englewood Cliffs, New Jersey: Prentice-Hall, Inc., 1942.

———. *Child Psychology*. 6th ed. Englewood Cliffs, New Jersey: Prentice-Hall, Inc., 1968, p. 376.

Jones, M. B. "Religious values and authoritarian tendency." *Journal of Social Psychology*, 48, 1958, pp. 83–89.

Jones, Molly Mason. *Guiding Your Child from Two to Five*. New York: Harcourt, Brace, and World, Inc., 1967.

Kagan, Jerome. "The child's perception of the parent." *Journal of Abnormal and Social Psychology*, 53, 1956, pp. 257–258.

———. *Personality Development*. New York: Harcourt Brace Jovanovich, Inc., 1971, p. 10.

Kates, S. L. "Suggestibility, submission to parents and peers, and extrapunitiveness, intropunitiveness, and impunitiveness in children." *Journal of Psychology*, 31, 1951, pp. 233–241.

Kaufman, Charles, and Rosenblum, Leonard. "The waning of the mother-infant bond in two species of macaque." *Determinants of Infant Behavior.* Vol. IV. Edited by B. M. Foss. London: Methuen & Co. Ltd., 1969, pp. 41–60.

Kelly, Earl C. "The fully functioning self." *ASCD Yearbook: Perceiving, Behaving, Becoming.* Washington, D.C.: National Education Association, 1962, pp. 9–20.

Kelly, George A. *The Psychology of Personal Constructs.* Vols. I and II. New York: W. W. Norton and Company, Inc., 1955.

Kessen, William, ed. *The Child.* New York: John Wiley and Sons, Inc., 1965.

Klein, Ted. *The Father's Book.* New York: William Morrow and Company, Inc., 1968, p. 270.

Koch, Helen L. "The relationship of certain formal attributes of siblings to attitudes held toward each other and toward their parents." *Monograph of the Society for Research in Child Development,* 25, No. 4, Serial No. 78, 1960.

Korner, Anneliese. *Some Aspects of Hostility in Young Children.* New York: Grune and Stratton, 1949.

Laing, R. D. *Self and Others.* New York: Pantheon Books, 1969, p. 117.

Landau, Elliott; Epstein, Sherrie; and Stone, Ann. *Child Development Through Literature.* Englewood Cliffs, New Jersey: Prentice-Hall, Inc., 1972, p. 154.

Landreth, Catherine. *The Psychology of Early Childhood.* New York: Alfred A. Knopf, 1958.

Larrick, Nancy. *A Parent's Guide to Children's Education.* New York: Pocket Books, 1966.

Lawick-Goodall, Jane van. *In the Shadow of Man.* Boston: Houghton Mifflin Co., 1971.

Lee, Catherine. *The Growth and Development of Children.* London: Longmans, Green & Co., 1969, p. 119.

Levine, Seymour. "Infantile stimulation: a perspective." *Stimulation in Early Infancy.* Edited by Anthony Ambrose. New York: Academic Press, 1969.

Lewin, K. A. *Resolving Social Conflicts.* New York: Harper & Brothers, 1948.

Liebman, Joshua Loth. *Hope for Man.* New York: Simon & Schuster, 1966, pp. 208, 210.

Lipsitt, Lewis, and Reese, Hayne W. *Advances in Child Development*. New York: Academic Press, 1969.

Livingston, Robert B. "Brain is molded by the age of twelve." *San Francisco Chronicle*, December 31, 1968, p. 4.

Longstreteh, Langdon E. *Psychological Development of the Child*. New York: Ronald Press, 1968.

Lovell, K. *An Introduction to Human Development*. New York: The Macmillan Company, 1968.

Lundin, Robert W. *Personality, A Behavioral Approach*. New York: The Macmillan Company, 1969, pp. 73, 267.

Madow, Leo. *Anger*. New York: Charles Scribner's Sons, 1972, p. 115.

Madsen, Charles. "Nurturance and Modeling in Preschoolers." *Child Development*, 39, 1968, p. 221.

Marcia, J. E. "Ego identity status: relationship to change in self-esteem, general maladjustment, and authoritarianism." *Journal of Personality*, 35, 1967, p. 118.

Marshall, H. R. "Relation between home experiences and children's use of language in play interactions with peers." *Psychological Monographs*, 75, 1961, pp. 1–76.

Maslow, Abraham. "A theory of human motivation." *Psychological Review*, 50, 1943, pp. 370–396.

———. *Motivation and Personality*. New York: Harper & Brothers, 1954.

Mason, William A. "Early social deprivation in the nonhuman primates: Implications for human behavior." *Environmental Influences*. Edited by David Glass. New York: Rockefeller University Press, 1968, p. 152.

Maynard, Fredelle. "What really matters when you're growing up." *Woman's Day*. July, 1969, p. 91.

McCandless, Boyd R. *Children: Behavior and Development*. New York: Holt, Rinehart, and Winston, Inc., 1967, p. 148.

———. *Adolescent Behavior and Development*. Hinsdale, Illinois: The Dryden Press, 1970, p. 145.

McClelland, David C. "Risk-taking in children with high and low need for achievement." *Readings in Social Development*. Edited by Ross D. Parke. New York: Holt, Rinehart and Winston, Inc., 1969.

McCord, Joan; McCord, W.; and Howard, A. "The family interaction as antecedent to the direction of male aggressiveness." *Journal of Abnormal and Social Psychology*, 66, 1963, pp. 239–242.

McKinley, D. G. *Social Class and Family Life*. Glencoe: Free Press, 1963.

Mead, Margaret, and Heyman, Ken. *Family*. New York: The Macmillan Co., 1965.

Medinnus, Gene R., ed. *Readings in the Psychology of Parent-Child Relations*. New York: John Wiley and Sons, Inc., 1967.

Mehrabian, Albert. *An Analysis of Personality Theories*. Englewood Cliffs, New Jersey: Prentice-Hall, Inc., 1968, p. 150.

Menninger, Karl. *Love Against Hate*. New York: Harcourt, Brace and Co., 1942.

Mergentine, Charlotte. *You and Your Child's Reading*. New York: Harcourt, Brace and World, Inc., 1963.

Meyer, William J., ed. *Readings in the Psychology of Childhood and Adolescence*. Waltham, Massachusetts: Blaisdell Publishing Company, 1967.

Mink, Oscar G. *The Behavior Change Process*. New York: Harper & Row, 1970.

Missildine, Hugh. *Your Inner Child of the Past*. New York: Simon and Schuster, 1963, pp. 20, 123.

Montagu, Ashley, ed. *Man and Aggression*. New York: Oxford University Press, 1968.

Mooney, Ross L. "Groundwork for creative research." *The Self, Explorations in Personal Growth*. Edited by Clark E. Moustakas. New York: Harper & Bros., 1956, p. 4.

Moore, Judith Ann. "Encountering hostility." *Perspectives in Psychiatric Care*, 6, No. 2, March–April, 1968, p. 58.

Morrow, William, and Wilson, Robert. "Family relations of bright high-achieving and under-achieving high school boys." *Child Development*, 32, 1961, pp. 501–510.

Moss, H., and Kagan, J. "Stability of achievement and recognition-seeking behavior from early childhood through adulthood."

Journal of Abnormal and Social Psychology, 62, 1961, pp. 504–513.

Moustakas, Clark E., ed. *The Self, Explorations in Personal Growth.* New York: Harper & Bros., 1956, p. 4.

Moustakas, Clark E. *Personal Growth.* Cambridge, Massachusetts: Howard A. Doyle Publishing Company, 1969.

Muller, Philippe. *The Tasks of Childhood.* New York: World University Library, McGraw-Hill Book Co., 1969.

Mussen, Paul H., ed. *Carmichael's Manual of Child Psychology.* Vol. II, 3rd ed. New York: John Wiley and Sons, Inc., 1970.

Mussen, Paul; Conger, John; and Kagan, Jerome, eds. *Readings in Child Development and Personality.* New York: Harper & Row, 1965.

Mussen, Paul; Conger, John; and Kagan, Jerome. *Child Development and Personality.* New York: Harper & Row, Publishers, 1969.

Mussen, Paul H., and Rosenzweig, Mark, eds. *Annual Review of Psychology.* Palo Alto, California: Annual Reviews, Inc., 1970.

Mussen, Paul, and Rutherford, Eldred. "Parent-child relations and parental personality in relation to young children's sex-role preferences." *Child Development,* 34, 1963, pp. 225–246.

Nash, J. "The father in contemporary culture and current psychological literature." *Child Development,* 36, 1965, pp. 261–297.

Neill, A. S. *Freedom—Not License.* New York: Hart Publishing Co., Inc., 1966.

Newson, John, and Newson, Elizabeth. *Four Years Old in an Urban Community.* Harmondsworth, Middlesex, England: Penguin Books Ltd., 1968.

Ojemann, Ralph H., ed. *The School and Community Treatment Facility in Preventive Psychiatry.* Iowa City, University of Iowa, 1966.

Painter, Genevieve. *Teach Your Baby.* New York: Simon and Schuster, 1971.

Palmer, James O. *The Psychological Assessment of Children.* New York: John Wiley and Sons, Inc., 1970.

Parke, Ross D., ed. *Readings in Social Development.* New York: Holt, Rinehart and Winston, Inc., 1969.

Patterson, Gerald; Littman, Richard; and Bricker, William. "Assertive behavior in children." *Monograph of the Society for Research in Child Development,* 32, No. 5, Serial No. 13, 1967.

Peck, Robert F., and Havighurst, R. J. *The Psychology of Character Development.* New York: John Wiley and Sons, 1960, p. 127.

Peirs, Maria W. *Growing Up With Children.* Chicago: Quadrangle Books, 1966.

Perkins, Hugh V. *Human Development and Learning.* Belmont, California: Wadsworth Publishing Company, 1969.

Piaget, J. *The Origins of Intelligence in Children.* Translated by Margaret Cook. New York: W. W. Norton and Co., Inc., 1952, p. 162.

Piaget, J., and Inhelder, Bärbel. *The Child's Conception of Space.* Translated by F. J. Langdon and J. L. Lunzer. London: Routledge and Kegan Paul, 1963.

Pikunas, Justin; Albrecht, Eugene; and O'Neil, Robert. *Human Development: A Science of Growth.* New York: McGraw-Hill Book Company, 1969.

Pitcher, Evelyn. *Helping Young Children Learn.* Columbus, Ohio: Charles E. Merrill Publishing Co., 1966.

Pollard, Marie B., and Geoghegan, Barbara. *The Growing Child in Contemporary Society.* Milwaukee: The Bruce Publishing Co., 1969.

Pulaski, Mary Ann Spencer. *Understanding Piaget.* New York: Harper & Row, 1971.

Redl, Fritz. *Understanding Children's Behavior.* New York: Teachers College, Columbia University, 1961.

———. *When We Deal With Children.* New York: The Free Press, 1966, pp. 386–389.

Redl, Fritz, and Wineman, David. *Controls from Within.* New York: Free Press, 1952.

———. *The Aggressive Child.* Glencoe, Illinois: Free Press, 1957.

Rheingold, Harriet L., and Samuels, Helen R. "Maintaining the positive behavior of infants by increased stimulation." *Annual Prog-*

ress in Child Psychiatry and Child Development. Edited by Stella Chess and Alexander Thomas. New York: Brunner/Mazel Publishers, 1970, pp. 1–18.

Rheingold, Harriet L., and Eckerman, Carol O. "The infant separates himself from his mother." *Annual Progress in Child Psychiatry and Development*. Edited by Stella Chess and Alexander Thomas. New York: Brunner/Mazel Publishers, 1971, p. 26.

Rich, Dorothy. "Payoffs used as education incentive." *Los Angeles Times*, November 18, 1969, Part IV p. 7.

Robson, Kenneth. "The role of eye-to-eye contact in the maternal-infant attachment." *Journal of Child Psychology and Psychiatry*, 8, 1967, pp. 13–25.

Rogers, Carl. "Toward a modern approach to values: The valuing process in the mature person." *The Journal of Abnormal and Social Psychology*, 68, 1964, p. 166.

Rogers, Carl, and Stevens Barry. *Person to Person*. Lafayette, California: Real People Press, 1967.

Rogers, Dorothy, ed. *Readings in Child Psychology*. Belmont, California: Wadsworth Publishing Company, 1969.

Rosen, B. C., and D'Andrade, R. "The psychosocial origins of achievement motivation." *Sociometry*, 22, 1959, p. 215.

Rosenzweig, M. R. "Environmental complexity, cerebral change, and behavior." *American Psychologist*, 21, Pt. 1, 1966, pp. 321–332.

Rosenzweig, Mark R.; Krech, David; and Bennett, Edward L. "Environmental impoverishment, social isolation, and changes in brain chemistry and anatomy." *Physiology and Behavior*, 1, No. 2, 1966, pp. 99–104.

Ross, Dorothea. "Relationship between dependency, intentional learning, and incidental learning in preschool children." *Journal of Personality and Social Psychology*, 4, 1966, pp. 374–381.

Rousseau, Jean-Jacques. "Emile." *The World of the Child*. Edited by Toby Talbot. Garden City, New York: Doubleday and Company, Inc., 1967, p. 369.

Rubin, Theodore Isaac. *The Angry Book*. London: The Macmillan Co., 1969.

Sandler, Joseph, and Joffe, Walter G. "A discussion of 'Psychoanalytic psychology and learning theory.'" *The Role of Learning in Psychotherapy.* Edited by Ruth Porter. London: J. & A. Churchill, Ltd., 1968, pp. 289, 291–292.

Sanford, Nevitt. *Issues in Personality Theory.* San Francisco: Jossey-Bass, Inc., 1970, p. 73.

Sawrey, James M., and Telford, Charles W. *Psychology of Adjustment.* Boston: Allyn and Bacon, Inc., 1967.

Schaeffer, E. S. *Infant Education Research Project.* Preschool program in compensatory education. Bureau of Elementary and Secondary Education. U.S. Office of Education: Washington, D.C., 1969.

Schaffer, H. R., and Emerson, P. E. "The development of social attachments in infancy." *Monograph of the Society for Research in Child Development,* 29, No. 3, 1964, pp. 1–77.

Schneiders, Alexander. *Counseling the Adolescent.* San Francisco: Chandler Publishing Co., 1967.

Schulman, J. L. "Management of emotional disorders." *Year Book.* Chicago: Medical Publishers, Inc., 1967.

Scott, John Paul. *Aggression.* Chicago: The University of Chicago Press, 1958.

———. "Critical periods in behavioral development." *Science,* 138, November 30, 1962, pp. 949–958.

———. "A Time to Learn." *Psychology Today.* March, 1969, p. 67.

Sears, Robert R.; Maccoby, Eleanor E.; and Levin, Harry. *Patterns of Child Rearing.* Evanston, Illinois: Row, Peterson and Company, 1957.

Sears, Robert; Rau, Lucy; and Alpert, Richard. *Identification and Child Rearing.* Stanford, California: Stanford University Press, 1967.

Seay, B.; Alexander, B. K.; and Harlow, H. F. "Maternal behavior of socially deprived rhesus monkeys." *Journal of Abnormal and Social Psychology,* 69, 1964, p. 345.

Skeels, Harold M. "Adult status of children with contrasting early life experiences." *Monograph of the Society for Research in Child Development,* 31, No. 3, Serial No. 105, 1966, pp. 8–10, 33, 40–42, 44–54.

Smart, Mollie S., and Smart, Russell C. *Children: Development and Relationships.* New York: The Macmillan Co., 1967.

Smith, Henry Clay. *Personality Development.* New York: McGraw-Hill Book Co., 1968.

Smith, Joseph. "The first lie." *Psychiatry,* 31, February, 1968, p. 62.

Smith, Leona J. *Guiding the Character Development of the Preschool Child.* New York: Association Press, 1968.

Sontag, L. W.; Baker, C. T.; and Nelson, V. L. "Mental growth and personality development: A longitudinal study." *Monograph of the Society for Research in Child Development,* 23, No. 2, 1958.

Spoerl, Dorothy T. *Tensions Our Children Live With.* Boston: Beacon Press, 1959.

Stagner, Ross. *Psychology of Personality.* 3rd ed. New York: McGraw-Hill, 1961, pp. 9, 106.

Stevenson, H. W. "Social reinforcement of children's behavior." *Advances in Child Development and Behavior.* Vol. II. Edited by L. P. Lipsitt and C. C. Spiker. New York: Academic Press, 1965.

Stolz, Lois Meek. *Influences on Parent Behavior.* Stanford, California: Stanford University Press, 1967.

Stone, L. Joseph, and Church, Joseph. *Childhood and Adolescence.* New York: Random House, 1968.

Storr, Anthony. *Human Aggression.* New York: Atheneum, 1968, p. 80.

Stott, D. H. *Studies of Troublesome Children.* New York: Humanities Press, Inc., 1966, p. 164.

Strang, Ruth. *An Introduction to Child Study.* New York: The Macmillan Co., 1959.

Streitfeld, Harold, and Lewis, Howard. *Growth Games.* New York: Harcourt Brace Jovanovich, Inc., 1970, p. 44.

Suomi, S. J.; Harlow, H. F.; and Domek, C. J. "Effect of repetitive infant-infant separation of young monkeys." *Journal of Abnormal Psychology,* 76, 1970, pp. 161–172.

Sutich, Anthony, and Vich, Miles. *Readings in Humanistic Psychology.* New York: The Free Press, 1969.

Swift, Joan W. "Effects of early group experience: The nursery school and day nursery." *Children's Behavior.* Edited by Rita E. Bergman. New York: Exposition Press, 1968, p. 153.

Symonds, Percival. *The Dynamics of Parent-Child Relationships.* New York: Bureau of Publications, Teachers College, Columbia University, 1949.

Taylor, Charles, and Combs, Arthur W. "Self-acceptance and adjustment." *Journal of Consulting Psychology,* 16, 1952, pp. 89–91.

Tharp, Roland G., and Wetzel, Ralph. *Behavior Modification in the Natural Environment.* New York: Academic Press, 1969.

Thomas, Alexander. *Temperament and Behavior Disorder in Children.* New York: University Press, 1968.

Trieschman, Albert E.; Whittaker, James K.; and Brendtro, Larry K. *The Other 23 Hours.* Chicago: Aldine Publishing Company, 1969, p. 92.

Trotter, Robert J. "Let it all out: Yes or no?" *Science News,* 102, October 14, 1972, p. 254. (Comments on a pilot study by Berkowitz and Buvinic.)

Tucker, Irving F. *Adjustment Models and Mechanisms.* New York: Academic Press, 1970, p. 154.

Ullmann, Leonard, and Krasner, Leonard. *A Psychological Approach to Abnormal Behavior.* Englewood Cliffs: New Jersey: Prentice-Hall, Inc., 1969.

Voeks, Virginia. Personal communication, 1973.

Wahler, Robert; Winkel, Gary; Peterson, Robert; and Morrison, Delmont. "Mothers as behavior therapists for their own children." *Behavior Research and Therapy,* 3, 1965, pp. 113–124.

Waldrop, Mary, and Bell, Richard. "Relation of preschool dependency behavior to family size and density." *Child Development,* 35, 1964, pp. 1187–1195.

Washburn, Ruth Wendell. *Children Know Their Friends.* New York: William Morrow Company, 1949.

Weill, Blanche. *Through Children's Eyes.* New York: Island Workshop Press Coop., Inc., 1940, p. 96.

Weinberg, Carl. *Social Foundations of Educational Guidance.* New York: Free Press, 1969.

Weiss, Paul, and Weiss, Jonathan. *Right and Wrong.* New York: Basic Books, Inc., 1967.

Westley, William A., and Epstein, Nathan B. *The Silent Majority.* San Francisco: Jossey-Bass, Inc., 1969.

Wheeler, L., and Levine, L. "Observing model similarity in the contagion of aggression." *Sociometry*, 30, 1967, pp. 41–49.

Wheeler, L. and Smith, S. "Censure of the model in the contagion of aggression." *Journal of Personality and Social Psychology*, 6, 1967, pp. 93–98.

White, Burton L. *Human Infants*. Englewood Cliffs, New Jersey: Prentice-Hall, 1971, p. 132.

White, Burton L., and Held, Richard. "Plasticity of sensorimotor development in the human infant." *The Causes of Behavior*. 2nd ed. Edited by Judy Rosenblith and Wesley Allensmith. Boston: Allyn and Bacon, 1966.

White, Dorothy K. *Teaching the Child Right from Wrong*. New York: The Bobbs-Merrill Company, 1961.

White, Robert W. "Motivation reconsidered: The concept of competence." *Psychological Review*, 66, No. 5, 1959, p. 320.

Winder, C. L., and Rau, Lucy. "Parental attitudes associated with social deviance in preadolescent boys." *Journal of Abnormal Psychology*, 64, 1962, pp. 418–424.

Woody, Robert H. *Behavioral Problem Children in the Schools*. New York: Appleton-Century-Crofts, 1969.

Yarrow, Marian; Campbell, John; and Burton, Roger. *Child Rearing*. San Francisco: Jossey-Bass, Inc., 1968.

Ziman, Edmund. *Jealousy in Children*. New York: A. A. Wyn, Inc., 1949.

INDEX